ADVENTURES ON THE HIGH SEAS

ADVENTURES ON THE HIGH SEAS

by

CAPTAIN H. G. KENDALL, R.D., R.N.R.

With 28 *Illustrations*

SECOND IMPRESSION

*Publishers
since·1812*

LONDON
HURST & BLACKETT, LTD.

First published 1939

Made and Printed in Great Britain for
Hurst & Blackett, Ltd., Paternoster House, London, E.C.4, at
The Mayflower Press, Plymouth. William Brendon & Son, Ltd.

LIST OF ILLUSTRATIONS

5

CHAPTER I

WHAT precisely can be the reason which makes a lad choose the sea as his career? To find a clear answer to that question is not too easy, and certainly in my own case I should have great difficulty in selecting one influence more than another as decisive. I was born in the Borough of Chelsea on 30 January 1874, but though the Thames ebbs and flows through this district bearing barges and lighters, tugs and coasters, every day of the week, London's river never touched my juvenile imagination. Nor, with one solitary exception, had any of my relatives been connected with shipping.

True, there once lived a Captain John Kendall, who went down with his ship off the Cornish coast nearly a century ago. His Bible floated ashore, together with other flotsam, and for many a long year was prized by the family until my parents lost it during a railway journey. Certainly this ancient mariner's life and death exercised no effect on me who, like thousands of other children, was early thrust into a sailor suit. Whilst it is just possible that immediate environment may have done something towards developing a trend unconsciously, more likely the fact that two old aunts started calling me 'Jack the Sailor' first put the suggestion of a nautical life bluntly into my undeveloped mind. On the other hand a natural desire to roam, encouraged by an unhappy period at school, finally shaped longing into something definite.

Fifty years ago a boy's educational days were harsh and unbearable, compared with modern conditions. Our head master relied on the cane as a regular principle, but his surname happened to be 'Thrasher,' so what else could be expected?

This drastic attitude was the cause of his pupils not infrequently running away, and I remember a boy named Campbell who managed to hide in seclusion for three whole weeks. When at length his parents discovered and brought him back, we inquired if Campbell's father had killed the fatted calf to celebrate the fortunate return.

"No," came the immediate reply. "But he pretty nearly slew the prodigal son."

My own father died when I was ten years old, leaving me as the only boy, and my mother always insisted that I caused her more worry than all her other offspring put together. The truth is that the longing to wander had become irresistible. Just as the turtle, which is hatched on a sandy beach, afterwards makes straight for the sea; so I was waiting till I could use the world's oceans as my playground, and nothing less would satisfy.

Unfortunately my mother was opposed to the idea whole-heartedly. Mischievous and a regular scamp, thoroughly deserving all the thrashings which came my way, I knew my own mind even if it was impossible to win her approval; till, finally, being now aged fifteen, I took the matter into my own hands. It was December, 1889, and I had obtained a berth aboard the Inman liner *City of Berlin*, but before sailing I paid a visit to where my mother and sisters were living. The whole family gave me a good send-off from Euston station. An uncle, who had not long returned from fighting in the Sudan, came along together with my grandfather. The latter presented me with a thin gold chain which he had worn round his neck throughout the Crimean War, and now wished me to carry that gift for luck in the same position.

The usual farewells had been made. "Good-bye, Jack—don't forget to write," was being impressed upon me; the Guard had blown his whistle and waved his flag; when, suddenly, my mother put her head into the carriage window and presented a parting wish:

"Now that you're going to sea, whatever you do never

drink intoxicating liquor, never be tattooed, and never chew tobacco."

Well, I didn't see her again, for she died shortly afterwards: but right to the end of my seafaring I respected her sound advice.

Now the *City of Berlin* was quite a famous ship. In 1874 the White Star liner *Britannic* had been built, and she caused a sensation by breaking the Atlantic record with her 16 knots speed; but then followed this Inman liner which wrested the pride of achievement by crossing in 7 days, 14 hours. The *City of Berlin* was the first steamer to be fitted with electric light (in 1879), and though of only 5491 tons, measuring 520 feet over all, such a size at that date seemed impressive.

Barque-rigged, she carried full sail during favourable winds and, since westerlies are generally prevalent in the North Atlantic, her eastbound passages were performed in remarkable time. It was because of her graceful lines that they used to call her the 'Yacht of the Atlantic,' and her commander knew how to get the best out of this fine vessel. Captain Land was a fine seaman of the old school, but his name could never be separated from the inevitable joke. "Land always in sight," they would remark.

The couple of voyages that I made under him were continuously boisterous, one gale following after another. For a boy starting his career, the wintry North Atlantic is not the most encouraging sea, and on arrival back in Liverpool I decided that some other route would suit me better. Having found that the S.S. *Agamemnon* was shortly bound away 'where the flying-fishes play,' I signed on within a week and found this ship likewise to be of more than ordinary interest.

Built so far back as 1864, she used her sail almost as much as her steam, and had made her way round the Cape of Good Hope to China five years before the Suez Canal was ever opened. She belonged to that historic trio—*Achilles, Ajax, Agamemnon*—which formed the nucleus of the famous Alfred Holt fleet which he used himself to design. The curious feature of these steamers was that the propeller was abaft the rudder, an idea which has been again experimented with by designers quite recently.

On sailing from the Mersey we were bound via the Suez Canal for the Orient with the finest Manchester goods. The few days of bad weather in the Bay of Biscay were soon forgotten after passing between the Pillars of Hercules into the Mediterranean and brilliant sunshine. Our voyage to Port Said could scarcely have been more pleasant, and as we dropped anchor I felt that I had struck another world. Soon we were coaled by the Arabs, and started on our journey through the Canal, where progress was less efficient than it is to-day.

Ships were not allowed to steam at night unless fitted with a searchlight on their bows, but since only half a dozen of these lights were at any one time available, it often meant that a steamer must make fast alongside the bank during dark hours. The *Agamemnon* succeeded in getting through expeditiously and, after Suez, we made our way south with Biblical lands on either side calling to mind the story of how the Red Sea waters were divided to allow the Children of Israel's crossing.

Some persons are able to connect present with past very realistically, like the old tramp skipper who anchored abreast of Mount Sinai. When the time came to weigh, something had evidently fouled the ship's anchor.

"Must be one of the wheels which belonged to Pharaoh's chariot," he dismissed lightly.

Well, we steamed out of the Red Sea through Hell's Gate and the Straits of Bab el Mandeb into the Arabian Sea; whence it is a long drag over the southern part of the Bay of Bengal till reaching Singapore. At the latter we discharged cargo, coaled, and received a number of Chinese passengers bound from the Straits Settlements to their homes. Not unusually these returning emigrants died aboard ship, wherefore the custom was for plenty of coffins to be carried; for no Chinaman liked the thought of being buried at sea. Such, however, was the exceptional mortality during *Agamemnon's* voyage, that the coffins ran short and we had to do some embalming before Hong Kong could be reached.

At Kobe we found the Japanese celebrating completion of their first thousand miles of railway, and it was indeed a great occasion. Every naval country had sent a man-of-war, the Duke and Duchess of Connaught halted on their voyage round the world, and altogether an immense joy prevailed. Since those days the Oriental character has become far less simple. I recollect once giving a Jap an old pair of trousers, in exchange for which he gave me: three canaries, three cages, together with an afternoon tea set.

Nowadays such a man would be far more sophisticated.

Coaling ship at Nagasaki was done by Japanese women, of whom the married were wont to lacquer their teeth black. Why? Doubtless it was the idea of a jealous husband to make his wife look so unattractive that no other man would ever stop to take note. We were to carry several hundred coolies from Hong Kong for Singapore, and at one time the practice was to give each Chinaman an advance of wages in silver dollars as soon as he had been brought aboard. The wily Oriental would then wait quietly till the steamer had started and got nicely clear of the town. Suddenly a crowd of them would then leap over and swim ashore, well knowing that these silver dollars would never have to be earned. But at last the Western mind thought out a scheme which so thwarted John Chinaman that such tricks became impossible.

Now when the *Agamemnon* arrived back in the Mersey, and docked one Sunday morning as the church bells were ringing out over Liverpool's city, I was rather like an audience who had been present at a moderately interesting play. Undoubtedly this voyage was a worth-while experience, and it taught me many things: yet what I longed for chiefly had not been granted so far. Romance of the sea! That summed up my yearning in those youthful days, and somehow a steamship failed to produce the romantic touch, even by voyaging thousands of miles through all kinds of weather.

Still unsatisfied, I knew that a sailing ship with her white wings spread, her hull yielding to the trade-winds as she flew like a bird above the wave-tops, appealed to me irresistibly. I had spoken about it to the *Agamemnon's* Captain, and he agreed. "If you want to become a sailor, you must serve in a sailing ship." That sounded reasonable, and the result was that thanks to his influence I was within a few days taken to Captain Russell, Marine Superintendent of the Alfred Holt organization. Shortly afterwards followed the order to join as apprentice the sailing ship *Iolanthe* then lying at Middlesbrough, so away I went north.

I was met by the Captain's son who took me and my belongings to this windjammer where the night-watchman greeted me and installed me. Apprentices' quarters? The place had been formerly a donkey-boiler room, but that didn't matter. Next morning *Iolanthe* was placed alongside the loading berth, where we began taking on board steel rails and sleepers for building the first railway in north Australia, to run from Normanton, in Queensland, a distance of less than a hundred miles till it reached the Croydon gold-fields.

By the time our cargo was stowed about three weeks had passed, which afforded me a good opportunity for learning many things about the ship. In the meanwhile the Captain had left for Liverpool to engage a crew. He wanted coloured seamen, who were more readily procured in the Lancashire port, and their wages would be ten shillings a month less. In those days an A.B. was paid £3 a month, so that when these sailors had left behind half their pay to their white wives, precious little remained for themselves.

Most of them were West Indians and American negroes. Fine seamen, and as good a crowd for handling a ship under sail as anyone could desire, they were frequently preferred to a white crew. Many a captain was only too glad to have available such abnormal primitive strength when dirty weather struck the ship and fast passages depended largely on how smartly tacks and sheets were hauled. Other Master Mariners would carry a 'chessboard' crew: that is to say, one half being black and the other half white. The latter would compose the starboard watch, so it was a case of working them in keen competition against the coloured men. Naturally this led to considerable trouble, and the scheme in most cases had to be discarded.

When the *Iolanthe* sailed, we made not via the Dover Straits, but north-about past Scotland to go between Orkneys and Shetlands. A south-westerly wind gave us a good slant, so that ere long we were out in the Atlantic making for the Equator. Here was a life very different from that in *Agamemnon*, and every pound or pint according to strict Board of Trade scale. The rations were one pound of biscuits a day—but so hard that they would have made good circular saws for cutting sheet-iron; three-quarters of a pound of salt pork one day, and a pound of salt beef for the day after; 14 ozs. of the worst quality brown sugar; 7 ozs. of butter and the same of marmalade, each week; and 3 quarts of water issued daily at 4 p.m. to cover all drinking purposes, including tea, pea-soup, and coffee. Washing of person or clothes had to be done in salt water, except when the rains came.

On Sundays, Tuesdays, and Thursdays, a small half-pound loaf was served out and had to be regarded as a considerable luxury. That strong Atlantic air created a vigorous appetite in healthy bodies, and despite the hard fare I doubt if you could have found a more robust crowd at the end of many days. So long as a sailor is at sea, able to do his work, to eat and sleep, he suffers comparatively little illness. Moreover, his powers of endurance are exceptional because of the accumulated reserves. Only thus can be explained the survival to ripe old age of those shellbacks condemned for years to serve in unhygienic fo'c'sles.

When once the British Isles had been left well astern, we seemed to pick up the Trade Winds fairly quickly. Heavy sails employed for high latitudes were then unbent, and old ones sent up in their stead, because in the doldrums —those calm patches so often met with in the area 5 degrees North and South of the Equator—the amount of chafing is very great. The ship rolls lazily to the swell, sails keep flapping against masts and rigging, a light air comes and goes, spars creak, braces and sheets tighten with a jerk or suddenly slack. But the want of steady persistent strain is a great test of sound gear.

Not till the southern edge of the Southeast Trades is reached are the best sails brought forth again to survive the storms of Atlantic and Indian Ocean, or that severe trial through which a ship passes when running her easting down in the 'roaring forties' between the Cape of Good Hope and Australia. *Iolanthe* crossed the Equator on the thirtieth day after leaving port: not a fast passage, but just about an average. The customary ceremonies with Neptune, the shaving-brush and razor, the capsizing into a canvas bath, were all observed.

But the thirtieth day out was also a cause for rejoicing. Before leaving harbour sailors were given a month's pay in advance, which of course they spent in a final jollification ashore. The first four weeks at sea were regarded as unprofitable—just so much 'dead horse': but, that period having passed, they were in a happier mood and now they could 'bury' the dead horse as something entirely finished with.

An effigy of canvas and straw (vaguely reminiscent of the quadruped) was borne along the deck accompanied by the well-known shanty 'Poor Old Man' sung by all. The versions of this song differ very slightly, and it has been suggested that it derives from an old negro ballad, though such a theory is hard to establish. 'Burying the dead horse' was essentially a British institution not found aboard American ships.   The words were as follows:

SOLO: 'I think, old man, your horse will die.'
CHORUS: 'And they say so.   And we hope so.'
SOLO: 'And when he's dead, we'll tan his hide.'
CHORUS: 'And they say so.   And we hope so.'
SOLO: 'We'll hoist him up at the main yardarm.'
CHORUS: 'And they say so.   And we hope so.'
SOLO: 'And now he's dead, we'll bury him deep.'
CHORUS: 'And they say so.   And we hope so.'

The routine was to hoist the dead 'horse' to the yardarm during the chanting, when three cheers would be given for the Skipper and others.   A sailor on the 'horse's' back, who had been hoisted in a separate bowline, then took out his knife and cut the effigy adrift, allowing it to drop into the sea.   Gradually the sailor was lowered to deck whilst his shipmates began singing that most famous of all sea-shanties, 'Blow the Man Down.'

'As I was awalking down Paradise Street,
With my way, aye, blow the man down,
A Liverpool bobby I chanced for to meet,
So give me some time to blow the man down.'

The Captain then called all hands aft, gave them a tot of grog, and the incident had concluded with the beginning of a new phase in the voyage.

Having at last finished with the southeasters and reached the zone of westerlies, we went bowling along past Cape of Good Hope running our easting down.   That part of the Indian Ocean lying between South Africa and Western Australia is one of the world's loneliest shipping tracks, but midway are those strangely situated islands of St. Paul and New Amsterdam.   Seventy or eighty years ago, when sailing ships used to call at remote places, and romance had not been swept off the sea by accurately scheduled steamer voyagings, vessels sometimes would call here to obtain fresh fish; for it is as excellent as abundant.   The glittering St. Paul rock cod, weighing six to eight pounds, was much welcomed after the ship's menu had become inordinately monotonous. And there was no little pleasure in the catching or cooking. Boats would be lowered and sent to this volcanic creation, where the unique pleasure could be enjoyed of holding the fish on the same hook in the springs that were always at boiling heat, as nature kept going a huge furnace down below.

This tiny uninhabited corner of the globe has been the graveyard of many a fine sailing ship and many an able seaman, so that long ago a relief station stored with food and clothes to last twenty men during three months was established. We made towards the locality not for the purpose of stopping, but in order to verify our position and rate our chronometers, then headed away in a north-easterly direction for that part of Australia called North West Cape.

Gradually each day's sail was bringing us finer weather, and we were glad of it. After having been wrapped up in oilskins and sea-boots for thousands of miles, with very little sun, you may guess what it felt like to be basking in real warm weather on deck and to begin drying clothing that had been soaked in salt water. For no fires or heating could be allowed us. In the Captain's quarters stood a small stove, of which he alone enjoyed the benefit; and the cook was allowed twenty wooden bucket-fuls of coal a week for his work in the galley. That was all.

But now that we sighted North West Cape, there set in a series of light airs and calms which lasted day after day, so that we kept chasing every catspaw on the waters, whilst sharks of varying sizes could be counted swimming about by the dozen. Well, here was the Australian continent, and on the whole there had been little to complain of the coloured crew's behaviour, yet it was impossible to disguise a not-too-friendly feeling which existed between the West Indian and the American negroes.

With regard to one point emphatically they were in

accord: theirs was the original colour of the human race!
And they were proud of the fact, as I soon learned. It
may have been the tropical weather, but something provided me with an over-supply of freckles. And one day,
when I stood at the port side of the galley by the door
receiving my rations, a French West Indian who was
drawing his at the starboard door greeted me with a
significant remark.

"Well, Baldy,[1] you see this colour?" he placed a finger to
his cheek.

"Yes?"

"This colour's 'riginal—no damn freckles about this."

And the man was so black that a piece of charcoal
would have left a white mark on him.

But a great drama was about to happen in our tiny
cosmos. Belonging peculiarly to the marine environment, it originated and developed unforced yet with a
dread destiny. Many a great novelist has shown the fateful
and fatal influence of surroundings on human character;
the prison-like inevitability which holds men mercilessly.
Here, however, was real-life tragedy on the high seas
against a colourful background, needing neither
exaggeration nor emphasis.

And, because of its stark simplicity, its intense
emotional appeal, there was left on the spectators an
impression which years could not efface.

---

[1] 'Baldy' was a term used by the negroes specially for white men,
possibly suggested by the latter's bald heads.

CHAPTER II

THESE calms and indefinite winds, coming at the end of a long monotony, had caused a certain feeling of restlessness to manifest itself. During five months we had been away from the amenities of shore-life, dissatisfaction was sweeping through the ship, and on everybody's lips—from the 'Old Man' down to the youngest sailor—a grumble everlastingly murmured.

Messmates were hating the sight of each other. Every ship in which they had previously served was heaps better than the *Iolanthe*. Petty grievances became ridiculously magnified, discussions grew into violent arguments, and fights were getting all too numerous. However, after gradually working our way through the Timor Sea, past Australia's northern extremity, we found ourselves running before a good breeze down the vast Gulf of Carpentaria which is about four hundred miles at its widest but more than that in its length from Normanton to Thursday Island. This was to be our last lap, *Iolanthe* having been sent to the Norman River which flows out of Queensland into the Gulf's southern corner. Being 166 days from Middlesbrough, we let go anchor about midnight.

But if the journey had ended, something more thrilling was well under way. Three days previously a West Indian and an American negro, after displaying no little contempt for each other, ultimately fell to blows, but then came knife-play. The American stabbed his opponent in three places: once between the breasts, once on the left breast, and once below the latter. The victim collapsed from loss of blood, but the Captain came along, immediately rendered first-aid, and then placed him in a spare cabin. That was the climax of a warm Sunday afternoon, and the West Indian's life remained too uncertain for more than conjecture.

Now this assault took place amidships, and in the presence of but two witnesses. One was a French West Indian from Martinique named Louie. The other chanced to be myself, for I had been sitting on the main hatch reading. When presently the Captain required us to make a statement, we both gave our opinion that the attack was done with deliberation. This assertion we uttered in the American negro's presence, which so infuriated the man that he swore to have his revenge. Forasmuch as the accused was not placed under arrest, but permitted to carry on with his work, it seemed not unlikely that he would carry out his threat at the first opportunity. Both Louie and I resolved to keep a weather-eye open.

The *Iolanthe* had been compelled to bring up some ten miles short of the Norman River by reason of the water's shallowness. Orders were given for us to climb aloft and make fast the sails, but a certain possibility darted into my brain. Approaching the Captain, I asked that both Louie and myself might be allowed to go up any other mast than that where the American was working. Doubtless the stabber had meant no empty menace.

My request having been granted, Louie and I were sent up the mizzen-mast together with the Captain's son. We were doing our job, furling the upper topsail on the starboard side, leaning over the yard. I was out towards the yardarm, Louie next to me, and next to him stood the Captain's son, when without the slightest warning something occurred. Louie became curiously ill, and began making a strange gurgling noise.

Hanging there limp across the yard at that height, the West Indian was in grave danger of tumbling to his death, so we hailed the deck, made fast a line round Louie's waist, worked him gradually towards the mast, and managed by various methods to lower him down. The Captain and Chief Officer having taken charge of him and begun to render aid, we resumed furling sails and, after coiling up all ropes, retired for the night.

At 7 a.m. all hands were called, coffee served, and the day's work began, and I was making my way aft to the poop when a great surprise filled my eyes. On the booby-hatch lay something covered with the Union Jack.

It was the dead body of Louie.

Apparently he had succumbed whilst aloft on the yard, for there was no sign of life by the time of reaching the poop. But here was a true mystery of the sea. A young man of thirty years, three days previously he seemed in the best of health. What had happened in the meantime? Stabbed? No. Shot at? No. Poisoned? Most probably. There could be no other explanation, yet time had failed to produce more than a strong suspicion. By ten o'clock that morning they buried Louie's body overboard in five fathoms (30 feet), of water, a bag of coal having been used to make it sink.

All this came as a great shock, because the unexpected had happened so quickly. And the hurried burial seemed illegal. Virtually the ship was in port, the body should have been landed and a post-mortem inquest held. Later on the Captain had to undergo some questioning, but his defence was that since the nearest town was some miles up the Norman River along which a small steamer proceeded once weekly; and forasmuch as we were lying only 18 degrees south of the Equator, it was impossible to keep the body in that terrific heat. The authorities accepted this explanation, so that part of the incident closed. 'Dead men tell no tales.' But most of us longed to know the precise cause of poor Louie's death.

Meanwhile justice had still to be done. It was on the third day following our arrival that the river steamer came out to meet the mail-boat due from South Australia. The former called alongside *Iolanthe* to fetch prisoner, victim, and Captain. Into hospital the wounded man was transferred, whilst his aggressor they lodged in prison ready for trial. Normanton during those early days consisted of 700 inhabitants, and the only coloured people permitted to live there were aborigines. Previously Chinese, Japanese, and Malays had also lived there, until the murdering of some whites brought about a crisis and the yellow men were shipped away south.

The Normanton white pioneers were hard as nails, very much wide-awake, but amazingly hospitable. A British stranger could rely on everybody extending a sincere friendship, and into this out-of-way territory I was to come by force of curious circumstances. The preliminary court proceedings had ended with an adjournment of fourteen days in which to prepare the case. When the trial was gone through at Normanton, I as the sole surviving witness had the unique chance of going ashore—a privilege that my shipmates much coveted after all these months.

But the case was not disposed of finally. Committed now for trial at the assizes, due to be held two months later, when the Judge during his visitation of the Queensland ports would come this way, the prisoner had to wait, and meanwhile I went back to my ship. The weeks dragged by till again I was taken up to Normanton, where the court house consisted of a wooden bungalow large enough to hold about one hundred people. The first case was one in which a man found himself accused of knocking a local policeman's eye out. The alleged culprit received acquittal, and then came the *Iolanthe* trial.

This lasted one day, and the defence stated that, at the time of the assault, prisoner happened to be employing the knife for whittling some wood ; the West Indian then struck the American, whereupon the two men closed, and the actual stabbing evolved rather as an accident than a deliberate effort. This version the court now accepted, and the accused was found not guilty.

But the wounded West Indian succumbed to his injuries all the same. But the story did not finish there. After the trial I was met outside by that negro who renewed his threats with determination, and I set to work deciding what to do. We were due back aboard, and the chances seemed that I should be at least another year in the *Iolanthe* before reaching a home port. What would be my fate in the meantime? How many hundreds of opportunities would my enemy be afforded for carrying out his menace? That same mysterious fatality which befell Louie might happen to me any day or night?

No: to go back aboard would be to take the worst chances. Desertion! That was the wisest, if the least pleasing, course to pursue.

At nightfall, when our Captain and others were joining the river steamer to reach *Iolanthe*, I was betaking myself to the bush. Knowing that the road had been well cleared for the sleepers and rails from Normanton right up to Croydon, I decided to make for the latter place. In between were no half-way houses, but there was adventure and I should enjoy that, whatever the hardships. So, existing chiefly on a kind of wild date, and sprinting along for considerable periods, I at last covered most of a hundred miles none the worse for hard going. Here at Croydon, where a pioneering population was trying to get riches from the goldfields, I began doing all kinds of work as a living. Nor was there much difficulty, or any lack of kindness. If you wanted employment, they gave it you. If you couldn't work, plenty of friends would see that you never ran short of food.

After a while I met in Croydon another runaway apprentice. The son of a bishop, he had quitted his ship whilst lying in Cooktown, a port on the eastern side of Queensland, then crossed the intervening 250 miles, hoping to make a fortune at the goldfields; but already his opinion coincided with mine. The possibility of valuable nuggets coming our way seemed remote.

A little later we fell across a young Irish sailor named

Kenna, who likewise had forsaken a British vessel; wherefore, having talked the matter over, we decided to go 'on the wallaby' together. A wallaby, of course, is a kind of small kangaroo, but when an Australian speaks of being 'on the wallaby track,' he means tramping. Our intention was to reach the coast by wandering overland day after day, being convinced that thus we should find better fortune.

The custom out here provided that every man 'on the wallaby' was to be given rest for the night, fed, and allowed the necessaries of life for helping him on his journey to the next place. Thus when, at the close of our second day, we reached a sheep-shearing station, no sort of reluctance hindered us. On the contrary, they were most anxious to entertain us with every hospitality. Supper being over, out came accordion and concertina, dancing began, and the maid-servants were allowed to join in. It was now, in this distant peninsula, that once again was to be proved that truth can be far more wonderful than any fiction.

Kenna, who happened to be our senior by two or three years, became infatuated with one of these maids. She was a pretty creature of nineteen, but at the end of a conversation he discovered that this was none other than his own sister! When a girl of ten, she had been sent out from Youghal in Ireland to an aunt in Australia, though for years no news reached home. So here at last the fact emerged that after having left her aunt, the girl drifted from place to place in service, till by the queerest coincidence she again met her brother in what was little better than the bush.

At daylight we set out to resume our journey, yet without Kenna. Since a job was offered him on the station, he remained behind. Nor did we make much progress, for the road turned out to be full of dangers and the rainy season was just commencing. What to do? Retrace one's steps first to Croydon, then to Normanton, so as to reach the east coast by water. I knew that on a certain date the monthly steamer was due to reach the Norman River's mouth, that the tender *Dugong* with passengers and mails would depart from the wharf after dark; so, being now alone once more, I decided to secrete myself aboard.

Everything at the right time worked out according to plan. Not only was I able to hide in the *Dugong*, but when she came alongside the mail-steamer before sunrise I managed to conceal myself in the latter. Over there still lay the *Iolanthe*, and I could see her riding-light, but it gave me no pleasure. If I were to be discovered during the next few minutes, they would send me back to where the American negro would rejoice to see my face. The suspense seemed unending. Would the mail-steamer never get under way? Was I to be caught at the last minute after all these land miles of wandering?

Suddenly I heard the Captain give his orders to heave up the anchor, then the propeller started its vibration, but not till we were gathering speed up the Gulf and *Iolanthe's* light dipped in the distance, did I dare to loose a sigh of relief. Now, indeed, whatever troubles might have to be faced in the future, nothing could be worse than the anxieties of these last nine months. I couldn't be dumped overboard, and my shoulders were broad enough to support any punishment that might result from being a stowaway. They would surely never send me back to the sailing ship?

Daylight broke about 6 a.m. Out I came forth from my hiding-place, walked along the for'ard deck towards the bridge further aft. The Chief Officer, who was on watch, immediately recognized me; for we had met before the murder trial, and he had since heard of my clearing away. Instead of treating my appearance with resentment, he behaved exceedingly generously, saw that I was immediately provided with a meal, and told me to stroll about decks until the Captain interviewed me during the 10 a.m. inspection.

Four suspenseful hours passed until at 10.30, his

inspection completed, the Captain made straight to where I was sitting on the hatch.

"Well, young man, what're you doing here?"

I immediately saluted, related my story, and explained that I wanted to reach the east coast. He listened attentively, then sent all my hopes down to zero.

"No," began his reply, "I'm afraid your chances of getting there in this ship are out of the question. In the first place, you're a runaway apprentice from a British vessel. If I were to take you beyond my first place of call, which is Thursday Island, and your Captain by some means were to learn you were on board, he could telegraph for you to be detained and have me up for harbouring a deserter. Now the best thing I can do is to land you on Thursday Island, place you in the hands of the authorities there, leave you till I return a month hence, pick you up and take you back to your ship, sending your Captain a bill for expenses."

Imagine my feelings!

The thought of being delivered up in this manner was terrifying, and I expressed a willingness to do anything rather than that.

The Captain reviewed my problem afresh.

"I'll do what I can for you," he promised; "but past Thursday Island it's impossible to take you. Meanwhile you will live in the 2nd Class."

That was fair enough, and a quick change, after having crept aboard at 3 a.m. as stowaway stealing a passage. Everybody was wonderfully kind, and several of the passengers offered to pay my fare round to South Australia, but the Captain declined to be moved from his decision: I was to be left ashore at the Torres Strait.

Now the distance from the mouth of Norman River to Thursday Island is roughly 460 miles; or two days' steaming, since the S.S. *Yaralla* could not be regarded as a fast ship. At first my thoughts were filled with dismay. To be left on an island would not suit by any sort of appeal, and daylight of the second morning found me scanning the horizon to obtain an early view of the Torres Strait group as they hove in sight. When Napoleon first looked out towards St. Helena, he could not have been more dismal than I was feeling. Soon Booby Island flashed by, next Prince of Wales Island slid past our starboard side, and then came Thursday Island. We made fast alongside a hulk that once had been a Dutch East Indiaman, cargo and mails were taken off, other goods brought aboard.

I was beginning to think that Captain Ussher had forgotten me, but five minutes before *Yaralla* was ready for sailing, he sent for me, wished me all kinds of good fortune, and added that he had written to the ship's agent on the island, asking him to do what he could. So, standing on that old hulk, I watched the mail-steamer cast off and begin her southern course. Then the world seemed full of loneliness and uncertainty.

At daylight next morning I went ashore to look for work. Having been ordered to visit Messrs. Burns Philp's store, and inquire for Mr. Bowden, I arrived to find that he was the Agent. Captain Ussher treated me well, for I now learned that he had asked Mr. Bowden to get me away, should there be any question of sending me back to the *Iolanthe*. I gave the Agent an account of my doings, and the reason for having deserted. He appeared well satisfied, and likely to arrange for me to remain in Torres Strait where not too many white people at that date were living.

"Go back to the hulk, and stay there till I require you," he instructed.

But only a few days sped by ere he sent for me.

CHAPTER III

DURING recent years Thursday Island has become slightly better known to the public by reason of the long-distance aviation voyages from Europe to Australia. Lying some thirty miles north-west of the mainland at Cape York, it contained not more than 1600 inhabitants even just before the Great War. Thursday Island's claim for notice was of a twofold character: a place of call for mail-steamers bound from England to North Queensland, from China to Australian ports, with a Government coaling-station in Port Kennedy, it was also the centre of a big pearl-fishing industry.

During the 'nineties this pearling employed a fleet of luggers whose size ranged from 10 to 20 tons; the divers comprising Japanese, Malays, and Roturnah Islanders who came from a district several hundred miles east of the Torres Strait towards the Solomon Islands. Of remarkable physique, highly skilled in the art of diving, the Roturnah men were straight-haired and seemed more of a mulatto type. Missionaries had been very successful among these people, who took keen delight to read their Bibles during spare time.

On Thursday Island resided the Hon. John Douglas, Governor of Torres Strait and North Queensland. One of nature's gentlemen, full of kindness, he was always ready to perform a gracious act no matter whether the recipient be black or white. There were three hotels on the island, of which the 'Grand' was owned by an Irishman and his wife named McNulty, two of the earliest settlers to arrive here. Besides Mr. Bowden, Agent for the Burns Philp Line, there was his brother carrying on a business for himself, and both were known for their hospitality.

27

When presently the former summoned me to his office
I found there a tall Roturnah Islander; but the latter had
brought with him his white wife, widow of an English
Captain who some years previously lost his ship on the
Coral Reefs. The job offered me was to go in one of the
luggers owned by the coloured man, so though I knew
nothing of the life I signed an agreement binding myself
for a year, and two days later began my first experience
of pearling: a most interesting and exciting time.

The crew consisted of two men from Tanna Island in
the South Seas, where not so long ago cannibalism was
rife; two more from Jesus Island in the Solomon group
(also notorious for cannibalism); two Roturnah Islanders;
and myself. Having provisioned the boat, we set out for
the Warrior and Wappa Reefs, 70 to 90 miles north-east
of Thursday Island, over towards the New Guinea coast.
Perhaps you may wonder how the first four mentioned
natives had ever reached Torres Strait, but they were a
relic of bygone practice. At one time a vast and flourishing business in the South Seas was carried on by white
men who arrived with their schooners. They would
leave Australian ports with plenty of rifles and tomahawks,
sail for the various islands, begin palavers with the tribal
Chiefs, and engage in what was euphemistically known
as 'Blackbird Catching.' In exchange for one rifle and
one tomahawk, the Chief would deliver up one cannibal.
Further conversation would multiply the business, until
the schooner had all the 'blackbirds' she could carry.
Then she would make for the continent where the cargo
would be sold in a sort of slavery to work on the Queensland sugar plantations for the next three years.

Some of these compulsory emigrants had thus remained,
and during my pearling career, though I met a good many
'blackbirds', never once did I hear them speak unkindly
either of those whites who had 'caught' them or of those
planters who worked them. Humanely treated, and
assisted by missionaries, their lot was by no means
unhappy.

On reaching the Wappa and Warrior Reefs, we prepared for a month's hard work, which began each day at 6 a.m. and continued till 6 p.m. From sunrise to sunset all of us were kept busy, and the diver had no easy time. The depth of water was anything from 6 to 12 fathoms (36 to 72 feet), and he would remain down for as long periods as three hours, coming up only for meals. The custom was for the boat to let go anchor with not too much cable out, so that she would gradually drag stern-first over the bottom in a north-westerly direction before the prevailing south-east wind, whilst the diver walked.

Taking it in turns at the air-pump, we spent each day under the broiling sun, while one of the Roturnahs tended the life-line; for all instructions from below were made by pulls or shakes of the rope. Another man would be sitting on the rail, looking after the air-pipe, keeping his eye on the bubbles, noting their direction, hauling in or slacking out this pipe lest it should be pierced by coming in contact with the sharp coral.

So the routine would go on daily until at spring-tides (that is to say when the moon was new or full) the water became dirty. Usually no diver would then work, for too many lives had been lost under such circumstances. Imagine him in his dress walking along the ocean-bed, which is by no means level as a billiards-table. All kinds of beautiful coral pinnacles and deep lakes contrast with each other, and he has to beware lest his pipe get foul of the former whilst his feet drop into the latter. Real danger threatens whilst the boat drifts to a strong current one side of the coral crest and the diver is stumbling to get round. Unless quick enough to improve his position, he may find air-pipe and life-line attain their fullest extent . . . then snap! He is left to die a quick death.

The greatest affliction that I found among these divers was deafness, due to the risks taken in deep water where shells were more numerous. Here there might be 18 fathoms, and the heavy pressure was bound to ruin ear-

drums. Sometimes, in fact, I have seen divers hauled up
to the surface paralysed, but in any case theirs is a short
life, and only the strongest can endure such conditions.

During the days when the sea was dirty, we would
hoist sail and visit Yam Island, Saddle Island, or some
other of the group, where we could obtain drinking-
water, wild-fruit, and vegetables. Many of these isles
were uninhabited, several possessed lagoons, so that when
the tide had gone out lots of fish remained for us to spear.
Altogether, what with the fish and fruit, pumpkins and
yams, the delicious mummy-apple and custard-apple, we
fared very well, but it was the freedom of life which we
relished.

For about two months of the year pigeons flew to this
region, attracted by the fruit, and we brought down
plenty of these birds with our Winchester repeating-rifles.
We discovered signs of some islands having been
inhabited. Partially cultivated ground, dilapidated wig-
wams, indicated that there had been an exodus by canoes
to where better opportunities offered.

But at one isle we came across an old sailor, who must
have come to grief in the Coral Seas by means of a sailing
ship years ago. On landing, I was greeted by him and
taken to his tropical hut, inside of which were six native
women.

"My wives," he explained. "All true as steel, and no
jealousy either."

They toiled for him, speared his fish, cultivated his
vegetables, prepared his food; yet, for all that, I could
not understand how a man could thus bury himself on a
South Sea lonely island.

"Are you really happy?" I asked. "Wouldn't you
rather be back at sea again?"

The old shellback smiled, and pointed to his six wives
squatting on the ground.

"This," he answered, "knocks the spots out of going
to sea."

Next morning, when the sun had just risen above the

horizon and we sat gazing shorewards from the deck of our pearl lugger, we could see silhouetted on the hills against the skyline this ex-mariner taking his wives for their morning walk; himself leading the way, each woman following in single file, about 10 feet apart. Then, presently, they would return, squat down again, smoke their pipes, and resume their jabbering.

We likewise went back to our reefs and diving, but during this month shells were not exceptionally numerous. Our haul actually amounted to about 600 shells, the weight of each being from 5 to 10 lb., making a total of not less than 4000 lb. It was generally considered a bad month's work if we did not obtain at least 2240 lb., that is to say a ton, which could be sold at Thursday Island for £100; or, if placed in the hands of an agent and shipped to the London market, would fetch £170, provided the shell was in good condition and not too much worm-eaten.

At the end of a day's work, generally half an hour before sunset, diving-dress would be washed down and hung up to dry; all gear stowed away, pump examined and oiled. Then we would set sail for some snug anchorage and begin our evening meal consisting of the centre of the pearl-fish turned into curry with the addition of rice; but every shell would first have been cleaned and examined to make sure no pearls remained inside.

Each of us took it in turns to cook, and make bread in a camp oven; and I still have doubts as to whether a baker's loaf to-day is superior to that made by South Sea natives in their cruder fashion.

The month's diving having been completed, we set sail for Thursday Island, where a boat would remain for a week or ten days : it all depended on how long the diver required for enjoying himself on a jamboree. Where the lugger was owned by a large company, the stay was normally shorter, but I was lucky that this one belonged to a one-man proprietor. And during our stay a member of the crew stole £3 from another. The owner,

anxious to make the culprit an example to the rest, handed
him over to the authorities and once more I was called as
witness. But before the tall Roturnah Islander commenced his evidence, the Clerk of the Court asked him:
"Are you a Christian?" this being the usual preliminary
question put to any coloured person.

"No," was the surprising reply. "I'm a Wesleyan."
Loud and prolonged laughter caused the owner much
annoyance, until I was allowed to spend some time
convincing the Islander that it was all right, and explained
the meaning of words. White men could exercise great
influence over coloured people; and no matter what sort
of solution the former should put forward, it was always
accepted.

In some ways this might be open to abuse. This man's
wife, we have already seen, was a white. She proved
herself also quite a formidable character, and very much
'all there,' but now she set out to extend her sphere.
Having instilled the possibility of his luggers being one
day taken from him through enjoying too much credit,
she pressed the idea that the only method of safeguarding
such property would be for him to place it in her name.
She further dragged me into the plan, with instructions
to lose no opportunity for convincing him of the advantage
to be gained. Admittedly, I did work very hard to that
intent, and finally the whole concern was turned over to
this grasping woman.

Little did I realize what a hornets' nest I was helping
to create.

We provisioned ship for the next pearling cruise, but
the 'darling wife' elected to come with us, and now the
fun began. She had sent aboard liberal supplies of rum
and *Schnapps*, which resulted in a competition as to who
could lower away the most. All the time I wondered
what this would lead to, and how soon the natives might
throw me overboard; but that which restrained them
was the fear of punishment. If any coloured man laid
his little finger on a white, the authorities at Thursday

Island would deal with the delinquent so thoroughly as to leave little opportunity for mercy.

A curious delusion of this tiresome female persisted just so long as the rum lasted. Quite unwarrantedly she would spend hours trying to persuade me her brother-in-law was Lord Halsbury, that famous Victorian legal luminary and Lord Chancellor. Of course I never believed a word of such statements, but it was not wise to exhibit my incredulity. During this merry-making we had been anchored behind an island, but at length we set sail for the waters of New Guinea where we hoped to engage two or three natives whom we needed as assistants in working the diving pump.

Navigation out here was certainly very casual: although compass and charts formed part of the luggers' equipment, I doubt if anybody on board understood the meaning. The procedure consisted of relying on the trade winds, departing from one island, keeping a good look-out in the hope of making a satisfactory landfall at the next. So trustful were these people in their ignorance, that they never realized the risks.

At the end of three days we sighted the New Guinea coast-line, which was about all that we knew. Reefs abounded, but by watching the shaded waters we managed to skirt hidden dangers till, finally selecting another island, we anchored for the night abreast of it. Exactly where we had arrived, or which this isle might be, not one of us had any idea. What I chiefly recollect was being disturbed by millions of mosquitoes, which never quitted us till daylight, by which time our eyes had been bunged up by the poison inoculated.

Thankful to get under way and leave this spot, we continued our guess-work and after a few hours sighted on the port bow yet another of these islands. Whether inhabited, whether controlled by cannibals, whether anybody was willing to accept work, not one of us could hazard, so we came to anchor and lowered the dinghy into which dropped the owner, his wife, and myself.

c

We pulled towards the sandy beach.   Not a soul in sight!

We rowed still nearer and when within quarter of a mile, there suddenly appeared fifty natives who began a sort of war dance, some entering up to their waists in water.   None of their movements tended to make me feel too comfortable, so I immediately turned our boat away in order to assess the strangers at a distance; when, behold, a coloured man in European dress, his head covered by a straw hat, waved us encouragingly.

As we made for the beach, a group of natives just picked up out of the water the dinghy with ourselves all in it, carried us to a dry patch where we were greeted by every man, woman, and child.   Our friend in the European clothes turned out to be a Malay missionary, but after the reason for this visit had been announced, we quickly suffered disappointment.   Unless we put the lugger under New Guinea regulations, and did our diving in those waters, no help could be forthcoming. So constant were the local wars, during which the tribes up-country were always trying to fight their way coastward, that not a man could be spared from the seaside.

I was impressed by the appearance of our new acquaintances.   Well-built, muscular fellows, they had terribly disfigured themselves; nostrils and ears being cut in strings, a bone skewered through the nose, large blisters stretching diagonally from the shoulders across the chest, and tattooed in various colours from waist to knees.   The women in many cases were not less awesome, but they seemed very friendly and, before we set out, took the trouble to have our boat well stocked with all kinds of fruit.

On putting to sea, we resumed our pearling in different waters and got back with our haul safely at Thursday Island.   The *Schnapps* having been all consumed, our difficult woman passenger became no more amenable. Now that everything was in her name, she did not hesitate to show her authority, or to abuse her husband, reminding him that he was just a coloured coon, and that he was working for her now as a servant. How this dominant woman regarded me may be appreciated by the following incident.

In those days a small weekly paper, no bigger than the size of an ordinary theatre programme, and called *The Thursday Island Pilot*, used to appear. It contained all the local news, court cases, paragraphs concerning the residents, together with some account of all vessels which called. Judge of my surprise when a small paragraph appeared stating that if the boy Kendall, who ran away from a ship in north Australia, would call at the editor's office, the former would hear something to his advantage.

All kinds of ideas flashed through my mind. Could it be that some unknown person had left me a legacy?

Straight off I walked up to the hotel kept by the kindly Mrs. McNulty, asked her to tell me what this meant, and she being in the know at once satisfied my curiosity. The editor of this magnificent journal had become tired, which was natural enough considering that he likewise combined the duties of compositor, proof-reader, printer, and indeed of all else connected with its publication. Wherefore he had decided to take a holiday for six months in southern Australia and, from what he had heard about me, considered I should be the right person to run the paper in his absence.

So that was the notion!

It seemed quite attractive, and the more I pondered over the suggestion the more I liked it. Away I marched to the office, only to find that it was already too late. That white wife of the pearler had also read the notice, and wasted no time inquiring of the editor. "Oh!" she warned. "That would never do. By the time you come back from your holiday, young Kendall will own the paper."

Evidently the editor became nervous of such a possibility, for his interview with me was remarkably short and of a negative nature. Instead of becoming a journalist, I resigned myself to pearling, and now the lugger was being provisioned for another trip. Among the crew was a remarkable character named Price, and many a good yarn was related concerning this old adventurer.

CHAPTER IV

PRICE was born in the United States with a certain amount of white blood in his veins. A sailor by choice, he had served many years both in American and British vessels until shipwrecked on the Coral Reefs. Then he took to the life of a beachcomber in the South Seas, where his easy disposition made him a general favourite.

He had travelled far, his experiences were as varied as numerous but, like most ancient shellbacks, he remembered only the smooth paths through life and forgot the others. His one failing was drink, and if not away at sea pearling these days, Price would be ashore in jail, which he always regarded as 'Simpson's Boarding House'; Simpson being the prison warden whom Price always spoke of as 'my pal.'

On one occasion when Price got back from pearling he set out for 'Smyth's bar,' where he found plenty of divers and *bêche-de-mer* fishers all enjoying the reward of their labour. It did not take long before beginning to feel the stimulating effect of neat spirits, and this would generally lead to the same result. Inspired with a longing to clear up the place, either with a chair or anything handy, he could not refrain from smashing all the windows; but amid this *mêlée* arrived a local policeman. Result—three months' compulsory residence in 'Simpson's Boarding House.'

As already noted, the Governor in this part of Australian territory was the Hon. John Douglas, before whom Price most frequently had to be brought; yet this old gentleman did not disdain to shake hands and have a yarn with the prisoner on completing the sentence. Since the jail happened to be adjacent to the Governor's house, offenders were often sent to work in the latter's garden or to do odd jobs at the back of the building.

It was during one of these compulsory periods that Price excelled himself. Lord Brassey in the famous S.Y. *Sunbeam* arrived and anchored off Thursday Island, came ashore to pay his respects, and the Governor subsequently invited him to breakfast, the morning's cool being regarded in those latitudes as the pleasantest time.

The day arrived, the meal began, but prefacing it Lord Brassey had sent as a present to his host a case of old brandy, which was temporarily deposited at the back of the house. Well, you can guess the rest. Scenting liquor, along wandered Price, who made no hesitation about opening the case and disappearing with nine bottles. When into the Governor's ears this sensational news was whispered, a great hue and cry began, and two policemen were detailed to find Price drunk or sober. Twenty-four hours elapsed, and only then did they discover the thief some distance away, well hidden in the scrub, but very pleased with his exploit. Carried back to jail, considerably mellowed by large quantities of Lord Brassey's eighty-year-old brandy, Price was really proud at having enjoyed such a privileged carousal.

Next day, the *Sunbeam* sailed and Price was brought before the Governor.

"What am I gong to do with you?" asked the latter in desperation.

"I don't know, sir," the man blandly replied.

Finally His Excellency delivered himself of this decision.

"You still have two months of the three to serve. You're a sailor and, I believe, a good leadsman, so I shall send you away to sea for a month in the *Albatross*."

This vessel was the Governor's surveying ship, which used to pay visits periodically to all the islands east and west of Torres Strait. Having ended the inspection, she would return after a month with a report to the Governor.

Thus the time worked round for the *Albatross* to come steaming back. Anchor was dropped, crew went ashore for the night after their four weeks' cruising, leaving on board an officer plus engineer, with the boat's painter made fast to the ship's stern. Price sat gloomily on deck. One month's liberty still denied him.

But when the sun went down, and the sounds of revelry rose from the forbidden shore, this enforced captivity proved irksome. Gazing across the water in the direction of old haunts, he began to ponder the glorious times enjoyed by his pals and all the fun he himself was missing. Meditation enlivened imagination, and ultimately stirred up his will. Let the consequences be what they might, Price could not remain apart from such jollification: he must be there among the boys.

Unobserved, he stealthily dropped over the stern into the waiting boat, shoved off, rowed ashore, and gained the bar. Then the wild night commenced, the tempo quickened, and everything seemed to happen at once. The company of old friends cheered him greatly after these dull weeks of sober respectability, drinks were being accepted readily enough, and ere time could lag Price had worked up to his usual standard. Suddenly he began smashing up everything, and making a clearance in the grand manner. Triumphant over captivity and such items as glass windows, he stood there still wearing his prison clothes defying the whole world.

But now strode in the policeman doing night duty. He looked in astonishment, not so much that Price was again uproariously drunk, but that the fellow should be there in jail garb. Law, however, prevailed over disorderliness; firm hands seized the liberty-seeker, who was led back to the 'Boarding House' where he best belonged. Next morning the Governor had another surprise when this hopeless offender appeared before him, and now to the month's imprisonment which yet needed completion there was added further sentence.

But the incorrigible Price had no regrets. He had

enjoyed himself thoroughly, and was willing to shoulder any penalty.

Next time that we went pearling it was in a different direction, where a fresh patch of shell had been discovered; and we made a fairly good haul, though it might have been wiser to leave the area untouched for another three years. Lacking maturity, the average weight of shell was only about 5 lb.; and because the sea-bed happened to be good, with not more than 10 fathoms of water, sandy bottom, no coral dangers and very little tide, the fleet forsook Wappa and Warrior Reefs for this region, with the result that it soon became overworked.

When the advent of spring tides enabled us to visit the mainland around Cape York, we used to come in contact with groups of Australia's aborigines. These Queensland blacks seemed to me the lowest type of human being; unclean, ugly, so lazy that they would not build themselves any shelter, preferring the roughest sort of existence. Their food comprised speared fish, wild pigs, but also lizards, snakes and other reptiles. Frequently, on landing, we gave them a little rice and flour together with some tobacco. Sometimes we spent hours in their company, and with amazing frankness they often informed me that, being white, I should make very good 'ki-ki'—which is to say, food!

As I always carried either a revolver or tomahawk, they would have been compelled to fight pretty desperately first. I noticed that each aboriginal seemed to have but one possession—a blanket. On examination I further observed, in the centre, a crest with the words: 'A Gift From Queen Victoria To Her Queensland Subjects.' Once a year this present was bestowed, and every native felt favourably disposed to the Great White Queen. As a dying race, these people will soon be extinct. Civilization, aircraft, and wireless have all hastened the transformation that Australia was destined to receive so rapidly.

One night, about 8 p.m., I was lying stretched out on

the lugger's deck. We had brought up till dawn behind a reef, and my mind set to wondering about old England. How was the homeland faring? What were people now doing? Suddenly I felt a sharp pain. Something had stung or bitten my hand between thumb-joint and first finger; but whatever the creature might have been, I immediately shook it off. Being pitch-dark, I could see nothing, yet was conscious that blood oozed from two places close together.

I accordingly summoned the native crew's aid, and forthwith they understood. Pricking the place to produce more blood, they started sucking out the poison, then extracted from the fire-box a piece of red-hot charcoal which they laid on the wounds; lastly adding a bit of tobacco-leaf as covering. A light was obtained, diligent search made about the deck, and after a few minutes it became obvious that my enemy must be a scorpion. His presence on board connected with our visit to the mainland, where we had cut down a mangrove-tree and split it up to make firewood for our cooking. In that timber had we brought off the pest, and true to custom he remained secreted till emerging after dark looking for prey.

Some of these species are six inches long, their bite being notoriously painful and troublesome. With me the pain became intense, hand and arm gradually swelling to a great size, working up to the shoulder and down to the breast, till I imagined the worst kinds of sequels. Presently the heart would be reached, and that would be the end. Here, a hundred miles from any medical assistance, suffering the greatest agony that drove me almost mad, I could do nothing save pacing the deck all night.

Not till daylight did the suffering ease and the swelling begin to subside, but twenty-four hours must pass ere I felt normal once more. Never do I expect to forget that sting, or the gratitude towards natives who, by their crude and efficacious efforts, saved my life.

At Thursday Island active preparations were now being made for welcoming the Australian Auxiliary Squadron, which had been built in England and would call on their way to Sydney. From the latter, to meet them, steamed north the flagship *Orlando*. To celebrate the unusual event of *Rangarooma*, *Katoomba*, *Boomerang* with two other new cruisers reaching this outpost of Empire, festivities were planned on a large scale, and I remember a big fair that lasted two days. Everything passed off happily, everybody looked back on that visit with genuine pleasure—all, with the exception of Price, the lover of fights and turbulence. Just before the squadron departed, he was mixed up in an argument with an English blue-jacket, and words led to violence. To-day Price met his Waterloo and Trafalgar combined. Quick and decisive came the finale when the beefy bluejacket laid him out after a few seconds, leaving Price unable to get up and watch the ships steaming away.

For a long, long, period no one at the island ceased to talk of this incident. Price himself often would refer to it.

"The shortest fight I ever had. Only a couple of blows. And there was me lying on the ground," he freely admitted.

Such events between pearling cruises introduced a certain variety, and now we sailed to the neighbourhood of Albany Island and Mount Adolphus; the former lying between the latter and the mainland, thus creating two passages known as the Outer and Inner. If the deep water and strong tides made pumping harder work, the trip was more interesting for us; though for the diver, compelled to grope about in 15 to 18 fathoms, too many dangers threatened. A hundred feet cannot be lightly dismissed, the pressure is considerable, and the man could endure it only a short time: yet on each occasion he succeeded in filling his bag fairly full.

On the mainland facing Albany Island, situated up a hill, stood a small house or bungalow where for years lived a Scotsman named Jardine who was the first to explore the

whole of Cape York peninsula. Married to a Samoan
wife, by whom he had two boys and a girl, his existence
was none other than lonely; for, during most of the year,
these children remained away at school in southern
Queensland. Very good-looking they were, despite being
half-caste, nor did they lack a keen adventurous spirit
which during their visits at home inspired a desire to take
long horseback rides miles into the primitive bush.
Risky? Had they fallen into the hands of aborigines,
death would have followed swiftly in all probability.
These blacks simply could not be trusted, many a white
family having been wiped out between sunset and dawn.

Jardine was owner of pearl-luggers, as of *bêche-de-
mer* boats too. Now the *bêche-de-mer* is a sea slug, in
size measuring from six inches to a couple of feet long;
being in shape akin to a cucumber or large sausage. It
abounds off north Australia and the East Indies. Collected, boiled, split open, then dried in the sun, this sort
of snail is in great demand among French and Chinese,
who regard it as a great delicacy.

When setting out, the boats carry chiefly native women,
who at low water search among the reefs, but there was
an occasion when more than sea slugs were found.
Whilst wading over a reef the women came upon several
bags, and inside the bags were Spanish dollars, said to
have come out of a sixteenth-century Spanish galleon
wrecked hereabouts. The Australian Government claimed
25 per cent of this treasure, Jardine receiving the rest.
Soon many of these coins reached Thursday Island, where
the Chinese jeweller earned a nice sum turning them into
brooches. This part of the continent is supposed to have
been discovered not till the first half of the seventeenth
century, by the Dutch, but I leave others to discuss the
exact date when Spaniards sailed hither.

Like so many of the early settlers, Jardine was the
central figure in all sorts of odd stories. It used to be
said that, having so frequently been the target of the
aborigines' spears, he took to wearing beneath his

clothing a fine chain-mesh. In the end, these blacks were too much for him, set fire to the bungalow one night, and so destroyed the whole family.

Some localities seem destined for tragedy, and it was in the Outer Passage, between Albany Island and Mount Adolphus, that the S.S. *Quetta* many years ago suffered disaster. This liner, homeward bound from Brisbane to London, was in mid-channel steaming at full speed when without warning an awful thud shook the ship. She had struck an uncharted pinnacle. The *Quetta*, badly holed, soon foundered and only four beings ever lived to tell the tale. Two were young ladies, who managed to remain on some wreckage for several hours, but eventually reached Albany Island. The third was a coloured passenger who hauled on to the raft a baby girl floating on the sea. The infant was brought to Thursday Island, where a Captain and Mrs. Brown, who kept a store, took care of the little survivor.

Now, the parents had perished; in fact nothing else than floating wreckage drifting through the channels ever was seen. Captain Brown (himself a pilot for the Torres Strait) and his wife, having no children of their own, adopted the girl who grew up as 'Quetta' Brown until some years later she was married to an Australian banker.

Yes, that part of the world, with all its uncertainties and excitements, was full of fascination, and after a while a man felt himself part of the untamed country. In the water were sharks, alligators, stone-fish, stingaree, turtle: on land existed snakes, scorpions, wild boars, kangaroo. Whether out for a swim or a walk, always there would be plenty of nature's lower life to keep the mind alert. I once heard the story of a white man who thought he would have a bathe.

"Any sharks about here?" he inquired.

The native shrugged his shoulders and answered: "No, sah."

So into the water dived the white man, had a good swim for half an hour, and then landed.

"Why," he further demanded, "is it that no sharks ever come this way?"

The native smiled.

"Too many alligators, sah."

I call to mind a certain day when we had anchored within a hundred yards of the beach. Our dinghy was ashore with the boys, who had gone to cut down wood and obtain drinking-water. After shouting, and failing to make them hear, I finally dived overboard, leaving a native boy on deck in charge of the lugger. I was swimming towards the shore, and had reached half-way across, when he began calling, but I ignored it and continued. Half an hour later, on my return, he explained that a large shark followed all the way behind me, keeping about ten yards off. I was wearing a pair of dark, drill trousers, which may have so puzzled the shark as to let me alone.

On another occasion I was with others in a lagoon, walking with the water up to my waist, holding my spear well above the head, prepared to spear a fish that I was slowly following. Something touched the back of my left leg. A shark all right, which the ebb tide had relinquished. Immediately I turned, drove my spear into him, and the last impression was of the voracious brute disappearing at terrific speed, the spear's shaft cutting through the water like a modern submarine's periscope.

It was difficult to convince some people to believe that which they couldn't see, but a certain Dutchman had to learn a lesson. This proprietor of a pearl-lugger did not employ diving dress or pump. Relying on the simpler method, he hired a dozen natives to leap into 4 or 5 fathoms alongside the reef and remain down as long as their breath permitted. A hard bargain-driving master, this Netherlander, who insisted on making substantial profits, and if any shell existed below he made sure his men brought it up.

Then one day these experts returned to the surface with remarkable celerity and fear. An alligator was asleep, lying on the bottom. This the Dutchman refused to credit, thinking it to be just a wheeze for idling on board; so he would speedily show them. Throwing off his wide-awake hat, removing his shoes, he took a deep dive down and down, investigated, then floated up to the top. He had seen for himself that ugly somnolent alligator, so now the anchor was hove in, and sail hoisted to resume proceedings several miles away.

In like manner I, also, was to move on.

CHAPTER V

WE had got back to Thursday Island at the end of a trip; all shell had been cleaned, packed, and landed. I came ashore, and it was whilst looking up some friends that I met a stranger.

He was a Norwegian, Master of a small barque that lay just now about 150 miles off at Raine Island loading guano for the United Kingdom. During the voyage out, unfortunately, he lost a couple of his men overboard: one an A.B., and the other an Ordinary Seaman. He inquired if I would accept the latter billet.

The prospects of seeing England again made a powerful appeal, and I began to bargain with him. I asked £3 a month, but he dwelt on the fact that his Second Mate was receiving only £2 10s., so that I as an Ordinary Seaman would get 10s. a month more. Nevertheless, I knew that since no one else around here could be obtained, there was sound justification for my demand. He finally concurred, provided that I should prove capable of steering, but I pressed for an agreement to that effect.

This he appeared reluctant to concede, because of the expense. When he expressed himself as short of money, I told him that whatever the cost I would bear the charges, being then flush with cash. The remark somewhat opened his eyes. Doubtless he had looked upon me as a thriftless South Seas beachcomber, so he then asked what had I been doing.

"For the last twelve months, pearl-fishing."

That roused his inquisitiveness. He wanted to know if there was much profit to be made, and how much I had acquired.

"My wealth," said I, "amounts to £50 or £60,

four large pearls, four small pearls, and one big blister."

"But what do you intend to do with the money?"

"Take it with me."

He then made a proposition. Could I lend him that amount to buy stores for the homeward voyage? If so, he would give me a receipt now, and on arrival in the United Kingdom would hand back the cash.

Under the impression that I was dealing with an honest man, I handed over my savings, and we then made for the office of Mr. Bowden, the Agent. An agreement was drawn up, Mr. Bowden keeping one copy, the Captain another, and myself the third. Preparations were then made for leaving the next day, for a steamer was due to pass through Torres Strait, who would drop us off Hannibal Island, 82 miles from Thursday Island. The barque's lifeboat would then pick us up, and convey us the remaining 70 miles to Raine Island.

So the last morning dawned, hurried calls were made bidding farewell to all those who had befriended me during my year's sojourn. To Mrs. McNulty and the Bowden brothers I owed many thanks for their kindness. These months had been varied, sometimes a bit wild, sometimes otherwise; but the great hospitality from almost everyone had been the principal factor which caused me to look back on those pearl-fishing days with happiest memories. And now, when I boarded the steamer in company of the old Norwegian skipper, together with freshly purchased stores, I began looking forward to new experiences.

We cast off, steamed away, and another milestone in my life's journey was passed. Next day off a headland we transferred ourselves to the barque's boat which had been waiting about for a couple of days, and set sail to reach our vessel. A tedious trip! Owing to light winds and calms, we spent 48 hours covering those 72 miles, but there she was; lying to her anchor off Raine Island. All which mattered was that I was bound home!

Well, she looked old, this wooden vessel. Of 350 registered tons, she carried eleven hands all told, but there were nearly as many nationalities. Let us count them up. Captain, a Norwegian. Mate, a Swede. Second Mate, a Dane. Cook and Steward, a Russian Finn. Carpenter, a German. The rest comprised Portuguese, German, Dane, Norwegian, and myself the Englishman. Frankly, I had not been too impressed on finding myself in the boat, whose four men were unable to speak a word of English; so the only conversation was with the Captain.

Within twenty-four hours of joining the barque, however, I had taken full measure of my new shipmates, and was convinced that this combination would pull well together. I was going to learn a great deal about other nations through association with these sailormen. Presently the Captain decided to warp the barque close to the loading jetty, ready for taking cargo in bulk. The crew had to do the loading, and this meant considerable amount of labour, for 500 tons must needs be stowed.

Raine Island, low and sandy, had during generations been the home of sea-birds; and, as everyone knows, guano simply consists of the excreta from fish-eating fowl. Its value as manure for general fertilization is high, though nowadays the best supplies are practically exhausted. All over this island guano existed in layers, going down several feet. But here, too, green turtles came to deposit their eggs. These reptiles existed in large numbers, weighing anything up to quarter of a ton, and each would leave from 75 to 120 eggs in a hole several feet deep, which had been first dug by the turtle and then filled up again.

Thus, during a stay of nearly a month, our diet chiefly consisted of turtle flesh and eggs, together with fish caught at the reefs. The men in charge here came from southern Australia, with only an occasional sailing ship to relieve the dullness. Most to be pitied was the white wife of a Manager. She passed away, and her body lies buried on this solitary abode.

D

At the southern end of the island was a stone tower, whither I used to wander when off duty. Standing about 60 feet high, with a doorway or entrance, its carved inscription on a slab reads: 'This Tower or Beacon was built by convicts brought here from Botany Bay by H.M.S. *Royalist*.' Each piece had been marked and put together again, and navigators owe undying gratitude to those—often trivially convicted—unfortunates whose edifice stands as guiding mark for ships making approach towards the treacherous Great Barrier Reef.

Our barque was now ready for sea, but the supply of drinking-water had been quite a problem. Inasmuch as it had to be obtained from a small condenser ashore, and the coal for this must be fetched expensively from south Australia by schooners, this simple fluid actually cost more to produce out here than beer in London.

We set sail with the intention of reaching England via Cape Horn on a 13,000 miles voyage. Steering a southerly course, we hoped to pass round the south of New Zealand, and then pick up the westerly winds in those latitudes known as the 'roaring forties.' Favoured by moderately fine weather, we reached New Zealand's north-west side when heavy westerly gales and high seas set in.

Wallowing along, riding victoriously over immense seas, the little vessel was doing well, but because of shifting winds we had to modify our plans by sailing through Cook Strait, which separates North from South New Zealand. In the heavy weather we had the bad luck to lose our mizzen-mast, which was serious enough, yet with fore- and main-mast still standing, strong following winds and seas, she required little sail to keep reeling off her steady 10 or 12 knots.

This sea-area between New Zealand and the Horn possesses an unenviable reputation, and it certainly treated us with scant courtesy; for now we lost our main-mast from two-thirds up the lower-mast, so we had to make a rough jury-mast. Instead of rounding Cape Horn as a barque, we looked more like a wreck, and she was leaking like a basket. Being Norwegian, she carried a windmill pump, and that kept her afloat. Moreover, the wind shifted to south, which helped us considerably when once in the Atlantic.

Yet the poor old ship was in a more or less hopeless condition, food began to run short and the Captain would have gone into the Falklands for replenishment. Calling the crew, he finally suggested that we take advantage of the fair winds, and carry on to some South American port further north. With these we all agreed. Two British sailing ships sighted us bound in our direction, and bore towards us. Soon they began signalling: 'Where are you from?' 'Where are you bound?' 'What is your name?'

Our Captain had no wish to answer their inquiries, well knowing that both would reach the United Kingdom before us and exaggerated reports would be spread concerning the barque's condition. When, at length, our questioners gave up the task, one ship ran up signal to the other asking: 'Can you see the name of wreck?' Then both dipped their ensigns, and sailed onward, much to the amusement of everybody aboard our vessel, from Captain downwards.

Southerly gales continued for days to our great convenience, but we kept well over towards the South American coast so that should the worst happen and the ship founder, we should not have far to pull in our lifeboats. The food difficulty, however, developed seriously. During the past month we had been living almost exclusively on biscuits and beans, other stores having been consumed. The only meat which remained was 'Dennis,' the ship's pig, but to kill him was out of the question. He had been a good shipmate, his habits were excellent, and his closed-in sty was the only warm place aboard now that coals were nearly finished. It was to 'Dennis' that we looked for dry clothes, since on him we laid our saturated garments as we went down below off watch. Even if they never properly got rid of the salty dampness, they would at least be nice and warm before going on deck to spend another four hours.

The Captain's object was to reach some port on the coast not fever-stricken, whilst using every help of the winds. Some little cherub must certainly have been sitting up aloft watching over us, for the southerly gales persisted happily till we picked up the South-east Trades in Lat. 25 degrees south, and now the balmy weather was ours. If appetites were not quite so keen as during the cold regions, we still needed food. Such ports as Rio, Santos, Bahia, had all to be avoided. At that time they were known as 'The White Man's Graves.' Dozens of British sailing ships lay therein without a soul on board, all having passed to the Great Beyond.

Many were the stories told of the conditions reigning in those yellow-fever ports, but let one yarn suffice. A certain sailor, stricken down with this illness, had been landed from his ship and brought to the shore hospital where for many days he lay precariously. Eventually he passed the delirious stage, became conscious of his surroundings, yet one thing annoyed him intensely. Except for brief intervals, a continual thump-thump-thump kept going on outside the door of that small ward where he was confined. He complained to the nurse, but she provided no satisfaction and took care to see that the door was always kept closed.

Now one day the nurse unexpectedly had been called away, and the door accidentally left open. Feeling a little stronger, the sailor was able to turn in his bed and stretch forth in eagerness to ascertain what was going on outside. You can imagine the effect when his curiosity was satisfied. There moved the figure of a big buck negro stepping down the stairs from the ward above. In each hand he held the foot of a sailor who had just died, and the thumping was caused as the deceased's head slid from one wooden step to the other. It was considered the simplest method of transferring to the mortuary. In our enlightened times these ports are as healthy as anywhere else. Scientists have banished tropical disease from their midst, modern sanitation and fine new buildings have done the rest. Passengers even go 'rolling down to Rio' on pleasure cruises.

We aboard the hungry barque now hoped to call in at Pernambuco, but the wind decided the matter. Those fine breezes, which had brought us north so wonderfully, vanished shortly before we sighted Cape Frio. The latter lies about a hundred miles beyond Rio de Janeiro in Lat. 22, 40 south of the Equator. Light winds and calms so hindered our progress that, after all, into Bahia roadstead we made. Having anchored, the Captain proceeded ashore, ordered the necessary provisions, and wired his owners. If we had some difficulty to get here, with plenty of 'nip and tuck,' as the sailor calls chasing gentle airs and making the best of it, our stay was to be limited.

Biscuits we especially needed, but they were not in stock, and would have to be made. Since that meant waiting three days, there was no alternative and we must stay so long. Meanwhile sufficient salt beef came aboard, yet the quality would have received criticism from any landsman: inasmuch as it had been dried in the sun, its texture seemed more akin to that of a leathery hide. Such was our longing for food, we could have eaten anything, and complaints just vanished. We had time, too, for obtaining a few luxuries to vary the sameness of ship life. All of us subscribed to buy a big accordion, out of which our German messmate was able to produce topical tunes. Then, the three days now terminating, we set sail with a fair wind, and a general feeling of thankfulness that no one had left his bones to rot in Bahia.

The voyage, which had begun so eventfully, gradually eased up to pleasant, peaceful progress, so that at long last the coast of Cornwall loomed up and into Falmouth's spacious roadstead we safely glided. We had been 197 days out from Raine Island. Seven months! A large slice out of a youngster's year. Yet none of us was really the worse for this experience, and all of us had learnt a lot.

"If you should wish to become a sailor, go to sea in a sailing ship."

Well, I had now sailed across the world twice.

The River Fal, with its green slopes and rural beauty, was a great change after tropical scenery and coral reefs. For generations this Cornish anchorage vied with Queenstown and Sydney as the place where full-rigged ships or barques could always be seen waiting for orders. Now such a sight is comparatively rare, although even just before the Great War it was not unusual for a dozen such vessels to be counted landward of St. Anthony Lighthouse. German ocean raiders, German submarines, and German mines were chiefly responsible for bringing the sailing ship era to a close.

After a few days our Captain received orders that our vessel should proceed in tow for the Thames, and the final act took place in London Docks. The crew were paid off, the old Norwegian Captain handed me the cash which I had lent him at Thursday Island, but to this sum he added a small present. Yes: he was honest, and one of the whitest men who ever sailed the seas.

But along came the artful Boarding Masters, who in those harsh days used to do a flourishing business at the expense of simple sailormen. On the arrival of a vessel from over seas cunning fellows would come down to the quayside, decked in their best, smoking a fat cigar, plenty of money in their pockets ready to use as a bait for the strange seaman in a strange port. Happily our crew in the barque were too wide-awake for these guiles, declined to be gulled, and departed on their several ways.

For myself, having been away from England all this while, I made tracks towards home. Mother being long since passed away, I was greeted by my two sisters.

"Fancy seeing you! We thought you'd been drowned."

Perhaps it was a natural enough assumption. Two and a half years! I had never written once. But I remained for a couple of months, during which all dangers of the ocean might have been as nothing compared with the perils which now awaited me ashore. I had succeeded in winning that accordion from Bahia, but this I now exchanged with an old schoolmaster for a bicycle—one of those very ancient affairs with an enormous wheel at the front and a tiny one behind. Together with a chum (also home from the sea) I used to spend most of the time on this tall velocipede trying to break my young neck, and nearly succeeding. That friend of youthful days is now a London Trinity House pilot, and we never meet without talking of those thrilling escapades.

CHAPTER VI

MY next ship was the full-rigged four-master *Liverpool*. Built in the year 1890 of iron, with steel beams, she measured 333 feet long with 47¾ feet beam. This magnificent creature of no less than 3333 registered tons enjoyed the reputation of being the largest British sailing ship of the time, although the celebrated French five-master built on the Clyde in the same year for a Bordeaux firm, and named *La France*, became still more notable because of her 3784 tons, 344 feet in length by 49 feet wide.

To serve in the *Liverpool* meant a privilege no less than a rare opportunity for acquiring further knowledge. Moreover she happened to be a new ship. As the reader will observe from the accompanying illustration, she was a good-looker and her sail-spread demanded many thousands of square yards; for handling which no fewer than twenty-seven of us were carried.

When I joined her, she lay loading salt in the port whose name she bore, and our destination was India. It used to be said in those days that most British ships were for 'Hunger and Ease.' This packet, however, deserved the title 'Hunger and Work.' We set out from the Mersey under tow of a tug which was cast off in the Irish Sea, but on the same tide another interesting vessel also departed from Liverpool. This was the *Shenandoah*, America's biggest sailing ship, so you may guess that the present occasion would be regarded as exceptional.

Many had been the arguments on both sides of the Atlantic as to which of the two possessed the greater speed: to-day there would be a chance of settling the discussion for all time. Both were in splendid trim, a fine fresh wind blew from the north, and ere long the rivals had set every inch of canvas. A magnificent sight never to be witnessed again! Hands were busy trimming yards constantly, officers and men sought to get the very utmost out of their respective vessel, but now the *Liverpool* began to show a definite superiority. By nightfall the *Shenandoah* was hull down astern. During twelve hours the lead increased to as much as 10 miles, and by daylight the American had dipped out of sight. Somehow she failed to prove herself as fast as certain critics foretold.

We sped on our voyage, and settled down to routine which can be summed up as strenuous rather than placid, brutal in many respects, but such was the established method for Captain and Mates in their handling of men. Survival of the fittest! Only a strong individual could endure the life, and a weakling soon went under; but everyone growled, cursed, and sometimes rebelled, whilst still getting on with the hard job.

There are few spots more fruitful of rumours than aboard a ship, and concerning the *Liverpool* a persistent yarn was told: there had been both a murder and suicide during her maiden voyage out to Australia. Nothing could check that story, she became a haunted ship wherever the wind brought her; and whenever sailors met ashore or afloat the four-master *Liverpool* could never shake off that reputation. Consequently many a seaman refused to sign on, and very great difficulty had to be undergone before obtaining a crew.

Captain Whiting, already past his seventieth birthday, was one of the toughest old sea-dogs who ever trod a deck; and his officers had to be of that same calibre. The former's principle was to 'plug' the crew from the moment they left port, as he reckoned that thereby a better means for exercising authority could be contrived. Having come aboard after a last 'jag' ashore, more drunk than sober, fuddled and dull, they would be given a thorough good hammering at the very first, with something to tame them for the weeks to follow. In other words, raw discipline was to begin without an hour's delay.

Now during most voyages everything used to work out according to plan, but on this trip the 'Old Man,' with his Mates, were destined for a big surprise. The universal bullying tactics simply wouldn't do: by an amazing coincidence Captain Whiting had chosen a crew of teetotallers, and not one of them was going to stand this sort of treatment. Thus, within a remarkably short time, they brought the Mates along to the Skipper 'like herrings on a plate.' The Captain's face was a picture! No more bullying on that voyage. The men had got to windward of him.

Well, they soon realized their strength, and gradually tried to work their way still higher.

Even during the 'nineties the scale of food remained very miserable, wherefore Jack never minded what risks he took to supplement his fare. A hungry man is not susceptible to conscience, and at sea the temptation under the particular circumstances was not easily resisted. Aboard the *Liverpool* the men schemed to raid the cabin stores in the lazarette at the after part of the vessel fronting the wheelhouse-door. That locality, be it noted, was where the supposed murder had occurred. Also this after-deck was always deserted by night, for in such a great four-master the steering was done not on the poop, but amidships.

Dark and dreary, thoroughly lonely, the stillness broken at times by the flapping of a sail, here in the stern existed the very environment for some mysterious deed; some blood-curdling drama of the high seas. It was during one of these dim interludes that the men inaugurated a series of visits, well-conceived and cleverly executed. The ghost was said to come out of the wheelhouse at different times of the dark hours; parade up and down in front, then finally return inside. Therefore the first intention of the raiders' visits was less to steal stores than to become hardened against the apparition; and by a series of nocturnal adventures the crew were training themselves towards more perfect achievement.

But at length truth revealed itself: stores were missing. Captain and Mates had learned it undoubtedly. Next night the First Mate, after being on watch from 8 p.m. till midnight, went below for his four hours, having been relieved by the Third Mate. Not feeling too well, and hating the noise made by the steering-wheel's chains passing through the sheaves above his cabin, the First Mate resolved to seek his rest in the after wheelhouse right at the stern. Here, then, he remained till 2 a.m. clad in his pyjamas, dozing quietly within the limits of an old cane-chair.

Four bells! Two o'clock!

He heard them struck, leapt to his feet. Restless, he would now wander back to his cabin. Four bells! This also was the hour for heaving the log and finding the ship's speed.

It may be explained for the benefit of the modern generation that the old-fashioned apparatus consisted of four items: log-ship, line, reel, and sand-glass. The first-mentioned was a flat triangular board, weighted so as to float vertically. At two corners were holes, and the log-line was fastened to one of these, but in the other was a peg connected to the line by a span. The procedure for ascertaining the ship's speed was to drop overboard the log-ship and allow the line to run out from the reel simultaneously with the sand-glass being capsized. Now since the log-line was marked off by knots at intervals of 47¼ feet, which bore the same proportion to a nautical mile as the 28 seconds of the sand-glass did to 60 minutes, it followed that the vessel's rate was the equivalent of so many knots or so many feet being accomplished within the time. In actual practice the first 10 fathoms were mere 'stray line' to enable the log-line to get clear of the ship's wake.

Picture, then, aboard this barque the Third Mate and his four men coming aft; log-reel and sand-glass being brought from the fore part of the wheelhouse. Keeping together, the little crowd were ascending to their position in the extreme stern, when all of a sudden from the wheelhouse stepped a mysterious white figure.

That confounded ghost!

Five pairs of hands attacked him with determination. The sand-glass was smashed to pieces on his head, the log-reel struck him such a violent blow in the chest as to send him tumbling back into the wheelhouse. Next, thoroughly terrified by this apparition, both Third Mate and his men fled for their lives, making the night hideous with their cries. A fresh courage fetched them back to the scene, after arming themselves with belaying-pins and obtaining lamps. Nothing to be found! The ghost had vanished for the present, and doubtless would come again with as little warning as before. Was the ship haunted? Five serious, honest men could answer that question from personal experience.

Next morning a thoroughly anxious crew came to ask of the Captain what steps should be taken; but the 'Old Man' had no suggestion. The First Mate in the meanwhile had made him privy of the whole affair. Forgetting entirely about the alleged spectre, this officer in his white pyjamas had ventured forth to receive a shower of blows. True, he recovered himself and followed for'ard along the deck his assaulters without their seeing him; and, whilst they were busying themselves with belaying-pins, he quickly slipped inside his cabin amidships. But the incident taught him a lesson, and the truth he was compelled to hide from all save the Skipper.

"Yes," commented the last-mentioned with dry sarcasm, "that's all right about the explanation, but what annoys me so much is the ghost didn't make his appearance before the stores were stolen."

Ship-life settled down once more and the voyage could scarcely have been more satisfactory for, after rounding Cape Hope and standing across the Indian Ocean, we arrived off the River Hooghly 84 days out from the

CAPTAIN H. G. KENDALL, R.D., R.N.R.

THE *LIVERPOOL*

Of 3333 tons (reg.), this four-master was the largest sailing-ship in the world. I served three years in her. Fastest passage Liverpool to Calcutta via Cape of Good Hope, 84 days.

THE *MASHONA*

Lying off San Francisco in 1896 when I was Second Mate in her.

Mersey. We were boarded by the pilot, bringing with him a retinue of coloured servants and a surprising amount of clothing: but that was an Indian characteristic always. The Bengal Pilot Service is the finest in all the world, the best paid, with its own dignified traditions; but these experts earn every penny of their pay in waters notoriously dangerous.

A tug brought us up to Calcutta, where we moored to buoys off Eden Gardens, and six long months lay ahead of us discharging our salt cargo, waiting for the jute season. A totally different life from seafaring, it gave me opportunity at the end of a day's work to wander ashore and become acquainted with India, to study its people, to learn something about its strange fascination. Dozens of the world's crack sailing ships, in tiers of four and five deep, all the way from Eden Gardens to Kiddapore Dock and on to Garden Reach, would impress the beholder every day of the week. A sincere and overwhelming pride of ship made men and boys convinced that their own vessel surpassed, for good looks no less than speed, all rivals.

There might be as many as four, and even eight, young apprentices aboard each. Leading citizens of Calcutta endeavoured to show interest and prevent these evening strolls from developing into a display of youthful exuberance, but such items as sacred concerts were not likely to attract—until some organizer included coffee and cakes. Then the boys rolled up in numbers.

But Father Hopkins, himself the son of a Rangoon pilot, started the Order of St. Paul with special consideration for sailor people, and the Priory at Garden Reach was open to all of us. No seafarer ever need go hungry. Here was a real friend to mariners of any age or rating. But a man named Ben Lyness, known as 'Holy Joe,' we regarded in the nature of an opposition to Father Hopkins' efforts. Poor old Ben! Every Thursday he used to provide a concert with plenty of buns and tea, though his great difficulty was in obtaining enough talent to complete the programme. Shortly after my arrival I was taken along by an apprentice named Lacey from a ship called the *Indore*, being introduced as 'Mr. Moriarty.'

"And which part of Ireland might ye come from?" was the first question.

"Dublin," I invented.

"Put it there," Ben shoved out his hand. "I come from Belfast. Now you'll sing at the concert to-morrow night?"

"With pleasure," assent had been compelled.

But you can imagine my feelings on arriving, and being handed a programme. It was Lacey who had dared to set down: 'A Chinese song and dance by Mr. Moriarty.' However, something had to be done, so on reaching the platform I gave them a sentimental ditty with a twist to parody it in the last line; which so sharpened the wits of boisterous apprentices that about fifty buns came pelting from across the room.

It was because of the hard existence and indifferent food afloat that we youngsters were usually up to some pranks on coming ashore. Most of the ships carried pets —often enough only dogs, but not always. Lacey and I, being without such an animal, resolved to see what we could pick up. To buy one was out of the question, as neither of us ever had any money; and to coax five rupees out of the Skipper would be akin to pulling out the 'Old Man's' back teeth.

Someone living ashore would have to lose a dog!

We made our plans, selected Kiddapore native quarters for our hunting ground, and after keeping a sharp look-out during an hour or so we spotted a small white animal, perhaps a month old, running in and out of a coolie's dwelling. It was one of those windless evenings and very hot, the quiet broken only by the jabbering of natives inside and the singing of crickets without. Placing ourselves in a suitable position, we waited till the pup came out again, grabbed him, and thrust the little fellow out of sight within my double-breasted white jacket.

Walking quietly away, Lacey and I feigned unconcern, but in a short time we realized that retreat was going to be difficult if not impossible. A native had been witness of our theft and gave the alarm. Before we knew much else, dozens of Indians armed with stones and bamboos came after us. We hastened our pace, we sprinted: so did they. We made in the direction of Hastings Bridge and Princeps Ghat, where Lacey's ship was lying: but the mob kept up a close chase. It was anybody's victory until at the very end we succeeded in reaching our sampan before being captured. Quickly pushing off into the stream, assisted by our old native boatman (who always used to enjoy our escapades), we got alongside the ship, went aboard, and made for the *Indore's* half-deck where her apprentices lived. Safe now, we could afford to breathe easily and admire our prize. I opened my coat, took out the 'pup,' held him up to the lamplight . . . only to discover after all it wasn't a dog. The creature was a small white goat!

In those days the Master of a sailing ship was monarch of all that he surveyed: even his owners regarded him with an awesome respect. Good freights had to be obtained, fast passages depended on smart working of tacks and sheets; which, in turn, meant that an able captain could shorten voyages to a minimum by driving his men. On arrival home, the ship's commander would be welcomed by the owners, congratulated on having made a fine trip; for, in contradistinction to the mechanically-propelled vessel, speed to no small extent was associated with the Master's personality. Uniform was hardly ever worn by the men, but photographs taken in the 'nineties show that at least in port it was put on by officers. When going ashore to transact ship's business, the 'Old Man' would dress himself up in square-shaped, hard, top hat, claw-hammer coat, plus collar and tie these two last-mentioned being known in sailor parlance as his 'gaff topsail.' Whilst in some examples it was 'different ships, different customs,' yet at sea the officers generally adopted a wide-awake hat and had their shirt sleeves rolled up. If you looked a real 'hard case,' both owners and captain were pleased. Not smart appearance, but toughness and driving ability, the skill to get the last ounce of work out of a crew, gained the most approbation.

One day Admiral Lord Charles Beresford during a visit to India arrived at Calcutta, and the merchant-ship captains decided to entertain him at dinner. Among these hosts happened to be a certain Captain Beresford, Master of a sailing vessel.

The latter went up to the Admiral and said:

"As you spell your name in the same way that I spell mine, quite likely we might be related."

The Admiral looked him up and looked him down.

"Not at all improbable," answered the Marquis of Waterford's son. "I shouldn't be a bit surprised. For my father was a fair old devil."

CHAPTER VII

WHEN the *Liverpool* had reached Calcutta, all able seamen were paid off after sails were unbent, stowed away, and all running gear taken down. Thus only the officers and apprentices remained for carrying on the work. Actually we youngsters were kept pretty busy cleaning, scaling, painting both holds and hull, yards and masts. Frankly, what with the intense heat and very little food, toiling away from 6 a.m. till 6 p.m., it was pure unconditioned hell. Yet, I doubt if any of us belonging to that hard school look back with regret. Such strenuous training gave each lad the chance of doing a man's work, and of learning a sailor's profession in all its branches.

The jute season now was at hand, and loading commenced, but we took care to protect all iron-work, such as stanchions, with sacking or burlap. Bales of jute were screwed down tight in order that they might occupy the smallest space; and you will realize how valuable every inch must be when I assure you that *Liverpool* actually stowed away no fewer than 28,015 bales before putting on the hatches. That last week was chiefly spent as to the evenings bidding farewell to apprentices in the other ships. All would soon start off homeward bound, like ourselves, and some we should meet again in the United Kingdom, though many we should never see after Calcutta.

For one of the inevitable tragedies was the disappearance of these beautiful vessels either in the South Indian Ocean during Mauritius hurricanes, or whilst rounding the Cape of Good Hope; and many a fine lot of young fellows vanished with them.

Dropping down to Garden Reach, taken in tow by the

tug *Retriever*, the *Liverpool* gained Sand Heads, set all sail, and departed across the Bay of Bengal. Soon the Trade Winds were met and the ship was flying across the Equator. In good time we rounded the Cape of Good Hope and made up towards the Island of St. Helena. Napoleon's place of exile detained us barely long enough to purchase a few sacks of potatoes, then once again we squared our yards to the South East Trades, and for still another occasion the Equator was traversed. The Atlantic region of north-easters followed till we got hold of the westerlies, but this time we were not bound up the English Channel. Our orders were to make for Dundee, so we proceeded by the north of Scotland, Pentland Firth, and at the end of 102 days from Calcutta arrived off the Firth of Tay, where an old tug—one of those wooden clinker-built types which survived for quite a long while on the north-east coast—met us.

She had a 'Geordie' skipper who hailed and offered to tow us in for the price of a pint of ale per ton. This signified 2½d. multiplied by 3333, which worked out at a nice reward, but it included also the use of a second tug to assist in docking. The bargain for nearly £35 was clinched, *Liverpool* a few hours later found herself made fast to a Dundee wharf, and her crew bade their haunted ship farewell. Me the Captain asked to remain, so, having no special reason for choosing otherwise, I accepted. During the next couple of weeks more ships from Calcutta with jute and some of my fellow apprentices kept arriving, so the time passed not unpleasantly till we ourselves had discharged cargo. Then it was back to Liverpool, loading more salt for Calcutta, another voyage—this time needing 130 days. In other respects everything was much the same as before, even to the ghost making his sensational appearance at the end of much gossip.

But this third voyage was to be for me apparently the last in that fine vessel. A fortnight before being due to sail from Calcutta the south-west monsoons with their heavy rains played havoc with the health of many, and I was sent into hospital as a fever patient. Weeks of careful nursing obtained final release, but the *Liverpool* had long since departed—this time for New York.

I set about looking for another berth, and found one, but the memory still remains painfully vivid. The *Bangalore* was to be one of the severest propositions which ever tried a sailor's endurance. She was, curiously, bound for New York, and her skipper belonged to Rhode Island. Yes: he believed in working his men, but giving them plenty of food. When we had got clear of Calcutta's river, sails being all set and ropes coiled down, he ordered the crew aft to the break of the poop. There he addressed us in no flattering terms, and with a rare bluntness.

First of all, he said exactly what he thought of us; then that which from now on he required. When the Mates gave an order, we were neither to run nor jump; but to *fly*. Next, this hardened old shellback put a choice before us. Would we have the Board of Trade scale for food—which in those days was very poor—or would we prefer 'full and plenty and no waste.'

A shout rose up in unison.

"Full and plenty, and no waste!" we answered.

"Right!" said the Captain, who confessed that he liked his crew to be well fed. "That'll do, men."

But as we turned to go forward, he called to the steward, and at the same time raised a couple of fingers.

"Steward, give the men plenty of potatoes. Give them two each. Two!"

This same martinet struck terror into our hearts in quite another way. He owned a big Senegalese monkey, a ferocious brute secured by a chain two fathoms long; but these four yards were quite enough for allowing the fierce animal to wander about the poop. Now one day the Second Mate was standing there making signals to a passing ship, when the monkey seized the signal book and began tearing out its pages at the rate of a hundred a minute. No one dared to approach, and we had no other copy on board. I was at the wheel, the situation somewhat uncertain, but the Captain had to be summoned that he might settle the problem.

Nor did that determined character hesitate to take firm action. By the time I was due to leave the wheel at the end of my watch, I couldn't be sure which he had most knocked hell out of—the Mate or the monkey.

The *Bangalore* was neither a slow ship nor handled other than smartly: moreover, luck favoured us. Consequently we were rounding the Cape of Good Hope on the 29th day after leaving Calcutta, and fortune still continued to give us strong fair winds. Thus at the end of 72 days we arrived off the Statue of Liberty, having created the second fastest record for that voyage. Here in New York was lying the *Liverpool*, so I rejoined, sailed with her to a Canadian port where we loaded timber, and crossed the Atlantic to England.

Now, however, I wanted a thorough change, so this time forsaking sail for steam and selecting a different route, found myself in the S.S. *Bathurst* bound for West Africa. By the time we reached Cape Coast Castle trouble up-country was fast nearing a crisis, and older readers will still recollect the Ashanti campaign. King Prempeh, who ruled a country of dense forest and difficult swamps (deadly to white men's health), was supreme over tribes notorious for their warlike nature and ghastly habits of human sacrifices. Their depredations on British subjects in the coastal regions had attained such a limit that now troops from England were being brought hither. It was quite an unusual ending presently, for scarcely a shot had to be fired, King Prempeh became a prisoner in Elmina Castle further up the coast and eventually was sent into exile on a Seychelles island of the Indian Ocean where many years were to be spent. Yet, though to-day Ashanti forms part of the British Empire, exporting large quantities of gold, rubber, and cocoa, many a soldier lost

his life through tropical disease: H.R.H. Prince Henry
of Battenberg, son-in-law of Queen Victoria and father
of Spain's future Queen, being one of the officers who
succumbed.

I found our steamer trips up these African rivers most
interesting, and at the end of two months spent about
here came home with a desire to see yet another corner
of the globe. This time it was to be the S.S. *Milton*,
and she set out for the west coast of South America. We
had an exceedingly instructive voyage going through the
Magellan Straits and Smyth's Channel, calling at all the
ports in Chile and Peru. Keen, concentrated navigation
was required in the 'nineties: lighthouses were scarce,
and many a ship met destiny whilst seeking a Magellan
anchorage after dark.

The savage scenery of that region, its perpetual bad
weather with gales of wind and excessive rain, impress
the mind deeply. It has yet to be charted thoroughly
and in detail, but ultimately exploration must be carried
out on a grand scale for revealing an undoubted wealth
of mineral products quite apart from its immense forests.
The primitive natives of the Straits—Fuegians and
Patagonians—are sparse, but their clothing despite such
severe cold and damp is likewise scant. When a steamer
passed a canoe of these nomads in Magellan Straits, the
custom of throwing overboard a sealed cask of food was
both expected by the natives and encouraged by mariners.
Shipwreck could never be ruled out as a possibility among
those strong currents and rocky pinnacles, so it were
well to encourage a friendly spirit locally.

Along South America's Pacific shores the trade was
carried on mostly by European sailing ships, nitrate being
especially the cargo fetched home. Steamers still were
singularly few, though in the *Milton* we spent five or six
months calling practically everywhere between Talca-
huano in the south and Guayaquil near the Equator.
Certainly, this period of becoming intimately acquainted
with the South American continent was not to be despised,

yet even now my wandering spirit had not found satisfaction. If one's brain had been expanded by so many
new sights, so much varied scenery, so many different
anchorages; I missed the romance and adventure which
belong only to sail. Steamship life was all very well in
its limited appeal, but it did not help an ambitious young
enthusiast to become a first-class seaman or to train him
for command of an important vessel that some day might
be his privilege.

So the year of 1896 saw me appointed as Second Mate
to the four-masted barque *Mashona*. How handsome a
vessel she was will be noted from the accompanying
illustration, and she must immediately suggest comparison with the *Liverpool*. Though at the time we failed
to realize the fact, this was one of the most notable
decades in the history of shipping; when a final and
heroic effort by builders no less than owners to retain
sailing ships, despite the competition by steamers, had to
be made. An imposing fleet they composed, though
space will not permit of a full list. When we think of
the above two examples, or of the *Olive Bank* (2824 tons
registered) built in 1892, the *Queen Margaret* (2144 tons
registered) built in 1893, and other four-masted barques
(most of them launched on the Clyde) of the 'nineties,
even the least sentimental person could not fail to regret
the passing of a golden age.

We left the Mersey on a 15,000 miles voyage for San
Francisco, the tugs towing *Mashona* as far as the Tuskar
Light (south-east Ireland). Here we set sail, but strong
southerly gales reminded us how dependent on wind and
weather even the finest sail-driven vessels would always
be. The *Mashona* could make no progress, but, in fact,
within the next twenty-four hours had lost considerably,
being driven so far to leeward up the Irish Sea as to sight
the Isle of Man. Admittedly this set-back made me
wish I was in steam after all.

Gradually, at the end of buffetings and heavy seas, the
wind veered round to north-west, which gave us a nice

slant, taking us well into the Atlantic till (well north of the usual latitude) we found the North-east Trades. The same old routine had begun, our Skipper this time being a man of about 56 years, the First Mate about 60, myself and the Third Mate being in the early 'twenties.' The latter was my fellow watch-keeper, and our aim was to keep in perfect physical condition, for which purpose we carried a punch-ball, Indian clubs, dumb-bells, and boxing-gloves. Every night throughout our watch up on the poop we were slogging at each other. The Captain used to sleep immediately below. A very strict disciplinarian, who expected his officers to keep things in motion, he never objected to the inevitable sound we two were making above. He said that he always felt uneasy if he couldn't hear us boxing.

But we carefully arranged that none of the men should practise with any of our gear, the principal reason being that, young as we were for our responsible duties, it was our considered intention to remain in a state of superior fitness. Not any other person in the *Mashona* should rival our standard. Result? Whether by night or day, we could have knocked the head off any stubborn mutineer, and the crew knew it: our orders were carried out implicitly, with never so much as a growl being uttered in protest.

Now the steward was quite a personality. He answered to the name of Joe. A very faithful servant-friend of the Captain, this fellow had been to sea with the Master in various ships for the last ten years, never failing when summoned to perform the most uncustomary jobs. Four of the Captain's children had been born afloat, and on each occasion the adaptable Joe played an important part. Perhaps all this had begun to affect his health, since during the last eighteen months a severe attack of brain-fever confined him ashore; and now that he was once more seafaring, his memory obviously lacked its previous grasp.

This quite suited our eight hungry apprentices, as

they all looked out for some opportunity to relieve Joe
of any eatables lying in his pantry. Now one morning,
before breakfast, Joe opened my cabin-door with a
doleful remark.

"There'll be one hell of a row to-day, when the Cap'n
goes in to breakfast."

"Why d'you say that, Joe?"

"Because I've made no bread."

This assertion seemed passing strange. I myself saw
him at 7.30 carrying along from the galley a couple of
loaves. But the truth was that the apprentices, following
in his wake, waited till he placed them in the pantry, then
immediately took the bread away with them. Meanwhile poor old Joe continued quite forgetful that he did
any baking that morn.

Throughout all ages since first ships doubled the
southern extremity of South America, the west-about
voyage has been a steady tussle. We read of Elizabethan
and later vessels spending weeks of hard battering in an
effort to get round the corner; but those were awkward,
clumsy cattle compared with the weatherly well-designed
four-masters such as *Mashona*. Still, we were to learn
painfully how the forces of nature remain fairly constant
in successive centuries.

Our voyage from the Irish Sea to Cape Horn took
about 70 days, but believe me it required over 30 days
before we could slip past the Cape into the Pacific. A
whole month fighting head winds and mountainous seas
without making progress! Wet, cold, and miserable;
dispirited and anxious; we had to keep on trying, and
only those who have battered their way through these
cruel regions know what it meant. Very different was it
punching through Magellan Straits in the steamship
Milton, or running with a fair wind eastward round the
Horn in that Norwegian barque from Raine Island.

Yes: the Panama Canal has saved modern mechanical
vessels a great deal of time, but likewise bad weather and
damage have been avoided thereby. Lying 60 miles

south-west of the Horn are some small islands, 'Diego Ramerias,' but commonly known by sailors as the 'Dago's Dungarees.' Unlit, they have caused many a fine vessel running before a westerly gale and high sea when home-ward-bound from Australia or Pacific ports to suffer disaster. When once a hull had struck, fate was settled: not a soul could ever be saved. For some indefinite period the world would not know anything. Perhaps at length owners and relatives would be able to note one short announcement:

'Missing. Probably lost off Cape Horn.'

With what gladness we in *Mashona* eventually gained the Pacific, worked our way northward into latitudes where the sun blazed down on decks, may well be imagined. To have obtained warmth and progress after long chill and weariness raised our spirits immensely, and soon we were bowling along in the South-east Trades, crossing the Equator into the north-east winds, till finally the westerlies got hold of us beyond the Californian coast and brought *Mashona* to the Golden Gate of San Francisco.

A tug towed us into harbour, we made fast alongside Green Street wharf after a voyage lasting 182 days.

Six months!

A small community of men who, throughout this period, never once had set foot ashore.

CHAPTER VIII

SAN FRANCISCO at this date was a very lively city, where no event could cause much surprise. Any sort of man from parsons down to labourers might be shanghaied and placed aboard as able seaman when some ship was outward bound for England. The water-front fairly swarmed with 'wharf-rats,' as the boarding-house runners were always regarded. If any of us passed through this locality after dark, every eye-lash and hair of the head had to be watching; otherwise life, or at least liberty, was imperilled.

'Frisco rose into prosperity during the early days of California's historic Gold Rush. It was not till ten years subsequent to our visit that the city suffered destruction from earthquake and fire, when a hundred million pounds' worth of property ceased to exist. The climate and beautiful scenery are rivalled only by the Californian hospitality. To us British sailors the kindness extended could not have been greater, picnics and sports for our enjoyment being arranged till the ship was due to sail.

One night our Captain gave a dinner-party on board the *Mashona*, the guests including half a dozen ladies from the shore and a similar number of old skippers from vessels in the harbour. He invited also a couple of our apprentices (because they could play musical instruments); the Third Mate and myself. The menu consisted of: Pea Soup, Salt Beef (out of the harness-cask), Roast Leg of Mutton with onion sauce, followed by Sweets.

The party duly arrived, and by a good deal of squeezing in we all managed to sit down at the saloon table. I was quietly wondering how Joe the steward would behave, and whether his memory would hold out long enough to make the evening successful. However, everything promised well. The table's appearance looked excellent, every item in its place and no article missing. Soup was served by the Skipper from a tureen, next arrived the beef, and Joe removed the wreckage as we stood by for the mutton. Now came the plates, then Joe brought in a large sauce-bowl of onion sauce and returned to his pantry.

Minutes ticked by, conversation rose and fell, but nothing seemed to happen.

At the end of a long interval the Captain became irritable.

"Steward?" he hailed, and in blew Joe. "Steward, the mutton."

"Yes, sir," was the reply, but a curious bewildered look fell over the man's face and he vanished out of the saloon.

More minutes, and still nothing developed.

"Steward? The mutton," was repeated, but with rather more emphasis.

Of course I knew something unfortunate had happened, though exactly what I couldn't guess. Perhaps the cat had stolen the joint, whilst the onion sauce happened to be in transit?

Fire raged in the Skipper's eyes. Trouble, terrible and overwhelming, ripened. At last he could tolerate the delay not a moment longer, so leaving his guests he made towards the pantry, myself following.

The difficulty became immediately evident as we directed our gaze into a corner. There, hanging by itself, was the leg of mutton. Joe had quite forgotten to cook it when he made the onion sauce!

Scarcely without some embarrassment the Captain apologized on returning, and the ladies all made light of the matter. Not so those six hardened old Master Mariners, who winked at each other incredulously; and this worried him quite a lot, so that months later, during our homeward voyage, he would sometimes remark:

"Kendall, they never did believe I had any mutton. They thought I was just bluffing."

All the same, his party could not have been ranked as a failure. If the beef was as salt as Lot's wife, it gave us a wonderful thirst and encouraged us to drink the 'Old Man's' health pretty frequently.

The *Mashona* stayed here over a month discharging cargo, and then we moved out into Mission Bay awaiting orders. This did not prevent some of us from enjoying a few hours' shore leave, so together with the Third Mate a stroll was taken up Market Street, where we came to a fair with its swings, mechanical race-horses, and the like. But the 'big noise' apparently was the 'Barrel of Love.' This cask, fitted with two seats on one side and two more at the other, started from the top of a hill, was then rolled down to the bottom and up the next to a distance of a hundred yards.

The Third Mate and myself resolved to try the experience, and in we went to the accompaniment of the crowd's cheering, but two corpulent ladies followed likewise. The attendant strapped us all securely—body, legs, and arms. With a shriek of the steam whistle the barrel was released, and down it rolled at a terrific pace, striking an obstacle on the opposite hill before returning to rest. Altogether, it was a horrible adventure, and sea-sickness can be reckoned as mild compared with the sensations of being violently hurled through space. Far happier had we been at sea in bad weather.

When *Mashona's* orders instructed the ship to reach Portland (Oregon), we towed out through San Francisco's Golden Gate and sailed northward during the next fortnight. Barely had the ship been made fast to the quay than the treacherous boarding masters began their work. 'Blood Money' was their principle, so they managed to clear out most of our crew and dictated terms for a new one. One hundred dollars, plus two months' pay in advance, were demanded for each new hand to be signed on. Blackmail? There was no other alternative. If any captain declined to pay the extortionate conditions, he must go without a crew.

These boarding masters with their agents (variously known as decoys, 'runners,' or 'crimps') were super-tough bruisers, and whenever through them a group of sailors was dumped on board the latter had become no wilder than tame rabbits. There used to be one particular boarding-house in Portland, where a large gymnasium was located immediately over the seamen's dining-room, so that whilst the unfortunate men were trying to satisfy a breakfast appetite below, heavy thumps descended ominously from tough crimps practising knock-out tactics for future dock operations.

Two whole months we lay in this port loading grain, and then we were towed down miles of river to cross the bar on the morning's tide. We set sail for the sunny south and balmy trade winds, bound to 'Queenstown for orders.' Thus again the old routine started, although new faces took the place of our original seamen; also a couple of apprentices had deserted whilst at Portland, preferring some other career than that under sail. Down to Cape Horn our voyage continued uneventful, but now the fierce gales of wind and merciless seas awaited us. Many icebergs, too, were sighted, being much larger and more massive than those met with in the northern hemisphere.

We were not long in getting past into the Atlantic, and so away northward. The *Mashona* got hold of the land off Cape Clear (south-west Irish coast) about 140 days out from Portland. From Cape Clear to the entrance of Queenstown harbour the distance is not more than 60 miles, or a few hours' run normally. Yet, ridiculous though it may seem, it took us a whole week on this occasion, being tormented with adverse airs; and, having come to anchor in that magnificent natural port, we left four days later for Havre. There the whole lot of us were paid off, and I made tracks for England to pass another examination.

It was always one of the disappointing facts in seafaring life that officers and men after serving together in the same ship for thousands of miles, through all sorts of dangers and difficulties, should barely end the voyage than they became separated over the world, destined most likely never to meet again. Can you wonder that, suddenly freed from going aloft or hauling on ropes, no longer asked to endure hard circumstances, but with several months' wages in his pocket, the sailor so frequently walked into trouble on coming ashore? In these canvas-driven vessels he had been bullied by Nature driving round the Horn, daily drenched whilst rushing the 'forties' of latitude, scorched and baked on either side of the Equator, and (often enough) reaching the British Isles through more bad weather. Then, abruptly, it all ended. He became a victim to that vilest and hardest of all masters—drink.

At the end of three months I was now qualified for a better job some day, and meanwhile appointed as Second Mate to another exceptional vessel. This was the full-rigged ship *Ditton*. She was nearly, though not quite, the size of the four-masted *Liverpool*; but *Ditton*, being of 3003 tons register, possessed the distinction of being the largest three-master afloat. I went up to join her at South Shields, where she was loading coal and coke for 'Frisco. Yes, it was to be the same voyage, the same Cape Horn; yet no two ships are ever the same. The Captain (whose portrait you will notice in the group taken on board) was yet another of that fine old school. Brought up in sail, he had lived 72 years, and been in command during more than half a century, so the amount of practically acquired knowledge travelling more than a million miles at sea could not have been surpassed.

Assuredly he was unusually fortunate to obtain a command at 22, due to the death of a captain suddenly. Our Skipper, despite a venerable age, could not be regarded otherwise than able and active, but doubtless his bones had long been pickled by eating salt beef. In his time he had commanded some well-known vessels, including the passenger-ship *Mystery*, and also the *Great*

Britain; being the last of her captains. His five children were all grown up, most of them having been born at sea; for in those times, when a skipper was compelled to be away during such long periods, the owners nearly always allowed the Master to bring his wife from home.

Those, too, were the days when doctors were not carried in sailing ships, and only rarely in steamers: consequently, to their many duties skippers added that of tending any sickness. I recollect one steamship commander who for the first time did have a doctor with him, and this is how the former used to describe the result:

"For twenty-seven years I never carried a doctor aboard, never lost a patient; but during the very first voyage with a medico at hand we had three deaths."

This reminds me of the fine old poem written by a sailor, long since gone aloft. In describing the multifarious duties of the sea captain, it is remarked:

'In time of need he must be midwife, too,
    Or help to kill, as doctors do.
    And should a sailor sleep his last long sleep,
    As parson he consigns him to the deep.
    And if he has a tear or two to spare,
    He acts chief mourner, and bestows them there.
    Well up in cooking, and in skill profound
    At weighing tea and sugar by the pound,
    Should there be strife or enmity aboard,
    He drops the scales and then takes up the sword.
    But when the strife is over goes his rounds
    As surgeon then binds up the gaping wounds.'

On putting to sea from the Tyne, we could not foretell, as does the modern mechanical ship, how long would be the voyage. Starting off with fair winds, we soon got clear of the English Channel and headed for the edge of the North-east Trades, by which time I had become well acquainted with my new habitation. The *Ditton* differed from any vessel in which hitherto I had served. Designed to withstand the hardest gales, she was built up amidships, as the reader will have noticed in the photograph. Here at the waist a sailing ship usually has to suffer the heaviest seas that try breaking aboard, but this additional protection made a wonderful difference to general comfort, especially when we began beating round the Horn and took long tacks towards the Antarctic.

Whilst lying at South Shields, the Captain made it his business to purchase two dozen good class laying fowls, for he had brought his 21-years-old daughter to keep him company. He thought that a new-laid egg for himself, the girl, the Chief Mate, and myself would be an agreeable variation from the everlasting salt beef and pork, provided only the uncertain hens might do their stuff. The Chief Mate, by the way, was the nearest approach I have ever seen to the old-time red-faced London bus-driver, and every bit as hard a case. The *Ditton's* steward, a veteran who had been in the ship for years, belonged to much the same type, but one of his eyes was missing. Nevertheless, when it came to handing out stores by the pound or pint, this fellow lacked not one of his faculties.

Down to the Equator we made fairly good time, and the hens had not forgotten us: each evening four nice eggs would be ready for our relish. The greatest care of these feathered friends was taken, yet now one of them seemed to have become weary of the sea and yearned for the sight of green fields. She refused to lay, declined to eat, but just stood stupidly in the waterways pining; and all the other hens in passing took a peck at her.

It was 2.30 p.m., and I chanced to be walking alone on the after-deck during my watch. Something attracted me. I looked, and there prone in the waterways was the hen. It had passed away, which did not cause me much surprise: but something else did a little later in the afternoon. Passing along to see that everything was all correct, I observed the one-eyed steward sitting outside the cabin-door plucking the dead hen. Nor did he seem to have any intention of announcing the fowl's natural decease.

THE SAILING-SHIP *DITTON* AND CREW

(*Top*) The *Ditton* in 1897. Of 3003 tons (reg.), she was the largest three-master then afloat.
(*Bottom*) Standing on extreme left of back row is myself, next to the Captain. I was then
Second Mate.

S.S. *LUSITANIA*

I was wrecked in her on the coast of Newfoundland.

"Hullo, steward!" I remarked. "Have you killed her?"

"Yes: to save her life," he answered somewhat illogically.

I then foresaw that the body would be cooked for to-morrow's dinner: either the four of us must eat the worn-out hen, or starve. I dared not give the truth away, or the Chief Mate would have killed the steward, and the Skipper at least would have put the man in irons. Still, the thought of consuming the remains of an invalid was revolting: I must sit on the fence and watch proceedings with secret knowledge.

So when the midday meal was prepared, and the aroma of roast fowl made us all think of an English country-side, we took our places in the little saloon, everyone save me wearing a smile of anticipation. Then, on the table, I rejoiced to see a 'Harriet Lane' pie—that is, one made of preserved meat—so it would be my choice beyond question. The septuagenarian Skipper set to work carving the fowl, handed one portion to his daughter, a second to the Chief Mate, and one to myself.

"No, thank you, Captain," my hand refused, "I never eat chicken."

"What? A sailor? And you never eat chicken?"

"No, sir. Never in my life."

"Good heavens! That's funny! You're the first man I ever met who . . ."

"Since I was a child," came the stammering falsehood, "I've always thought it cruel to kill a fowl."

"Never mind—eat it!"

"Honestly, sir, I'd much prefer the pie."

This obstinacy quite upset the others. The 'Old Man' much regretted that I should miss the best meal in months. His daughter, sitting opposite, gave me a series of black looks and kept trying to convince me how nice the chicken tasted. As for the Chief Mate, he said nothing just then, but I was thinking all the while how much trouble would ripen if I were to speak freely.

F

The meal being ended, the daughter strolled along deck and approached me for a yarn. Something on her mind!

"Why are you vexed with father?" she demanded.

"But I'm not."

"Then why did you refuse to eat the fowl?"

I tried to explain that, being a bird-lover, I couldn't endure the thought of a hen suffering death to provide human food.

Somehow that explanation failed to convince. A large part of the carcass was being kept for the evening meal, and I did not wish to upset the girl till it was quite finished. But some day she would have to learn the truth.

As to the Chief Mate, his greeting made it hard to reply.

He asked:

"What the hell is the matter with you? And why didn't you eat some of the bird!"

Again I protested that I always refrained from such sustenance.

"That's a ruddy lie," came his flat contradiction. "I once saw you having chicken in a Newcastle hotel. Why the hell d'you eat the Captain's eggs if you . . . ?"

But I could see it was useless to argue the point, and I let it go at that. All this bother, merely because I tried to save the steward's skin.

Gradually the incident died a natural death, but now a new anxiety was being hatched.

The Captain promised that after rounding the Horn, and having got well into the Pacific, he would kill one fowl a week before reaching 'Frisco. This set me thinking deeply, and I began working out plans; so later on as we sailed northward the daughter and I used to sit on deck discussing various topics, and I bided my opportunity. It would be difficult to convince a woman against her will, yet some attempt must be made.

Since she had been born at sea, and was becoming

daily hardened to seafaring, it gave me a good opportunity for talking of the hardships which belong to a sailor's life. Then I went on to remind her how sometimes mariners have been cast adrift in a boat without food, compelled to eat their own shoes for nourishment, and each example I tried depicting more gruesome than the other. Working up to a climax, preparing for a true and full narration of that dead chicken, I told her all about the notorious Chicago meat scandal. Yet with that waywardness of a woman the latter made not the slightest impression: she never batted an eyelid or turned a hair.

Finally, at a right opportunity, when she was in a suitable mood, I presented her with the full story, and it made a deep impression. The sailing ship on the lonely ocean is a tiny world of its own, independent of what may be happening elsewhere in empires, kingdoms, dominions, republics. Those items which ashore would pass unnoticed gain a primary importance among a small crowd of people isolated from external influence. Consequently this ridiculous chicken episode had become the equivalent of what, in modern slang, would be called 'front-page news.' Shocked as she now was, she promised faithfully not to repeat what had been mentioned. Her father would certainly fire the one-eyed steward after reaching San Francisco, and I should be given hell for not having reported the misdeed when it happened. Furthermore, since everybody excepting myself had enjoyed consuming the bird, why not let the matter drop?

Yes: but the future? That weekly fowl still to come? How could I make a complete turn-round?

The problem was solved simply. She was to persuade me—compel me to change my prejudices. At her personal request I was to begin eating chicken, and like it.

This ruse succeeded, and till the day of his death her father never knew the reason for the Second Mate transforming a dislike into a pleasure.

CHAPTER IX

WE crossed the Equator in the Pacific 140 days after departing from South Shields, and another 40 days brought us to 'Frisco. Dozens of the world's finest sailing ships still frequented the bay, some actually loading, some awaiting better freights, one of the favourite anchorages being at the back of Sansalito Island.

Nor had the city's character altered since my last visit, unless it were that the enthusiasm for boxing seemed keener. Bob Fitzsimmons was training for his fight with Corbett, and the former did many of his pugilistic exercises on Sansalito; wherefore quite a number of skippers used to be rowed off and landed at the island, where they not merely became spectators, but also friends of Bob. The latter, hearing that some of these visitors owned the reputation of being very hard cases and heavy-fisted, took them on as sparring partners. This created wonderful delight among apprentices and sailors, who were there too. The opportunity of seeing their 'Old Man' in a real 'set-to' was so rare that they willingly would have sacrificed a month's wages for the treat. One morning, Fitzsimmons tackled three of these maritime bruisers simultaneously, but within a few minutes had flattened out the whole trio—to the unbounded amusement of their seafaring onlookers.

During our stay within the Golden Gate several weeks went by before receiving fresh orders, but apart from the natural physical beauty of this environment plenty of exciting activity was around. It will be recollected that this was the time of the great Klondike Gold Rush, when get-rich-quick prospectors were leaving daily for the Alaskan coast at Skagway. From small schooners to steamers, any kind or sort of vessel that hadn't a hole in her was chartered. Men of normal sense lost their balance in this wild lust for wealth. Greed for gold, whether in Australia or north-west America, has been responsible for a whole category of crime culminating in brutal murders.

When I was serving in the *Liverpool* we had a sailor named Butler, who happened to be the only man that I've ever seen move his ears backwards and forwards like an animal. Now in course of time Butler found himself in Australia, where this gold craze inflamed his avarice so that he would stop at nothing. His technique was to advertise for a partner with £200 or £300, when they would join forces and go prospecting. Next Butler would set out with his companion into the bush, where the seaman's prospecting knowledge was expert. His artfulness, however, rivalled his local intelligence; for, all too quickly, he would poison his victim with strychnine, pocket the money, entice from civilization another unsuspecting person, and begin the scheme again. Thus did this series become known as the 'Bush Murders.'

Now the date arrived when Butler decided he must make himself scarce or be arrested. Choosing the name of Leweller—the last of his assassinated dupes—Butler re-adopted his former calling and signed on aboard the sailing ship *Swanhilda*, which was bound for San Francisco. The destination suited him perfectly, both because of the new Klondike possibilities and also for the opportunities of losing his identification in a different country.

But a rogue has to be singularly clever if he is to defeat fate and justice. The real Leweller had loyal friends, who determined that his murderer should be caught, and ere long it became established that Butler was on the high seas making towards California. This news was cabled to the United States authorities, who promptly made their preparations to prevent the fugitive from sneaking ashore. Selecting a suitable steamer, they ordered her to patrol night and day about 20 miles seaward of the 'Frisco coast, looking out for any sail that should come over the horizon.

Aboard this steamer were half a dozen policemen, but all dressed as Quarantine Officers, so that no suspicion might be aroused when they came aboard outside the Golden Gate's approaches.   At length the *Swanhilda*, having been 60 days under way from Newcastle (New South Wales), hove in sight, and everything was ready for her. Off came the pretended Quarantine men, and these six soon had the sailing ship's crew lined up on deck. Examination for smallpox.   That seemed reasonable enough.   From one seaman to another the inspecting process passed, and by this manner the desperate Butler was taken completely unawares.   Suddenly arrested, his indignation knew no bounds.

"Had I known this," he cursed his captors, "I would have poisoned the whole crew and scuttled the ship."

That the threat was not altogether boastfulness received speedy proof when after searching through his clothing, enough strychnine to kill a regiment came to light.   In due course Butler was extradited to Australia, where after being tried he suffered extreme condemnation, yet on his way to the scaffold he fought like a tiger, greedy for that to which he was not entitled, right till his last breath.

And now the *Ditton* was to bid farewell.   None of us would ever see San Francisco again as it then appeared. Richelieu Café, that popular resort of sailors, where with the foaming beer was presented a green cardboard disc entitling the customer to a free lunch and all for a nickel; Kearney Street; the Hall of Justice; Portsmouth Square, where Robert Louis Stevenson gathered some of his early inspirations and a monument was raised to his honour: these were but familiar landmarks which presently were to disappear in the terrible disaster when earth, air, fire, and water combined to destroy one of the most lovely, if lively and utterly reckless, cities of the American continent.

The earth trembled, the avenging fires broke forth

fanned by the wind, water gushed in torrents from the broken mains, whilst horror-stricken thousands watched the savings of a lifetime transformed into ashes. Yet plans for building a grander and better town matured immediately, and within six months a miracle more wonderful than the earthquake had wrought the vast change.

We had loaded with ballast and received orders for Tocopilla, which is nearly 2000 miles south of the Equator on the coast of Chile. At the end of 46 days we arrived, discharged ballast and began loading nitrate for a German port, all this work being performed by the ship's crew, one bag at a time. Finally we filled the *Ditton* with 4800 tons of this commodity. But west coast ports down along the Chilean territory were anything except attractive. Ashore it was just barren land. Rain being unknown, vegetation non-existent, all food imported, and the drinking water obtained by condensation, we all hated the locality which provided precious little opportunity for recreation. Nor were the inhabitants too cheerful themselves, every second person confessing that he was afflicted with heart-disease.

Through two weary months in company of other vessels we lingered, the chief excitement occurring when we all cheered that sailing ship which had taken aboard her last nitrate bag. The custom obtained that when this moment approached during daylight, and the final lighter was being rowed off to the anchored ship, with a Union Jack stuck on a pole into the topmost bag, each vessel in the roadstead would welcome the fact by vigorous applause. It was likewise usual for the last bag to be hoisted, with a sailor sitting on it, to the yardarm, whilst the crew sang a shanty, the lowering being accompanied by the familiar 'Blow the Man Down.'

Next Captain and officers would be given a cheer, the 'Old Man' produced a native spirit, costing about one dollar a gallon, but being intensely fiery. Each man was allowed a glassful, and that night there would be a general jollification to celebrate the completing of the preliminaries before setting out for home. Next morning, as the land breeze sprang up, welcome hands from the rest of the fleet would help to weigh anchor, sail would be broken out, then the time came for the dozen old skippers from neighbouring ships to cease drinking the Captain's whisky, get into their respective boats, and shove off. They had wished the departing vessel a happy voyage, and soon they also would be bound back to Europe.

During our stay several vessels let go anchor here from Australia, and some of these skippers were quite gay dogs, when 10,000 miles away from home; so their escapades were worth noting. In particular one barque, preceding three others, caused a certain amount of human interest. Owned by the Skipper's wife, this vessel arrived, however, with a very popular barmaid to accompany the Captain, but the latter next morning must go ashore to transact the ship's business, which necessitated a two-miles pull. With telescope glued to observant eye, each of three Master Mariners concentrated attention on the first arrived vessel, looking for a signal. By the time apprentices had rowed their commander near to the beach, the buxom but flirtatious barmaid made fast her handkerchief to the backstay. Whether before setting out from Australia this code had been prearranged, it is impossible to say; yet the result was immediate, and I never witnessed in all my career at sea a finer boat race than those three craft provided as three captains endeavoured to gain the barque first.

When the *Ditton* weighed, bound for Hamburg, she was to have an unusual experience. Our Captain intended to retire when once back in England, so quite naturally hoped to make a fast passage—something to take with him for future contemplation during the few years which remained. But winds conspired against the intention. I have frequently in these pages referred to the westerly gales which from time immemorial have prevailed round Cape Horn, yet once in a very long while the wind here blows from the opposite direction. And so it contrived for us.

Bad luck that we should on both occasions have to beat round 'Cape Stiff,' and these easterly gales were at least as vehement as the normal westerlies, which resulted in our boxing about off there for a month. I wonder how many ships in a double voyage ever experienced such a coincidence? Obviously we could now never expect a quick trip, but got to Hamburg in exactly 156 days. One voyage is never the same as any other, even though the same seas be traversed and the same landfalls made. Something unforeseen capsizes all generalization, and it was during this trip that our Third Mate developed 'bats in the belfry.' For his own sake, it became necessary to detain him in a secure place and keep him there till arrival in port, where also the crew were paid off.

Another important stage in my seafaring had now been attained. Having put in the required period afloat, and passed my examination as Master Mariner, I decided on a return to steamships. I had given sail a thorough testing, travelled many thousands of miles over the oceans, realized all the romance associated with the older species: yet too many disadvantages belonged to the canvas-driven vessel, and steamers during the late 'nineties were definitely establishing themselves as sea-transporters of the future.

What especially were the drawbacks even aboard such fine sailers as the *Liverpool* or the *Ditton?*

The answer is firstly the bad food, but secondly the dreariness of life. To be away on a six months' voyage in those days, long before the invention of wireless, was to shut oneself away from the world and cut off all news communication. So many important affairs might happen in half a year before getting in touch with the land, that the sight of any passing vessel was the cause of considerable excitement and we eagerly welcomed the chance of learning if any untoward movement had rocked the world. Inevitable, too, was the strain on tempers during such a

long period when a score of men made up our universe.
The Captain became irritable and overbearing because
of anxiety for his ship in heavy weather; his officers sorely
tried by a difficult crew; and the latter in turn, worn out
by ceaseless toil no less than indifferent food or the discomfort of a fo'c'sle, viewed the problem from not the
same angle.   Collectively, however, the merciless sea was
responsible for all their woes.

There is a strange simplicity about the sailorman not
always understood, and the most hardened is very often
influenced for good or evil quite easily.   Months of ill
treatment and scanty rations can be forgotten, during the
close of a long voyage, with a few days' liberal diet and
kindly treatment: by the time land is sighted and the
pilot picked up, once again the world seems a happy place
to inhabit.   As I often heard old mariners remark, the
way of a transgressor is not so very hard after all, provided
you know the ropes!

Of course, it was a real break saying good-bye to the
old sailing ship shanties; to realize that I should not hear
again 'Away Rio,' 'Blow my boys, I love to hear you,'
'Sally Brown,' 'Whisky, Johnny,' 'Blow The Man Down';
or that ballad: 'The pants I have on were made in Hong
Kong.'   One shanty stands out as the most inspiring of
them all, and brings back memories of those bygone
times:

> 'Up aloft and loose her topsails,
> Shake her white wings to the breeze,
> Think of those we leave behind us,
> So we sail our Southern Seas,
> Rolling home across the sea,
> Rolling home to dear old England,
> Rolling home, dear land, to thee.'

Yet with all these recollections I thought also of those
weeks together when my clothes were never dry; when
our Board of Trade scale was supplemented by such
horrible concoctions as 'hob scouse,' 'slumgullion,' or
'dandyfunk.'

Thus when, after a few weeks at home, I obtained an appointment as Second Officer aboard the S.S. *Aphrodite*, it was like opening a new book with a different story. This vessel had been ashore on the coast of Spain, but since been patched up and sent to England for permanent repairs. Her Captain and First Mate, having gone home for a few weeks' holiday, I was left in charge with a Lascar crew, who showed themselves an awkward crowd, disinclined to do their jobs. Well, not for nothing had I been serving all these years in sail, handling tough customers, and I made up my mind that *Aphrodite's* lot should each do a man's whole work.

To cut this story of everything save essentials, at the end of three days they defied me and walked ashore, which helped them not at all; for, within a few hours, I had the crowd in jail, after which they were returned to India at Government's expense. At least I managed to do the owners a good turn, since they had rid themselves of a disgruntled crew whose wage-bill would be unprofitable during the twelve weeks needed to make good the damaged hull. There still remained both stewards and cooks, so I was well catered for, whilst my accommodation notably contrasted with that in sailing ships. The rest and contentment, the quiet, and easy routine, were destined not to last beyond ten days.

Why? Because, previous to joining the *Aphrodite*, I had applied for a position as Junior Officer in the Beaver Line trading to Canada, and now was offered the chance of serving in the S.S. *Lake Superior*. Of course I accepted. The *Aphrodite* being a tramp steamer, whilst the liner *Lake Superior* would be away only four weeks at a time carrying passengers across the Atlantic, the matter demanded no long pondering. I began as Fourth Officer, and found that the Third Officer was an old friend. He had been an apprentice with me in sail during those Calcutta days already narrated.

The Boer War had broken out, and we quite expected that the *Lake Superior* would be employed transporting

horses to South Africa. Actually she proceeded to
Canada with 1000 passengers, most of whom were
travelling in the steerage from all parts of Europe.
Immense improvements for human comfort have taken
place in Atlantic liners during the past forty years, and
the modern generation would be amazed at the primitive
conditions which still existed in many a ship. Third-
class travellers had to put up with most elementary
environment, and the accommodation for officers would
be regarded as bleak compared with that in any typical
liner to-day.

In the first place, this *Lake Superior* was illuminated by
ordinary oil-lamps; for, whilst in an earlier chapter we
observed that the *City of Berlin* was the first to employ
electric light during the year 1879, this by no means had
become the general practice two decades later except in
crack vessels. Moreover, that old-fashioned design
existed aboard *Lake Superior* of berthing saloon passengers right aft in the stern, and well did they realize it.
This ship was of just over 5000 tons, built like an iron-
clad, but when she encountered a head sea, pitched her
bows and made her propeller race; or crashed down on
her stern with a mighty thump which sent a shiver through
the hull; only hardened travellers could make any pretence
of toleration.

Frankly my first few voyages in her did not at all appeal
to me. On this initial trip to Nova Scotia and New
Brunswick it became obvious enough that the route was
unrelieved by contrasts. In sailing ships, if there had
been Cape Horn or the Cape of Good Hope to endure,
at least there were periods of pleasanter latitudes. Now,
however, the cold weather of North Atlantic, the formidable fogs of Newfoundland made me seriously consider
whether I had chosen rightly. Should I not be wise if
I left this Canadian trade, and transferred to another
which would mean sunny seas and blue skies?

In every man's life occurs a big crisis, when the future
trend of his career is determined, and this voyage in the

Lake Superior must have been coincident with my own climax. Certainly it shaped the course of my marine destiny. Despite the longing to thaw out in pleasanter seas, I began to like this northern route, presently it gripped me, and eventually I was reluctant to be released. All the conditions and perplexities had become part of myself.

Now, on all homeward voyages from Canadian ports at that stage of history the cargo consisted of the usual produce in the holds, but with the addition on deck of 800 to 1000 head of live cattle. These were loaded the night before sailing, which meant that during the noisy embarkation very little sleep was possible for human beings. And there was plenty of excitement also. Wild bulls and obstreperous steers from the 'woolly west' required considerable effort to be expended ere being roped and secured to the head-boards. Ticklish job? Many a cattleman was gored to death during this duty.

CHAPTER X

MANY of these cattle tenders were serving as a means to get temporary employment. Drawn from all classes and occupations, they comprised chiefly medical students during the months of Canadian summer vacation. For them it meant tackling an awkward job, roughing it, yet not without profit. On landing in England they likewise received a return ticket, but before going home they would spend valuable weeks gaining knowledge in the hospitals of our big cities. To-day there are plenty of distinguished doctors throughout Canada who in their early years were glad to become cattlemen during an Atlantic trip.

A hundred humorous stories could be told describing the trials which the cattle imposed on all of us. It was customary on coming up the Mersey to discharge the animals at Wallasey, on the Cheshire side, when all hands endeavoured to get the duty finished quickly. Deck officers, engineers, stewards, firemen, sailors, all mustered armed with sticks and at the end of each stick was added a sharp pointed nail—long enough not to penetrate the hide, but sufficient for tickling the beasts up. Their head-ropes having been cast off, you can imagine what were the circumstances when a thousand wild creatures, after being in confinement for ten days, and driven still more furious by Atlantic buffeting, suddenly realized their liberty.

On one occasion we were working against time, with but an hour in which to conclude this discharging and then catch the tide into Liverpool docks. All was shaping quite nicely until it became evident that one ferocious bull had been left behind, and would not be coaxed ashore. Minutes were being wasted, the tide nearly done, and there was the ship held up by a quadruped. The great expert for inducing recalcitrant oxen into obedience was the wharf's butcher, whom we now sent for; and meanwhile our Boatswain with his mate thought they would descend to the deck and have a look at the bull.

Oh! it was amusing enough for everybody, except these two men. Hardly had they shown their noses round the corner cautiously, than Mr. Bull spotted them and made a magnificent onrush. Flee? They longed to be able. But how could escape be possible? Standing in the alleyway, they were up against a cul-de-sac, where a large hogshead of cold water barred retreat. Yet a race for their lives was on, and Mr. Bull, by his loud roaring, his smashing of head-boards, indicated a terrible temper.

And already he was increasing his pace. Something now must be done drastically, but immediately; and the Boatswain, though well over 60 years old, short and wiry, did some active thinking. To his mind the only way of salvation would be to jump into the hogshead, despite the chill of a December night, and this he had barely achieved than Mr. Bull arrived in his wrath. Thrilling seconds! Boatswain was safe, if nearly frozen. But Boatswain's clumsy, 6-ft., slow reasoning, 30-years-old mate found himself out of luck. With no effort at all the snorting bull picked him up and flung him through a trap-hatch above.

Then from this peak of excitement the incident became remarkably ordinary. Here on to the scene hastened the butcher prepared for lots of trouble. The beast blandly regarded the man, liked the look of him, felt ashamed. So the last act showed Mr. Bull with bowed head walking ashore most perfectly behaved, leaving two unhappy human figures to receive the laughter. Shivering with cold, water up to his neck, stood the miserable Boatswain, whilst his mate—stretched out along the deck above—meditated whether it was really true that some men had sold their farms and gone to sea.

I recall the day when, during the command of Captain Stewart, we brought the *Lake Superior* into Montreal as the first ship of the season after ice permitted. Our berth then used to be at the bottom of Berri Street, close to Sohmers Park, whence the portable sheds had been removed before winter's approach. Our advent synchronized with a strike amongst the stevedores, who were mostly French Canadians; consequently we began discharging the cargo ourselves.

This roused indignation. Not long had we been at our task than two or three hundred of them came down to the wharf with sticks and chased us all on board. Old Stewart had made up his mind they should not have the best of it, and now made preparations for the following morning, which doubtless would still be bitterly cold. Early enough he caused all hoses to be connected up, with nozzles screwed on, and disposed fore-and-aft about the ship covering the whole wharf-side. Our ship was wont to carry a couple of small brass cannon—one on the poop, one on the fo'c'sle head—which were to be used for distress signals.

He now filled these with the usual 1 lb. bag of black powder, then rammed them full of Indian corn and trained them towards the wharf in readiness. Nothing further developed until 8 a.m., when about four hundred stevedores swooped down with the intention of stopping us working. As all gangways were blocked up, the crowd could not get aboard, but contented themselves with clustering along the wharf, shouting violent threats. Captain Stewart was not greatly worrying, bided his time, but just waited till the mob had become well packed together. Then he issued two orders: one to fire the guns, and the other to start all pumps. Goodness! I never saw a crowd of men scatter with such swiftness. What with the cold water and the Indian corn hitting them all on the face, you might have imagined from the helter-skelter which ensued that machine-guns were pelting them with bullets. Up Berri Street they ran like greyhounds, and left the wharf to us. So the strike was ended, and we got on with our unloading.

Captain Stewart was quite a character, and I remember the time when he took a dislike to a young doctor from Ottawa. It may be mentioned that the latter, making his first voyage, rather proud of his new uniform, used to strut up and down the saloon deck in front of the passengers. One day an American lady strode up, whilst the ship forged ahead over a calm sea. "Say, Cap'n, is it always like this? When're we going to see a real Atlantic swell?"

"Right now," answered the Skipper: "just walk along this deck and take a glance at the doctor." Occasionally, however, some bright feminine was the smarter.

"What time will it be daylight in the morning?" was the silly question, and poor old Stewart had been asked too many for one day. So his response had in it no excess of politeness.

"I don't know," he registered annoyance. "Go and ask the cook."

"Oh!" apologized the woman icily. "I'm sorry. But I took you for the cook."

The Captain so admired her repartee, that for the rest of that voyage he made a great friend of this passenger.

After I had made several voyages in this ship to Canada, it was decided to lay her aside for a three-months' overhaul, wherefore the Third Officer and myself were transferred to the shore staff. Troops and horses for South Africa were pouring into Liverpool, where the greatest excitement prevailed. British forces had suffered a number of reverses, and reinforcements were now badly needed. In the North Docks we were hurriedly preparing for sea five of our company's steamers: *Montrose*, *Monteagle*, *Monteray*, *Lake Erie*, and *Montcalm*, all most suitable as transports. When a vessel became ready, brass bands would march the troops down to the quay. Popular airs, cheering women and children, would be the accompaniments of the tramping soldiers with rifles, fixed

G

bayonets, and a small Union Jack at the bayonet-end. As each steamship filled up and was about to shove off, the Mayor of Liverpool gave the troops a parting address, and I well recollect watching the Dublin Imperial Yeomanry embarking aboard the *Montrose*.

On the foredeck stood an Irishman bidding his chums farewell. It was: "Good-bye, Mick," " Good-bye, Pat," and "may those Boers knock the divil out o' ye." Next marched into view some Lancashire Yeomanry for other ships. "Look a fine, tough lot," I ventured to congratulate a young military officer on these men. "So far," he admitted, "I don't know very much about them— except this: if they ever storm a Boer town, they'll jolly well steal it."

Before long I was back on the Atlantic, this time in the S.S. *Wassau*, taking out passengers to Canada and bringing home cattle. When about in mid-ocean, eastward bound, we had a death one voyage. A cattleman passed away in his sleep—one of the case-hardened, desperado type. The Captain instructed the Boatswain to have the body sewn up in canvas, ready to be buried; but half an hour later came back a message that the sailors refused to carry out the order, because of the smell.

"All right!" said the Captain, "give them a bottle of rum. That'll help."

Meanwhile arrangements for the funeral were being made on the after-deck. Several passengers and myself proceeded thither, and the Skipper stood by with his prayer book. It was blowing fairly hard, and a heavy sea running, when the Boatswain returned to say the body had been partly sewn up. Not much longer delay would be necessary, now.

Suddenly the *Wassau* shipped a wave, which sent us in our several directions and the Skipper lost his prayer book. He would be thankful when the mournful task had terminated. We rescued ourselves, assembled again, but still no corpse.

The 'Old Man' was getting impatient.

"For heaven's sake," he ordered, "go and find out how much longer they'll be."

I hurried down to the lower fo'c'sle, where two sailors were sitting with the gruesome duty half done, but the rum all consumed. No! They positively refused to put another stitch in the canvas until they got more rum.

When I reported this, the Captain let the language flow, but finally agreed to send them another bottle, and the funeral party once more took up their positions.

Yet further delay reminded me of that incident when one-eyed Joe the steward forgot the leg of mutton. The *Wassau* was rolling and lurching, all of us were waiting for the principal item . . . still, 'nothing doing.'

Once more was I bidden to go and investigate, and you can understand my surprise on entering the fo'c'sle. There, completely and stupidly drunk, sprawled the two sailors singing ' Our Jack's come home to-day.'

"Where's the corpse?"

They seemed not to understand.

"Where is it—what you were sewing up?"

But glazed eyes could not answer, lips were busy with the chant, and I could get no explanation. Only when a fireman on the fo'c'sle deck was asked for information did the truth emerge.

"These two sailors," he said, "got the body, were carrying it along the deck, but at every step halted and remarked 'Phew.' Finally, when they got to the fore side of the bridge, they stopped altogether, took the corpse from their shoulders and hove it overboard."

So we had no funeral, and next voyage we no longer carried those two sailors, but we had a trying experience. Setting out in ordinary weather, we had barely rounded the south of Ireland than westerly gales with high seas were encountered. By the hour when 300 miles had been logged the fun reached its peak. The gale in mad fury swept decks, overboard went the main topmast, steering-gear collapsed, and dawn revealed an unfortunate vessel so battered about that to continue westward were madness. She could not possibly reach Canada in that condition.

The Captain accordingly turned round, made a fair wind of it, and ran into Queenstown. Instructions were telegraphed by the owners for the passengers to be made as comfortable as possible, and we were to bring them back to Liverpool next day. There the travellers transferred to another outward-bound steamer, whilst the *Wassau* was taken in hand for repairs. Thus it came about that I was sent as Second Officer to a vessel named the *Lusitania*. Very considerably smaller than the Cunard liner which a German U-boat sent to the bottom some years later, my new ship had been one of the Orient liners. At that period a favourite vessel in the Australian trade, she had been bought by the *Wassau*'s owners not to carry cattle, but first-class passengers.

She used to be square-rigged on the fore, main, and mizzen masts, though carrying fore-and-aft canvas also. Internal comfort, reckoned not by modern standards but according to liners of her day, could be described as sumptuous. We came out of dock into the Mersey to embark about 900 passengers, of whom 800 were a motley crowd from all parts of Europe travelling steerage, and by 5 p.m. were steaming down the river.

All went well down the Irish Sea and across the North Atlantic, until we reached the Banks of Newfoundland, when cold weather and dense fog set in. The Captain, knowing that the track was pretty well clear of ice, saw no reason why the ship's speed should not be continued. Good astronomical observations having been made, a safe and proper course was set with the intention of bringing the ship 15 miles well clear of Cape Race, which is the extreme south-eastern corner of Newfoundland.

Yet it was the old story. Since ships do not travel on railway lines but are subject to all the elements of weather and the influence of unseen currents, absolute certainty at sea cannot be guaranteed. The *Lusitania* piled herself on the shelving rocks of Cape Ballard about

1.30 one bleak May morning and became a total wreck, over 20 miles to the north of Cape Race.

Well, here was a nice situation. We had struck a barren corner in a remote part of the world, and even the nearest village lay 7 miles away. Working in the dark, hindered by heavy rain, the conditions were made no pleasanter by thunder and lightning; yet with such an able crew we managed to lower boats, take off every passenger, pull away seaward, and remain there till daylight before looking out for a decent landing-place. The Captain, Chief Officer, and myself remained by the wreck so long as practicable, but the surge and swell of the Atlantic, the long ocean roll which broke hammering and crashing over the doomed *Lusitania* compelled us to leave. We climbed into a boat, groped our way through the darkness, and found ourselves driven ashore to a sandy cove. This turned out fortunate, because when daylight broke we met the boats containing women and children. A bleak and cheerless coast revealed itself, but everybody was safely brought ashore and the Newfoundlanders ere long were doing everything in their power for our assistance.

Some 45 miles distant lay the capital, St. John's, with its fish industry and fine harbour, its shipping and dry dock. Thus the S.S. *Glencoe* arrived off the wreck about 2 p.m., fully prepared to receive our passengers and to supply them with warm clothing besides a hot meal previous to taking everybody into St. John's. Now an acute problem faced us as we considered how we might be able to transfer these people first through the heavy surf pounding on the beach, and then over the Atlantic swell alongside *Glencoe*. A steamer's lifeboat is a heavy, unhandy thing, more suited for open-sea work than for being launched from a beach through breakers. Trouble seemed certain.

Luckily, in the vicinity were many of the Newfoundland fishing fleet, and readers who are familiar with Kipling's *Captains Courageous* nautical novel, or have seen the film, need no reminding of those small boats named 'dories.' Double-ended, flat-bottomed, built so as to nest into each other on deck, they are readily dropped over the side and from them the fishermen pursue their job with long lines. The design of such craft makes them excellent for beach work and manœuvring alike.

Thus it was a prudent decision to employ a number of 'dories' fetching women, children, and men through the turbulent waters to where the deeper lifeboats were waiting at anchor well seaward of the sandy shore. When once filled, the *Lusitania's* boats were rowed alongside the *Glencoe*. The local fishermen by no means resented use of their 'dories,' for payment had been agreed at the price of a dollar a load.

Of course our chief anxiety was to get away the women and children first, that they might find warm comforts in the shortest time; and the work progressed quite satisfactorily as they crowded towards the white-foamed shore, eager to get away. But up on the beach sat a woman on an old box. She looked despondent, utterly miserable, her senses stunned by recent events. I shouted for her to come along into the 'dory,' but the effect of having been shipwrecked on a dark, rainy night evidently had been to unhinge her mind.

I called out again and again, but she made no response, so that the only alternative was to employ brute force. The last load was about to shove off through the surf, so I rushed up the beach, grabbed this poor demented Russian emigrant, threw her over my shoulder, and made towards the shallow boat. Then the worst happened. The woman howled and kicked, struggled to get free, but I held on till gaining the surf-line, where she had to be flopped down. However, before a few seconds had ticked along burst a great Atlantic wave thundering against the sand and swallowing up both of us.

On coming to the surface I saw her long hair just showing and the water receding. I was able to make a grab, seized hold, and then another officer helped me.

It was a fierce struggle, a desperate contest, to persuade her forcibly, matching our combined efforts against her determined obstinacy. Then a momentary interlude as she emptied her lungs of the Atlantic, and she gasped out something in English.

What was that? What did she say?

For a while I was dumbfounded. Then amazement gave way to understanding and embarrassment. No emigrant passenger from the *Lusitania*, this, but a Newfoundlander fatigued after her seven-mile walk from the village. She chanced to be watching her husband in one of the 'dories,' and reckoning up how many dollars the afternoon was bringing them!

At length the *Glencoe* with our passengers and *Lusitania's* crew steamed off to St. John's, leaving behind the Captain, Chief Officer, and myself, to salve anything possible from the wreck. Bitterly cold were the nights, and we had lost all our personal belongings other than what we stood up in. The only place for sleeping or protection from the blasts was a fisherman's hut, where we simply stretched our wearied bodies along the fishy floor. There existed no sort of covering—not even an old sail—so the Captain lay in the centre, the Chief Mate and myself on either side to keep him warm.

What a contrast with a few hours ago, when the 'Old Man' was distant and unapproachable, king of his bridge, regal in his domination over us. Truly in the strangest and most literal manner adversity had brought together strange bed-fellows. No comforts whatsoever, but the barest and wretchedest conditions.

When in the morning we sought warmth by exercising our limbs, we discovered that all sorts of articles had been washed ashore, and the Newfoundlanders were having a busy time helping themselves to whatever flotsam that came along. On the cliffs, staggering with his load, I met an old native who admitted with satisfaction this was one of the finest wrecks the island had been favoured with for years!

Poor old *Lusitania*, her remains were eventually sold for what they would fetch, about £600, the purchaser being the Premier of Newfoundland, (the future) Sir Michael Cashin. It so chanced that at this time Captain (afterwards Commodore Sir) Frederick W. Young, R.N.R., the famous salvage expert, was in St. John's, who, hearing of the disaster, hurried towards us in the old salvage steamer *Algerine*, but nothing could be done and in the latter vessel we three were carried to St. John's.

Here we took residence in lodgings to await the Court of Inquiry, but meanwhile Sir Alfred Jones, Managing Owner of *Lusitania*, impressed with the way we had all behaved and the fact that not one life had been lost, cabled out to the Captain awarding two months' wages for meritorious services rendered. And this came as a veritable windfall, helping us to replenish some of the belongings already lost. It was now arranged for the essential witnesses—that is to say, those who were on watch during the accident—to be retained whilst the rest proceeded to England.

But on the first morning of our arrival in Newfoundland's capital a local paper of the yellowest sort, with sensational headings related a thoroughly inaccurate account of *Lusitania's* loss. It described the 'terrible scenes,' the 'fighting for boats,' 'trampling on women and children,' 'officers using revolvers,' and other untrue details. Such disgraceful exaggerations were too much for our Skipper, who summoned me and several other officers together for conference. Having resolved to make straight for the newspaper office and demand of the editor an apology, we unanimously agreed.

On arrival at the building we demanded to see the editor, and presently the latter appeared in his shirt sleeves but with a scared look. Setting on him with our tongues, we demanded to be told why he had allowed such an article about us to appear in his paper. He tried to explain, and each time we shut him up. Our

combined wrath had risen to boiling point, and we
intended to accept nothing save apologies.

" If you attempt the slightest justification," we added,
"in less time than it takes for a lamb to shake its tail,
fifty sailors and firemen will come to throw you and
your machinery into the street."

The editor protested stoutly.

"I can assure you there's no such article in my paper,"
he averred.

"Oh, yes, there is," we contradicted.

"By the way," our Skipper put in, "your paper is the
Telegraph?"

The editor waxed indignant.

"Certainly not," he denied. "These are the offices
of the *Telegram*."

"Oh! My goodness! The *Telegram?*" repeated the
Captain. "I'm sorry for the mistake, but where does
the *Telegraph* live?"

"Across the road," snapped the man in shirt sleeves,
"and now you can go to hell, the whole darn lot of you."

We offered profuse apologies, tried to explain, yet it
was he who had become the injured party and too full
of abuse to listen any more. We withdrew, therefore,
crossed the street, and found ourselves interviewing the
Telegraph's editor. This time we certainly had found
the real culprit, and he received the accumulation of
our forceful remarks. It was no peaceful scene, yet the
purpose of our visit triumphed, for having listened to
our story he expressed his regrets, promising to make
full amends in the paper's next issue.

Nor did he disappoint the crowd. A marvellous story
did he print, proving that we were the world's finest
seamen, and in fact each of us felt as if on the head we
now wore a golden halo. Such was the rapid transformation from having been regarded as a questionable lot.
The *Telegram* went one stage better and came out with
the headline: 'A Lovely Liar,' piling his opinions of the
Telegraph's editor into something steep. The other

replied, and thus these two local rivals kept things going lively for some time. If we enjoyed the fun, we noticed that though our stay in St. John's became protracted, both these journals never omitted an opportunity to say the nicest things about us.

CHAPTER XI

DURING the weeks before the Inquiry was to be opened concerning the *Lusitania's* loss, we resorted to working up a strong case of defence. A careful study of local currents, and of positions wrongly ascertained through errors in observations, was made, so that by the time we learned that Judge Sprouse would be President of the Court and Captain English sitting as Nautical Assessor, we were ready with our points clearly martialled.

But the name of Judge Sprouse held out neither comfort nor hope, for he was known to be very severe when dealing with marine matters, and seldom did he try a case without some unfortunate officer's certificate being suspended. Also he used to sit in Police Court cases, where his favourite sentence was 'Thirty Days.' Indeed, so established had this become that men in every-day life throughout Newfoundland, when playing poker and holding three 'tens,' were wont to say they possessed a 'Judge Sprouse.'

The first witness to be called was the Captain, who after some searching questions was allowed to stand down. When it became my turn the old skipper was sitting at the back of me, and if I answered a question which he did not much like, he would tug the tail of my coat with a kind of 'Be careful' signal.

The Judge spotted these tactics.

"Now, Captain," he ordered, "stop pulling the tail of his coat."

This instruction being ignored and the skipper having been caught a second time, the Judge promised that if the offence were repeated he would put the delinquent out. My testimony pleased the Judge, who at its conclusion complimented me. "This," said he, "is the most valuable evidence we have had."

(Incidentally, at the time of the disaster I was in my bunk asleep!)

The verdict was finally given in our favour, Judge Sprouse complimented us on having saved all the lives, and indeed we should all be rewarded.

Thus ended another of life's episodes.

We travelled homewards as second-class passengers in the Allan Line *Carthaginian*, by which we reached Glasgow. Long, narrow, with inferior accommodation, this vessel left much to be desired, yet as shipwrecked mariners bound for the United Kingdom we gladly put up with any discomfort. On getting back to Liverpool, the owners, as a reward, appointed us all to their best and fastest ship, S.S. *Lake Simcoe*, then fitting out at Birkenhead. Beautifully decorated, the ex-German *Ems* was more up to date than any previous vessel in which I had sailed. This would be—so far as concerned her new ownership—her maiden voyage and we had a fine send-off; but barely had we reached mid-Atlantic than she broke down. Necessary repairs were effected for the time being, and she crawled into Quebec on one leg, so to speak. Several other voyages I made in her, and this reminds me of a certain surprising incident.

It was the year of King Edward VII's Coronation, the ceremony being at first postponed because of the Royal indisposition. London was full of Oriental personages, who had to while away their time till the delayed occasion should take place. Now one of these —Prince Ranji of Baluchistan—decided that he would fill up the interval by a visit to Canada in our ship, and it was considered by the owners to be a valuable advertisement for the Line. In every way the greatest attention must be paid to see that the Prince and his retinue were made comfortable. He arrived accompanied by twenty-seven servants and two *nautch* girls, was given the best suite, and seen off with no little homage by head directors.

All meals he partook of in one of his cabins, and the ship's doctor who attended was compelled, in accordance with Eastern custom, to taste his own medicine before the watchful Prince drank his apportioned draught. Naturally the doctor made his physic not too unpalatable, and expected that in return for his services a magnificent diamond might be presented. During this voyage the usual concert on behalf of the Seamen's Orphanage was held, and the Prince decided to be present, but not till everyone else had taken their places. As he entered the saloon and was conducted to a seat by the Captain's side, the audience stood up out of respect, and again when he went out. The two *nautch* girls gave an exhibition of their dancing, which won a polite rather than enthusiastic applause, and the evening ended.

As we steamed up the St. Lawrence, it was noticed that, for two or three miles before reaching Montreal wharf, the river-banks were lined with crowds of people, but this curiosity had been roused by a whale coming up from the sea and here remaining. Every time this creature rose to the surface for his blowing, dozens of people blazed away at him with rifles; yet, as one newspaper commented, although his body was filled with lead, his heart was light as ever, till finally at Hochelaga opposite Montreal, the whale succumbed. Certainly by the time when we made fast alongside the wharf, huge crowds had assembled to see the Prince land, though many doubtless expected him to appear on an elephant's back. Actually he drove off to the Windsor Hotel in an open victoria supplied by the shipping company.

Now when at last the India Office in London heard of all this fuss aroused by the potentate's progress, they suddenly bestowed most unusual interest. They had never heard of the Prince, and sent on the news to Canada as warning. There, alas! it came too late for the impostor with his retinue had already crossed the border into the United States. It turned out that he was a curry cook in a New York hotel, had been sent to fetch twenty-seven under-cooks from India, and now returned with them. Well did he bluff his part as Prince, and got to windward of us all.

Somehow ocean-going steamships bring together all sorts of unusual travellers. During that same voyage and among the saloon passengers were a Monsieur and Madame Vere Gould, with their niece. They were proprietors of a Montreal dressmaking business, and had been over to Paris for the latest fashions. Gould was a very quiet fellow, though fond of making friends on board with the officers, in whose quarters he loved to spend his spare moments. His wife was of a retiring disposition, choosing but few acquaintances among passengers, but their niece—a bonny girl of about twenty-three—happened to be more sociable.

On arrival in Montreal, and during our stay, the Vere Goulds gave us many invitations to their house and treated us right royally. Some months later, however, they decided to give up their business and return to Paris. Thence they proceeded to Monte Carlo with the object of trying their luck at the gaming tables. Fortune did not favour them, funds got low, but about this time they made the acquaintance of a beautiful Russian lady who owned considerable jewellery of great value. Furthermore, she became a guest in the Goulds' home. Money had to be obtained from somewhere, and they planned a terrible crime, murdering the Russian for her jewels, then cutting up the body and depositing it in a trunk.

As usual, however, a blunder was made, the man and wife were arrested, and after a long trial in the French courts both were found guilty. Sentenced to be guillotined, they were subsequently reprieved and sent to the French Guiana convict settlement for life. Six months later I heard that he died a raving lunatic, whilst Madame contracted typhoid fever and passed away likewise. From the time of their arrest, the niece had been lying at a friend's house, prostrated by the shock. Then the day came when furniture and all belongings of the Goulds were put up for auction. Souvenir hunters, and those strange people who love to secure anything connected with a notorious crime, flocked to the sale, and a most curious coincidence occurred. At the very moment when to the highest bidder this girl's bed was being knocked down, she passed away.

It was after making several voyages in the *Lake Simcoe* that I was transferred to the *Garth Castle*, which our owners had bought from the Castle Line for passenger service. The time worked round when she must be laid up, so I resolved to spend a couple of months studying for an Extra Master's Certificate which, as everyone knows, is the highest standard in our profession. I was glad to pass into that select circle, and now received appointment to the *Lake Champlain*, one of the Line's newest steamers. In her I spent four or five years as Second, and then as Chief Officer.

I went to that ship in 1902, so we were kept busy carrying back to Canada the troops who had come over to serve in the Boer War. In those days the Canadian Government always looked to the Mother Country for some noted Army officer to serve as Inspector-General of Militia, and the choice had fallen on the 12th Earl of Dundonald. He had served in the Nile Expedition of 1884–5, distinguishing himself at Abu Klea, and during the South African campaign served under Sir Redvers Buller. At the head of the 2nd Cavalry Brigade he was the first person to enter Ladysmith, after Buller had raised the siege.

When Lord Dundonald was appointed to command the British forces in Canada, he travelled with us in the *Lake Champlain*, and from the day he came aboard at Liverpool impressed us all as the real type of an English gentleman, urbane, lofty of character, fearless. It was the latter quality which led this Major-General into

difficulty.   Certain public utterances, reflecting with
frankness upon Sir Frederick Borden, then Minister of
Militia, created so much discussion that in 1904 the
Secretary for War in London recalled Lord Dundonald.
From that date Canada has appointed one of her own
trained officers to be Inspector-General.

The *Lake Champlain* was a comfortable vessel, though
built to carry cattle as well as passengers. Our Captain
had spent many years in the Canadian trade, being
looked upon by us as the 'Father' of this activity. Even
before steam conquered the route, he had commanded
sailing ships. As an experienced navigator of these waters
no Master Mariner could surpass him. It was customary,
when heavy bookings demanded it, for the Company to
hand over Officers' cabins for the use of passengers.
This might be continued during as many as four voyages,
but we were always paid £12 each time by way of
compensation. Since the Chief and Second Officers
normally had cabins to themselves, they individually
received the full cash. The Third and Fourth Officers
berthed together in one cabin: if therefore both berths
were let, the compensation was divided between them.

I still remember an occasion when only the Third
Officer's berth was reserved for a passenger, and the
Fourth Officer had no need to be disturbed. Provided
the traveller were the right sort of fellow, none of the
staff would have objected to sharing his cabin with a
stranger. In this case, unfortunately, the latter turned
out to be a weird being who belonged to a curious sect
domiciled in Michigan. Aged about forty, he was one
of the 'Sons of the House of David,' and he wore long
hair down to his waist. You can well imagine the Fourth
Officer's shock when he saw the appearance of his cabin-
mate. Fancy sending a 'Son of the House of David' to
a sailor! Nor did he hear the last of it for a long time,
though I believe the two got on together excellently.

But almost every voyage was marked by some unusual
characteristic.   Once, shortly after embarking our

passengers at Liverpool, news came down that a number
of wild animals for some menagerie in British Columbia
were to be brought aboard and housed in the after
shelter-deck. I saw that the cages were placed con-
veniently for feeding and properly secured; then, having
left a sailor in charge, I went about my duties to get the
ship away. All went well till we were half-way between
the Isle of Man and Rathlin Island (north of Ireland).
The time was 2 a.m., my watch being below, when the
Boatswain entering my cabin woke me up saying: "One
of the wild animals has got out of its cage and gone to
the steerage amongst the passengers. It's the leopard!"

For the moment I was half-dazed, firstly through
having been roused from a sound sleep, and secondly
because I was at my wits' end to know how I should
act in such a crisis. The old Bo'sun looked scared stiff,
so I thought of my revolver. Then I realized there was
no ammunition! But two of those Indian clubs employed
by athletes stood in my cabin, and I relied upon these,
handing one to the Bos'n. We set out towards the
steerage, being met on the way by the Night Steward
and six sailors, who informed me that the beast had
gone into one of the bathrooms where, owing to the
ship's rolling, the door-catch had slipped into action.
Thus, for the time being, aware that the brute was safe
we felt a certain amount of relief: had he escaped where
children were asleep, heaven alone knew what might
have happened.

The next thing was to secure him, and I got the door
unlatched; but each time it was opened, however slightly,
the animal snarled and made ready to spring. So I had
to think up how we could defeat him by some subtle
method.

Render him unconscious! How? By chloroform!

From the steward I obtained the key of the dispensary,
opened it, took out a stone mortar and half emptied into
it a chloroform bottle. Next, having obtained likewise
a big syringe, I was ready with the following aid: six

H

sailors, one Bos'n, one steward, two Indian clubs, chloroform and syringe, plus one lassoo.

Now for the bathroom!

As I opened the door, the same snarl as previously. Next I transferred charge of this entrance to the old Bos'n, whilst I made final preparations including filling the syringe full of chloroform. Through an opening wide enough to squirt the latter, I let our enemy have it . . . then waited a few minutes to see how he was getting on.

No result! He seemed to wink at me as if to say: "Go ahead. And do your damnedest."

Accepting the challenger, I gave him another dose, which also produced no effect, whereupon, leaving the half-dozen sailors on guard, I returned to the dispensary and tried a variation. Mixing half ether and half chloroform, I hurried back to the bathroom door and was about to administer the final dose when to my horror I found the six sailors in an abnormal condition, reeling about and apparently overcome by the fumes that emanated. The initial job accordingly was to rush the men out into the fresh air.

That being done, I relied on the assistance of Bos'n and steward. Hurling the new concoction at the animal, I was glad to see him reel. Quick! The lasso! Over his head we slipped it, and a few seconds later were dragging our prisoner back to his cage. The sailors, recovered by means of the sea air, now showed up, and each had a kick at him in passing, thereby to obtain some small revenge for the exciting and superfluous trouble during the middle watch. When about 7 a.m. the Captain was called and I went into his cabin to report, he simply roared with laughter as I related what had happened; yet had some of the children been attacked that night, not much hilarity would have remained.

The ship returned for her annual overhaul, during which period we stood by to superintend the work. Now one of the features of such a refit always included the visit of an official rat-catcher, who should make the best possible job of clearing out these pests. That they should come aboard was inevitable, for wherever cargo in bales or cases was dumped into a ship's hold the chance favoured possibility of a rat-nest being brought from land warehouse; and within a short time these vermin became grandparents. Also, further rat families would climb up by ropes and over gangways to visit their friends, even deciding to make a voyage with them should the society be found congenial.

The rat-catcher, be it mentioned, was paid at the rate of thirty shillings a ship. An additional reward accumulated from the sale of each live rat at fourpence to dog-fanciers who engaged in Sunday sport or wished to train puppies. Some of these catchers had their own tricks, and used to arrive not merely with cages and aniseed, but a pillow-slip or sack full of live rats, in case the ship herself did not yield her full quota.

One old fellow that we used to employ was quite a character, and did business with many firms, but the day dawned when to one of these was appointed a new, shrewd, extremely thrifty Scotsman as manager. The latter began to cut down expenses right and left, finally coming to the items of rat-catching. He was not satisfied at all. Why pay thirty shillings when the fellow sold his prey? Double profits! Making too good a thing out of it.

So when the catcher came into the office collecting fees for several ships, he was informed by the manager that the sums would not be paid. This sudden refusal nonplussed the old expert, who argued his point but could get no cash. Next day he called again, and he never omitted once throughout the whole week. Hopeless! The manager was resolute, unsympathetic, and denied him.

Not to be outdone, the wily catcher called for the last time, armed with the regular impedimenta—tin of aniseed, cages, sack of live rats.

"Once and for all," he demanded, "will you pay up for the previous lot caught in those other ships?"

"No," was the firm response. "And that's final."

"Final, is it? All right, then. Since you won't pay me, you can take your damn rats back."

And with this remark he shook the bag full of vermin on to the palatial office carpet.

Things have improved since then. To-day no live rat can be taken ashore from a vessel, but must be destroyed. All ropes and gangways are protected against this invasion, and once every six months the ship has to be fumigated throughout, before being passed by the port's Medical Officer.

CHAPTER XII

IT was not long after the Boer War, when trade became rather slack, that the Company made some modification in their Atlantic sailings till matters might improve. Several of the steamships were transferred to a more southern route and employed as freighters during winter months, fetching from New Orleans in the Gulf of Mexico cargoes of cotton.

Seeing that no passengers were carried now, and only a skeleton crew, we were not compelled to take with us a doctor; the Master having to deal with any case which might crop up. The dispensary still remained on board, and aided by the *Shipmaster's Medical Guide*, doubtless with sailorlike adaptability he could deal with quite a number of ailments. Luckily, during the voyage of which I am thinking, the sickness among all hands was very slight, yet this septuagenarian skipper—hard-boiled though he always seemed—used to make a habit of entering the dispensary every morning, spending some time there rubbing up the information which the *Guide* afforded.

One day, to his surprise and annoyance, on opening the door he found this place full of steam; for a pipe leading through had burst. When the thick, white, woolly fog had been cleared, he looked along the shelves of bottles, and another shock awaited him. There we were on the high seas, with all the fluids requisite for any illness, but despite the *Guide*, now of no practical value. Indeed they were a danger. For the steam had unstuck from the bottles every label!

In his dilemma he sent for me, but I felt not less bewildered than himself. Which label belonged to which bottle? That was the urgent question.

All the same, he was the kind of man who would acknowledge defeat from no set of circumstances, and this apparently hopeless problem wasn't going to keep him in suspense for long. There the bottles above, and below was the deck covered with soaked labels. He glanced where the latter lay. Then, "These damn labels must've dropped in a fairly straight line," he decided, "so that more than likely we shall be correct if we stick each to the nearest bottle."

And in that manner the keeper of the ship's health made a guess-work restoration. Yes: it was mighty fortunate the crew kept so free from illness that trip, for the 'Old Man' expressed himself as well satisfied with the job, though a serious result might quite easily have occurred. On arrival at New Orleans all bottles were landed, examined, and labelled afresh.

I have stressed in previous chapters what an extra-ordinary place is any ship for collecting contrasted types of humanity, and there is also an opportunity for noting these characters closely. To many of the younger generation to-day the name of Edward Whymper conveys little, yet their grandparents will not have forgotten such a human oddity. He passed away three years before the Great War at the age of seventy-one, after an adventurous life made famous principally as mountaineer and explorer. Even in his early 'twenties' he was making a name for himself climbing formidable peaks, but at the age of twenty-five to him belonged the honour of being, not merely the first Briton, but the first human being, to climb the Matterhorn. He likewise belonged to that mountaineering party in which another British subject lost his life, and gossip laid a slur on Whymper in this connection.

Of the incident he very rarely spoke, but whilst crossing the Atlantic he came into my cabin and told me the story. Because the rope between him and others of the party had broken and Whymper was saved, there had been suggestions by slanderers that he intentionally cut the rope. This my visitor strenuously denied, explaining that during the party's descent the Alpine guide turned round and placed the other Briton in a certain position ; but that when the guide was about to place himself in another position, Whymper's companion's feet slipped so that the whole party (excepting Whymper himself) disappeared down the slope, a sheer drop of 4000 feet. Nor have their bodies ever been found. Whymper made it clear to me that he survived solely for the reason that being alert, and the rope having parted as mentioned, he had enough presence of mind to take a quick turn round a boulder with what remained of the line.

Edward Whymper did not confine his adventures to southern Europe, but went north to Greenland, south to South America, investigating Ecuador and the Andes, but to Canada he came with us as passenger more than once. A particular occasion, when he was to sail home from Montreal, sticks out from my memory crystal clear.

At the best of times he might always be reckoned a little quaint, and wherever he went affected to be dressed as a mountaineer, a coil of rope round his shoulder and carrying a knapsack containing his gear. On this night of which I mention he seemed rather more than ordinarily odd. Our sailing time from Montreal generally was at 4 a.m., so that we might have the advantage of good daylight whilst going down the St. Lawrence River. His arrival on board at 10 p.m. showed how wisely he had chosen the time, but when I met Whymper at the gangway, one look at him (complete with mountaineering rig) convinced me that the climber must have been bidding a lot of farewells to his Canadian friends. His condition was something more than merry.

I conducted him down to his stateroom, where one porthole looked out on to the for'ard deck whilst the other looked over the side. Well, after we had yarned a short while, I left him and lay down on my cabin settee for a snooze till 4 a.m., when we got under way. At breakfast, to my astonishment, he was not there.

"Go and tell Mr. Whymper that breakfast is ready," I called to a steward.

But the passenger couldn't be found, and not till a little later was it possible to piece the story together with the assistance of his cabin steward.

Whilst still in a drunken stupor, the mountaineer was unpacking his bag when a large head thrust itself through the for'ard porthole and gave one dickens of a roar. The unfortunate Whymper, unaware that we were carrying as cargo hundreds of semi-wild cattle, released a yell, grabbed his bag, and fled like a rocket on deck, down the gangway to an hotel. There he spent the rest of that night (I learned later), and took the morning train to New York. He made neither complaint nor comment, never even asked for refund of his passage-money, but a year later when we met he put the blame on me with charming vagueness.

"It was your damn fault," he insisted. "You ought to have known."

Doubtless, as we have already observed, a maritime officer is supposed to know all sorts of things, but however faithful to his duty, however conscientious in its execution, some person will not approve. Take the following illustration.

We had arrived in a home port after being away from England, and a sailor came to ask of me a pass for his bag; a wooden tub which he had made; together with a 14-lb. tin of dripping. His request being granted, the man was walking through the dock-gates when the policeman examined the bag. Inside he found numbers of large pin-cushions made of different-coloured materials. Closer scrutiny revealed that these materials included tea, coffee, and cocoa. Arrest then followed, and I had to give witness before the magistrate, to whom I made it convincingly clear that the man had stolen ship's stores.

"Well," inquired the Justice of the Peace, "what about the tub? And the dripping?"

"These tubs are of no value, being normally thrown

overboard," I told him. "And the dripping is often the cook's perquisite. In practice it is given away or sold for a small sum to one of the crew."

The sailor, therefore, was acquitted with regard to these, but fined forty shillings for theft of ship's stores. Off he went home with tub and dripping. Next day I discovered what the dripping really comprised, and the scheme certainly could not be thought other than ingenious. True, at the top a layer of beef fat had been poured on warm, but only to conceal 14 lb. of ship's butter. This revelation upset the seaman considerably, especially when he learned of his dismissal.

Then, addressing himself to me, he fired his parting remark, which was neat and terse without being florid.

"Look 'ere," the dejected thief began. "If I was to tell you all that I think about yer, I'd have to engage a blinking large hall, pay the rent in advance, and shut out all the women and children."

I am sure that from among those fine old Master Mariners who commanded sailing ships in the last decade of the nineteenth century some of the most picturesque portraits could have been painted. Let us add to our gallery that of another septuagenarian who still stuck to the sea. His clothes seemed nearly as old as himself. When he landed in a foreign country, he wore the same suit as at home. No change he deemed necessary, and when his friends asked why he didn't wear better garments, his answer was always: "Why should I care? When I'm abroad, nobody knows me. And when I'm home, everybody knows me."

As soon as the ship got south of the River Plate, bound round the Horn, his greatest ambition was to drown his sorrows in Scotch whisky. Consequently very little was seen of him in those latitudes, though plenty was heard as he lay in his cabin singing songs at the top of his voice. The ship would then give a heavy roll, he would curse her for doing so, then quietness prevailed until he commenced shouting: "To hell with the Owners, and God Save the Queen." But when the case of whisky was finished, he would again bellow so that the Chief Mate and I could not fail to hear.

"Steward! Steward! Get me up another case of whisky. I want to give the Mate a stimulant."

This particularly infuriated the last-mentioned officer. Seven years had he been serving in that ship and never one drink from the Captain. She continued a thirsty and hungry vessel. Seagulls gave up following us: there was nothing left to be thrown overboard.

Another old skipper named Jock was on the point of retiring, after being at sea since his 'teens, and now he was trying to pile up his savings as much as possible so as to carry him on with the pension which his Company might grant. Every voyage, on leaving port, he was wont to confide in me his troubles, complaining how extravagantly his family seemed to be during his absence, and especially with respect to the gas bills.

One day whilst making the same statement to an American passenger, the latter inquired how often old Jock was at home.

"A week in every five," replied the latter.

"Well," said the American, "I will give you a good tip for reducing the bill, but you must keep it quiet, and don't let even your family know."

"I promise," Jock nodded.

"Now listen. At night, when everyone's gone to bed, stand on a stool, place your mouth on a gas-burner, and blow down the pipe."

"What'll that do?"

"Something very useful. Blow back the register of the meter. That's what happens."

Old Jock returned home, and at the end of each week in five he used to blow down the pipe as instructed, and the time drew abreast when the Inspector came to read the meter. It so happened that Jock was at home, sitting upstairs smoking his pipe, wondering why the Inspector was so long about it.

Finally the gas man stated the difficulty and consulted his book.

"Well, Captain, I'm not in a position to say why and how. But certainly we seem to owe you seven shillings and six pence."

When at last this old seafarer retired and settled down in his little house, 'The Poplars,' surrounded by a quarter-acre of ground, he hoped to spend his days planting flowers and doing odd jobs about the garden. One day I paid him a visit, to find him much upset.

"As I plant the seeds," he bewailed, "the damn birds come and pick them out."

"Why not have a scarecrow?" I suggested.

But this idea he dismissed.

"If there's to be any scarecrow here, it'll be me."

The following week, on going to see him again, I found him seated in his drawing-room with windows wide open as it might be with gun-ports ready for action. There he waited, smoking his pipe, but by his side was the ammunition for attack. All day long he kept a smart look-out, and whenever a bird swooped down to steal the seed this alert mariner put his hand into a bucket of small coal, and bombarded the feathery thieves.

Resourceful, independent of others' opinions, he had been accustomed to command all these years, nor did he relinquish the habit of being supreme within his sphere. Fond of dogs, each of them had perished one after the other by some strange canine, but the Skipper definitely suspected a certain Airedale. This belonged to a farmer, who every morning brought it down the footpath which ran alongside the Captain's house and at night the dog accompanied him back to watch the farm some distance out of the village. Annoyed by the mysterious worrying of his four-footed friends, the sailor said to the farmer:

"I'll never be satisfied till I get a dog that can beat yours."

"Well, Captain, you're welcome," agreed the other.

So days were spent searching for something cheap. The task turned out unsuccessful, till by accident a very rough sort of man was seen taking a big bull-terrier into a railway station. This seemed just the animal which would fight any Airedale.

Getting into conversation with the unkempt owner, the Captain made him an offer.

"I'll give you a pound for the dog, but on condition that you take it to my house."

The man demurred, owing to the distance, and asked twenty-five shillings.

"All right! I'll be there when you arrive."

An hour later the bell rang, and there stood the dog —hero of a thousand battles, with more scars on him than ever a pugilist carried, and (as the Captain described), 'with a head as big as a bucket.' So the dog was accepted, but minus collar and leash. These doubtless would be evidence that the animal had been stolen, so could be dispensed with.

The day waned, and at 6 p.m. there sat the Skipper waiting by his gate, his new dog well hidden inside the house. Along walked farmer and Airedale homeward bound.

"Hallo! There you are. Come inside and have a nip. You've got time."

The farmer assented, and followed up the steps.

"Well," resumed the proud new owner, "I always said I'd get a dog to beat yours."

"That so? You're welcome to it."

Upon which the Skipper opened the door and called the bull-terrier.

"What you think of him, Farmer?"

The latter looked at the head, tried to count the scars, but simultaneously formed a secret opinion. What he openly expressed scarcely conveyed the real truth.

"Fairly good. Yes, not too bad . . . yet I still believe my Airedale could lick him."

"Right! And I think otherwise. Still, when you come

past my gate I shall be there with the dog, and we can let the two decide between themselves."

But the contest was never allowed to mature. The farmer came that way not again. Preferring a long cross-country walk to the short cut by the path which skirted the sailor's house, he avoided the battle royal which might have ended in the Airedale's rout.

It was the hard school of seafaring which developed such sharp-chiselled characteristics in these sons of the ocean. With all its perils and difficulties, the sailing ship life for these shellbacks was irresistible until declining years forced them ashore. Then often enough began the steep tragedy: it was not practicable at that age to readapt oneself to new conditions and fit in with a new scheme of living. And during the final months afloat many a brave disposition has been haunted by this apprehension.

There was one, however, who by a certain age was quite looking forward to settling down within four brick walls. From boyhood to ripe years he had ploughed the angry main, revelled in it: beating round the Horn had long been to him a joy-ride.

Nevertheless increasing physical weakness hinted that he ought to be planning for some job away from boisterous seas and gales of wind. His name was not Murphy, but that will suffice, for an Irishman he certainly remained till the end. With £40, and after much puzzling of his brains all the way home from 'Frisco, he started a greengrocer's shop, at the same time purchasing a donkey-cart. For months he carried on, but against adverse fate, and there was too much in him of the reckless sailor for development into a money-maker: nothing could transform his original outlook. When, sometimes, I used to run across Murphy after one of my voyages, he confessed that things were going not too well.

"More at home on a topsail yard, rounding Cape Horn, than here in my own backyard."

One day, too, as I passed his shop there was Murphy

busy trying to effect repairs, or something, to the donkey-cart's wheel.

"What're you doing, Murphy?" I hailed him.

"Jambing up the steering-gear," he answered, and went on with his profitless work.

Months passed, and I returned from another voyage. Murphy came along to greet his old shipmates, but his slender business no longer existed, and he was broke to the world. Wearing that same old smile which had concealed many a disappointment, he had now to admit that drink was the principal cause of his downfall. As to the donkey, it had developed rheumatics in the knees through waiting for him in the cold wind outside public-houses. That might have been true, but the 'moke' was reputed to have more intelligence than normally possessed by asses. It used to be related that if Murphy had not emerged from the ale-bar by 5 p.m., the animal would go home and get some food before returning to wait for his master.

Then the climax ripened rapidly when the donkey died. With failure of the green-grocer's shop, the realization that time spent within a public-house got him nowhere began to make Murphy's mind concentrate more accurately. Back he must go to his seafaring. Thus his final years were spent like his earlier ones, wallowing about the North Atlantic, till at the very end they brought him to fade away on land.

The day of his funeral suggested little sadness, and on a bright summer's morning I witnessed poor Murphy's coffin on its way to the cemetery near the town's out-skirts. A few of his old friends and shipmates were following astern when, to my astonishment, the procession, instead of carrying on, suddenly halted outside a suburban 'pub.' Here all hands entered to have a drink, whilst the hearse hove-to outside.

This was rather too much for me, so I wandered across and remarked to one of the mourners as he came out of the bar:

"This is a curious way of doing things?"

"No, it ain't," he denied. "It's just as the corpse wished. He knew well enough we should all stop to have a drink on the way *back* from the funeral; and he left instructions that we should have that drink on the way there—so that he could be with us, like."

CHAPTER XIII

IT may seem incredible to some people, none the less, in many a ship with a large crew recently joined often for a few days some of the men below have never set eyes on their Skipper. Especially is this true as regards cooks, stewards, and firemen.

The subject of our present yarn happened to be another Irishman, but of a very different calibre. Let us call this genuine person by the fictitious name of Connell. Unlike Murphy, he was a lifelong teetotaller, a man of strong and upright character, who always walked through life by the straight and narrow way without deviation. His charity to all men was genuine, for he never lost an opportunity for doing anybody a good turn, and withal he possessed plenty of dry humour.

As a seaman, this Captain was unsurpassed: a finer example never trod a deck. As a navigator, his record was second to none of his contemporaries. He loved both the seafaring life and those who served under him. Throughout his remarkable career, despite the difficult problems of his own particular shipping trade that was full of pitfalls, he never made a mistake, but triumphed right to the finish, envied by all mariners but not less respected.

Among his habits at sea was to promenade the deck between 6 and 8 a.m. every morning. Things being generally quiet at this time, with few passengers about, he would wear not his uniform but an ancient greenish coat with a 'bucko' cap. The effect was to suggest a poverty-stricken individual who needed human pity. Well, one morning after recently quitting port for a voyage, and the ship full of passengers still in their cabins, Connell was taking his stroll. She belonged to the old-fashioned steamers where the galley was on deck, and since in his perambulation he kept passing the open door where the scullion was lighting the fire, this ill-dressed commanding officer could not help being noticed. His identity, however, was still hid from the scullion, who, taking compassion (and simultaneously wishing to do himself a kindness) called through the galley-door:

"I'll sell you a nice cup o' tea for threepence."

"No, thanks," answered the Captain, and continued his walk round the deck.

Presently again he was passing the galley, when the scullion—extremely anxious to do business—increased the offer.

"An' I'll throw you in a damn big bun."

Once more the offer had to be declined.

Shortly afterwards entered the second cook.

"Morning! How's everything?"

"Fine!" reported the scullion. "Few minutes ago tried to sell that poor old steerage-passenger a cup of tea. But 'e couldn't run to threepence—even with a big bun as well."

"S'truth! What! 'Im in the old coat and 'at? You've done it, m'lad. That's our Skipper."

The scullion collapsed, but Connell had many a smile to himself over this incident. Rising to the very top, he became Commodore of that company's fleet for many years until the date for compulsory retirement.

"When once you drop your mudhook for the last time," he often foretold, "you're forgotten. Nobody wants to know you in retirement, and everything's all over."

He was quite right, and it means a great effort making new friends.

But in the village, where Captain Connell settled down, lived several other splendid old skippers who, like the Commodore, had known every wave of the ocean by sight. Now you can imagine that when this little select

I

crowd got together, swapping yarns and with ample time on their hands, any injustice within the village would be discussed and endeavour be made to right the same.

Among the local inhabitants was a butcher with a dog, in some respects not less fierce than the previously mentioned farmer's Airedale. Curiously, the butcher's animal reserved his bitterest hatred for Dalmatians, and it was common knowledge that never had one of that breed ever passed through the village alive. Not less true was the butcher's local unpopularity, and these old Salts plotted to annoy him. After a few days' searching around within a radius of 40 miles, they were lucky enough to obtain just the quarrelsome savage cur likely to take on all comers. The only drawback was that this dog had a white coat.

A 'bruiser' he unquestionably must be, but during the first few days they took him for walks, treated him with great kindness, so that to them he would be not less docile than loyal. Then the ancient mariners prepared to give the villagers a grand free show, and first to effect the necessary camouflage. 'Pongo' was the name of this ferocious white animal destined for the greatest contest within recollection of the oldest inhabitant, but 'Pongo' must be made to look like a Dalmatian. Picture, then, three retired skippers making a concoction from burnt cork, persuading 'Pongo' on to the kitchen table, who allowed himself to be black-spotted all over.

A triumph of artistic ingenuity resulted, and the next thing was to hire an open carriage. The trio of Captains then were driven through the village with their 'Dalmatian' trotting enticingly behind. Unfortunately, though the butcher's shop was passed and re-passed, the local champion was not on watch. Most disappointing, after all this trouble! For the third time they made the attempt, and now they were filled with delight unbounded. At the shop-door, yawning pleasantly and fresh from his afternoon nap, lazed the butcher's pride, when suddenly the yawn died and violent activity flashed instead.

Another of those Dalmatians daring to invade the village!

Within a few moments the darnedest fight of canine history was in full swing, encouraged by the three promoters; but to the anger of the butcher, who used every article save his cleaver to rescue a situation already doomed, 'Pongo' disputed the onslaught and started his own counter-attack with such spirit that his rival was left on the field of battle mortally wounded. Off went the sons of the sea in their carriage followed by the spotted victor, but a sequel occurred a few days later.

Summoned to appear before the local magistrate, their conduct was investigated and the butcher looked for his revenge. It came not, for the verdict went in favour of the seafarers who, none the less, were warned never to spot their dog again.

I can remember one Captain in whom the spirit of fun was never manifested. Standing about 5 feet 6 inches, this little fellow more than any other commander in his line was responsible for getting many an officer 'sacked.' We might sum him up as suspicious and distrustful of others, yet vainglorious as regards himself, with something also of a strutting actor's attributes. A few minutes before the ship was due to leave port, he would send for each of his officers and utter a few kind words—but at the same time putting his face so close that it seemed as if he were about to impress a kiss. Artful old fellow! He was smelling an officer's breath to find out if the latter had been drinking.

This commander made himself a great favourite with the lady passengers, by whom in turn he was not a little flattered; and the high opinion which he had formed of himself he always endeavoured that others should share. His love of the spectacular and dramatic were much evident during the days of bad weather, when he made it his business to come down for meals in the saloon with oilskins and sea-boots still dripping water. Little did his worshippers know that he had thrown this over himself just previously. Still, as he stood at the saloon's threshold, disrobing with considerable ceremony whilst outside the gale raged and seas smote the hull, his feminine admirers were immensely impressed. Playing to his audience? Yes: he scarcely missed a chance.

Once he became slightly indisposed—merely some mild stomach trouble—but enough to start the women sympathizing.

"Oh, Captain, I do hope you're feeling better," they would tell him across the table. "Captain, you really must take better care of yourself. However should we get into port, if anything happened to you?"

"I simply don't know," he confessed unashamedly.

Now this last remark happened to be overheard by another wife sitting at the same table, and her husband was master of a large sailing ship aboard which she had made several voyages round the world. Woman-like, she inquired of the boaster with seeming innocence:

"But, Captain, surely all your officers have Masters' Certificates?"

"Well, yes. They have."

"Then couldn't they take over the command as ably as you?"

"They *think* they could," was his arrogant response.

And on a later date it seemed as if circumstances were to encourage his distrust of others. For that evening there was to be the ship's concert and, whilst sitting at the dinner-table, the ladies were asking him either to sing or to recite.

"No," he refused without excessive humility, "I'm good only at facing danger."

Barely had the words left his lips than a terrific bump shook the ship, and the 'Old Man' almost collapsed. The officer on the bridge had run the steamer into some field ice, unyielding enough to make the hull shiver from stem to stern. Luckily, however, it had been no berg, so that serious harm did not follow.

Perhaps the reader may never have heard of a woman

being skipper of a steamer? Many years before the San Francisco earthquake, already mentioned, the fleet of beautiful sailing ships might remain anchored in the bay waiting for the grain season month after month. Meanwhile, of course, provisions were essential and these used to be brought off by a tug commanded by a very decent man assisted by his wife who became so expert that she was practically First Mate. All the skippers of the fleet liked the tugmaster and gave him every encouragement: but, one morning, quite suddenly he died and this meant a serious financial outlook for the widow. She would have to hire a master, and thereby all earnings must suffer considerably.

In her own opinion, likewise that of the sailing ship skippers, she was quite capable of running the tug herself. The law, however, required that the master of such a tender must hold a proper certificate to navigate within the bay's limits. The sailing ship skippers sympathetically approached on her behalf the Commissioners, begging departure from any old custom and precedent that might ordinarily disqualify her. The result was that their petition received favourable attention, the widow after examination for ability won her certificate, and everybody felt happy.

The concession created no end of interest in San Francisco, local papers were full of it, she was photographed standing at the wheel wearing a peaked cap with goldleaf. Thick head-lines across the page called notice to the 'First Woman Skipper.' But almost without delay joy was again turned into sorrow. The tug lay alongside the wharf, filling up before beginning her round of the fleet, and meanwhile it seemed right to celebrate this unique occasion; wherefore the woman, her engineer, and the deck-hand, came ashore and marched along into the nearest saloon. One drink led to another, minutes sped by more quickly than was being realized, and at length three extremely jovial people emerged on to the wharf arm-in-arm.

Nor had they barely gained the water's edge than the shock of a lifetime sent them into complete helplessness. That which their eyes beheld, their fuddled brains tried to disbelieve. It was to them like the forthcoming earthquake and fifty additional troubles rolled into one.

The tug! The only portion now visible was the top of its mast showing out of the sea. For the engineer had carried the fresh-water hose on board to fill a big tank that was to supply the sailing fleet, but long sojourn in the drinking saloon had caused him to forget. Result? Unhindered, the water flowed over the tank, on deck, down the engine-room, into the bilges—in fact, everywhere, until the unfortunate tug could float no longer and down she went.

A regrettable beginning to a new command! A reminder of life's uncertainties!

But one of the best illustrations respecting the changes and chances affecting human fortune had for its background that Chilean roadstead, Tocopilla, where it will be remembered we lay some while in the *Ditton* loading nitrate. Within that bay, so long as man's memory could go back, the waters had always been amazingly plentiful of fish big as herrings. All you had to do was to lower a basket over the ship's side and haul it up immediately. Each of us is familiar with that careless phrase: 'literally alive with fish,' yet with regard to Tocopilla Bay this alone describes the condition.

Now, on land, adjacent to the beach were some works used for repairing locomotives that fetched the nitrate from the Andes. Most of the officials and men had come from Leeds, encouraged by that picturesque personality, Colonel North, who, when first he arrived out in the 'sixties, was bound by a contract of only £60 a year. Long before he died, North rose to be a famous million-aire, known universally as the Nitrate King.

The desire to amass wealth quickly often derives from envy or jealousy of another's success, and it may have been North's prodigious fortune which made these

locomotive people yearn to become equally independent.
'What man has done, man can do.' If one far-sighted
mind can scoop a fortune out of the ground, others might
take it from the sea. Fish manure should surely be almost
as valuable as nitrate for fertilizing, and fish oil would
find a ready market in the European factories.

So these ambitious men pooled their finances, sent to
England for machinery, had it erected ashore, obtained
a lighter that could so easily be filled with fish; and by
the simplest method of transport these constant cargoes
would be pressed or crushed into the oil and manure.
The plan seemed so feasible, the idea based on everyday
observation. Yet had they been more familiar with
history and the vagaries of fish they would have recollected that hundreds of years ago—for no apparent
reason—the silvery herring deserted the Baltic and made
the North Sea waters off Holland their future habitation.
Thus it used to be said that Amsterdam was built on the
foundation of herring-bones, and that from the herring
wealth were constructed the Dutch ocean fleets which
made the seventeenth-century Lowlanders such a
prosperous nation.

And all through the waywardness of cold-blooded
animals flicking their tails through the water in another
direction! Precisely the same phenomenon happened in
Tocopilla Bay. No sooner had operations been arranged
for a profitable industry than, without the slightest warning, these millions of fish swam off and were never seen
again. Instead of being a vast moving jelly, the water
became crystal clear and deserted below its surface: but
many a gloomy human being reflected on the strange
anomaly that some people have exceeding great luck
while others have misfortune thrust over them.

The mention of South America summons back to my
mind an old shipmate and brother-officer, Captain Gillies,
who rose to become General Manager of our shipping
company but passed away about a year ago. Early in the
present century Gillies was being given his first command,

for which reason the final instructions to him were about to be issued verbally by Captain Mowat, then General Superintendent. The latter can be visualized as a great, raw-boned Canadian from New Brunswick, sailor to his finger-tips, with a heart as big as a lion. 'Barney' Mowat, as we thought of him behind his back, was a man of few words and firm action: if we feared him, we likewise loved him.

Mowat, having sent for Gillies, informed the latter as follows:

"You will take the S.S. *Milwaukee* with her cargo of coal to the west coast of South America and there discharge, after which you will proceed to another Chilean port and load nitrate for home. Kindly note that having discharged the coal, you must keep part of the money for crew's wages, ship's dues, and other expenses incurred whilst off the coast. The rest you will send to the Company's head office in England."

Gillies reflected a moment, looked at 'Barney,' then inquired:

"But supposing there is no *rest*?"

"Well," answered Mowat, "all I can tell you is that, such being the case—there'll be a hell of a long *rest* for you after you get home."

Some years later we were running a passenger and freight service from Austria and Italy to Canada, and at one port our agent used to come down to see that the work of loading went ahead satisfactorily. His leading man, however, was much given to drink and in that condition appeared whilst on duty, though able to carry on with a certain amount of difficulty. By a certain day matters had gone too far, it was useless to pretend or shut an indulgent eye; so the agent, taking his trusted assistant to one side, rebuked him.

"You'll have to stop this sort of thing, you know. If, when I come down here for the next ship, you're found drunk, then out you go."

A fortnight intervened, another ship arrived, and

along came the agent who sought out his leading man.

"There you are! In spite of what I warned you, drunk again."

The man obstinately attempted to argue the point.

"I'm not," he insisted. "I tell you I'm *not*."

"You're talking nonsense, man. Look at you! Why can't you behave decently? What made you get drunk a second time?"

"I'm not drunk a second time," stammered the culprit. "I'm not drunk again. It's the same drunk as before."

One of our ports on that route was Trieste, where the Seamen's Mission was being looked after by an English parson. I had not long been in command of my ship when we arrived and he asked me if during the voyage we could raise a few subscriptions by means of a concert. Wishful to help his organization, I was rather up against a problem, since ship's concerts by well-established custom were ear-marked for the Seamen's Orphanage. However, inasmuch as we were away from England and our passengers though embarked in Canada consisted mostly of Americans, I had to think of a way for helping the parson.

Then the notion was born of making a collection during the Sunday morning service. After the usual prayers had been said for the Royal Family—petitions, by the way, which apparently did not interest American tourists —I uttered a very long prayer for the President of the United States, having also arranged for the stewards during this protracted period to pass round the plates.

The result worked wonderfully and, instead of 10-cent bits, the congregation handed out dollar bills. "That," congratulated our passengers afterwards, "is the first time we ever heard an English Captain pray for our President."

CHAPTER XIV

MANY years ago, during the days of sail, one of my shipmates previous to joining us had been serving as Second Mate of a small barque. Off the Equator a French sailing ship collided with her and the barque sank within a few minutes, only my friend and two sailors surviving from the British vessel. Luckily for the French ship, which happened to be homeward-bound, her forward bulkhead saved her though foretopmast and yards went tumbling down.

Now the homeless trio received every kindness, and were given what few clothes were available. In due course the shores of Cornwall were sighted, and a signal was made by the French Captain via Lloyd's Signal Station to his owners; so that almost simultaneously with the ship's arrival past St. Anthony Lighthouse into the River Fal orders were telegraphed for her to make for Havre in tow of a tug. The French skipper requested that the three British survivors might accompany him in order that their version of the accident might also be heard, and to this the owners wired their approval.

The latter treated the shipwrecked mariners with consideration and, before leaving Havre for London, gave the British Second Mate the sum of 500 francs (which in those days signified quite a lot of money) to cover the cost of new suits and travelling expenses across to London. It was impressed upon him that, whatever happened, he must hang on to the couple of sailors and see that they didn't get lost. These two seamen, on the other hand, were equally determined not to lose the Second Mate or the rare opportunity of getting an excellent rig-out gratis. In fact they so arranged that they did very nicely out of the bounty, with a result that barely enough francs remained for rail and cross-Channel steamer. Thus did the unfortunate Second Mate have to deny himself of purchasing clothes, but remain content with an old French hat and claw-hammer coat presented by the French skipper.

Odd? Well, this British officer certainly looked a 'proper tough' in such disreputable kit, and was well conscious of the effect; yet he cared for nothing so long as he could steer his pair of sailors safely home. Finally they reached England, he placed his men in the train for London, whilst he walked down the platform to buy a newspaper. Sitting in the railway carriage, smart in their new attire, they contrasted powerfully with their guardian's shabby appearance. As the Second Mate was returning, he noticed a railway porter speaking to them, but the conversation terminated immediately as the officer got nearer. Arrived in the compartment and about to read his paper, the latter could not fail to notice that his protégés were consumed with laughter.

"Well, what is it?" the Mate demanded.

They told him.

"That there porter," they shook their sides. "Slipped alongside to give us the tip. Thinks you're one of them cardsharpers. 'If 'e arsks yer to play crown-and-anchor, between 'ere and London, my advice is *don't*.' That's what 'e told us."

And went into fits of laughter again.

It reminds me of a sailing ship skipper who was so cool in emergencies that he could make too light of things. Once, after getting south of the River Plate into the 'roaring forties' heading towards the Horn, night descended and the weather looked none too good. The vessel was bowling, but hard pressed, and the Mate felt it his duty to go and warn the Captain who was lying in his cabin.

The 'Old Man,' however, failed to be anxious.

Time—approaching midnight. Wind—freshening rapidly.

"Don't worry," he advised father-like, possibly not too pleased at having been roused from sleep. "When the moon gets up, it'll scoff the wind."

"Aye, aye, sir."

Back to his watch went the Mate, and shortly afterwards a heavy squall burst from above, heeling the ship down, and away disappeared her royals, t'gallantsails, besides all her staysails.

Hundreds of pounds' worth of canvas gone!

Once more this officer descended, and this time woke the Skipper with a full announcement.

"Well, sir, the moon's up, she's scoffed your royals, your t'gallantsails, and all your staysails. Yes. And now she's looking mighty hard at your topsails."

But now let us quit yarning and get on with a notable chapter of steamship history destined to have a great influence on my future career as on the trend of North Atlantic shipping.

I was still serving in the Beaver Line, whose connection with the Canadian trade went back to the time when their sailing ships served that route. One evening, whilst in port, I was surprised to read the following head-line in an evening paper:

'Canadian Pacific Railway Company Negotiating For Atlantic Steamship Line.'

I knew well enough that already this enormous corporation owned five vessels on the Pacific: those three white ladies *Empress of Japan*, *Empress of India*, *Empress of China*; together with the *Tartar* and *Athenian*. Even in those pre-War days the trio of 'Empresses' were intended to become armed merchant cruisers should hostilities break out. Subsidized by the British Government, fitted with mountings to carry eight 4.7-inch guns, possessing a speed of 18 knots, they were unusually able ships for that date. They have long since passed out of existence, been replaced by larger, more magnificent creatures; yet mariners and travellers alike will not easily forget these stately queens of the sea.

Well, on continuing to read this newspaper article it amazed me when I realized that the fleet to be purchased was the Beaver Line. Daily the paragraphs were becoming more emphatic about the deal, and I became more uneasy; for the possibility of the new owners ridding themselves of existing officers in favour of their own staff could not be ruled out. Perhaps after all these sea-years I was going to find myself on a lee shore?

So I set out to inquire of the C.P.R. representative whether the story was true and, if so, to offer my services. Armed with my credentials, I sallied forth the next morning to call on Mr. Arthur Piers, the company's Steamship Manager, who received me with courtesy. Whilst answering my queries with considerable reserve, he informed me that any officer joining the C.P.R. must have an Extra Master's Certificate, besides holding a commission in the Royal Naval Reserve. I was able to acquaint him with the fact that I possessed both.

"Very well," said Mr. Piers. "You've no need to be anxious. Go back to your ship, and should we purchase the fleet, you will be all right."

A few days later followed the official announcement confirming that the fleet had been bought. So that's how I joined the Canadian Pacific. I hadn't stolen another man's job, nor seen my predecessor's body floating down the river, nor had I pushed anyone in. It was just as part of the ship, hanging on to my own job, that I went over to the new owners.

Arrangements were made for hauling down the Beaver Line's house flag, and hoisting that of the C.P.R. The latter's Marine Superintendent, Commander Walsh, R.N.R., came aboard; the Canadian Pacific's red-and-white chequers were bent-on and sent up to the mast-head; whilst the old flag bearing a beaver resting on a log was lowered by myself and another officer. Some modification of our uniform was made, and the Company immediately raised every officer's salary so liberally that the sudden severance from former ownership and old-established connections became softened. If new friends had to be made, within a few months we had not merely fitted into a different scheme, but realized that we belonged to one of the greatest corporations on earth, and its shipping interests were only an item among its vast concerns. Our arrival at a Canadian port, each voyage, brought us into closer touch with railway people, yet the Company was introducing something more than a mere ferry from England. Beginning with about fourteen 10,000 to 12,000 tons steamships for the Atlantic service, a notable precedent had been introduced and important developments would follow.

We met, as our passengers, some of the famous old pioneers responsible for that main railway line connecting Montreal right across Canada with Vancouver, to say nothing of its extensions to Quebec, Toronto, and in other directions. The stories related of how, in spanning a continent, one immense problem after another had to be solved put fresh enthusiasm into our seafaring lives. It was one long thrilling chapter in the history of empire-building, and, at the time of our transference, the Chairman of Directors (Sir William Van Horne); the President (Mr. T. Shaughnessy—later raised to the peerage); the Vice-Presidents (Sir W. White, Mr. McNicol, Mr. Ogden, and Mr. Bosworth); were inaugurating a bold policy. After a couple of years' running they determined to build two of the largest and fastest passenger ships anywhere to be found: the *Empress of Ireland* and *Empress of Britain*, which soon were to win a rare popularity on the Canadian route from England.

So, then, did it come about after a few months that I was appointed Chief Officer in the *Empress of Ireland* under Commander J. V. Forster, R.N.R. We were packed with a full list of passengers every voyage, and all things were done most efficiently to a high standard. Presently came the contract for carrying mails, and also a further undertaking whereby the Company was responsible for the landing in Japan of mails from England within

about 21 days. These two vessels would make the
voyage from Liverpool to Quebec in 6 days, 3 hours;
actually traversing the Atlantic—land to land—in 3 days,
19 hours. At Quebec a train with powerful locomotives,
and steam up, would be waiting at the quay; passengers
and mails for China or Japan landed immediately, so that
within less than half an hour of our arrival they were
being rushed towards Vancouver, the trip across Canada
lasting not longer than 90 hours.

If you look at all this imaginatively, there comes a
wonderful thrill. Speed annihilating distance, ocean and
land yielding to modern progress, valuable time econo-
mized and the world encompassed luxuriously. For at
Vancouver, alongside the quay, would be waiting one of
the C.P.R. 'Empresses' with a full head of steam, and a
few minutes after the train's arrival this vessel was off at
full speed for the Orient.

Romance? All this unity of purpose, this magnificent
organization combined with detailed achievement, brought
back to voyaging something which at one time belonged
to sail. The performances over the globe were truly
marvellous: every man, whether on ship or quay, or
train, being keen as mustard, each competing to beat his
opposite number for reliability. During the twelve
months that I was serving in the *Empress of Ireland* we
carried many illustrious personages, including Earl Grey,
Governor-General of Canada; Viscount Lascelles; Prince
Fushima, the Emperor of Japan's cousin; Rudyard
Kipling; Marconi; and others. But, during the trip
when the first-mentioned came with us, a Hungarian
emigrant travelling steerage suddenly died.

Arrangements were made for the funeral to take place
next morning at ten o'clock. By 6 a.m. the body had
been stitched up in canvas, and deposited within the after
wheelhouse; at 9.45 the six sailors who were to carry
the corpse on a grating from the wheelhouse stood by;
and I impressed the fat old Bos'n's mate with the necessity
to have all things prepared that no hitch might be

possible. Covered with a Union Jack, the body was to
be moved at a given signal, the six men assuming a
mournful aspect with head on breast and solemn tread.
On reaching a certain spot, I was to join the procession,
followed by the Captain, who would await the right
moment and then the last ceremonies would begin.

Nothing seemed to have gone wrong, everyone in his
proper station and the routine running smoothly, when
my eyes caught sight of an awful error. Just as I joined
to follow behind the Bos'n's mate, I glanced ahead. No
Union Jack! But Earl Grey's private flag, which consisted of a modified Union Jack with crest in the centre,
used by the Governor-General when in Canadian waters
and flown from the masthead. That confounded assistant
of the Bos'n had spent about ten minutes smoothing the
crest out neatly over the Hungarian's stomach, and my
remarks during the procession were not chosen for
kindly sentiment. I called the stupid fellow every name
that came to my tongue, promised to have him 'fired' on
return to Liverpool; yet it was too late for changing the
flag, and there was Earl Grey standing as a looker-on.
The funeral ended, so when all had been cleared away
I went up and reported to the Captain in his cabin. This
is what he said by way of comment:

". . . And when we have the next funeral in this ship,
kindly moderate your damn language."

Not long afterwards I was given my first command—
the S.S. *Milwaukee*, which had obtained a good deal of
publicity in connection with the Boer War by carrying
General Kronje to the island of St. Helena as prisoner.
Years earlier this vessel had passed through a curious
experience. She ran on the rocks off the north of Scotland, and became so tightly wedged that it was impossible
to shift her, wherefore the only thing was to cut her in
two, leaving the fore portion on land, but the after part
containing engines was floated free. This latter they
towed into the Tyne, where a new bow was later added.
Thus arose the joke that *Milwaukee* was the world's

EMPRESS OF *JAPAN*
This former C.P.R. liner was taken over as a hospital ship in 1914.

S.S. *MONMOUTH*
This was the second ship I commanded.

THE SHIP THAT MADE HISTORY

S.S. *Montrose*, which I commanded when the notorious murderer, Dr. Crippen, was arrested on board. Note the wireless aerial.

longest ship—her bow in Scotland, but her stern on the Tyne.

I brought this old vessel from Liverpool to London, left her there, and then went on to Avonmouth where I was to take command of the Company's S.S. *Monmouth*, which became by custom a sort of training vessel for young officers destined to be given command. Nor did many months elapse before she provided me with anxiety enough to last me a long while. Now, doubtless the reader has frequently heard about the Strait of Belle Isle, the northern outlet of the St. Lawrence Gulf separating Labrador from Newfoundland. Eighty miles long and only a dozen miles wide, this defile is used by vessels during the summer season, but throughout the winter months it is blocked up by ice.

One August midnight I had brought the *Monmouth* into the Strait, the weather being fairly thick, and my suspense was by no means lightened by remembering that during this day we had passed so many as 86 icebergs. But now, about one point on my port bow, I kept hearing the howl of sirens, and at once I knew whence they originated. Those two fine new battle-cruisers *Indomitable* and *Indefatigable* were homeward bound with H.R.H. the Prince of Wales (afterwards King George V) on board, having been to Quebec for celebrating the Tercentenary. That was in 1908.

The *Indomitable* had been launched only the previous year and now, with so distinguished a personage on board, she had set out to make a record run to the Isle of Wight. Fog or no fog, she certainly cracked on. Her official speed was 25 knots, but she maintained an average of 24·8 knots all the way to Cowes, which indicates plainly enough how little she allowed waves and weather to slow her down.

But Belle Isle Strait! And 25 knots!

By the approach of sound I inferred they must be travelling at utmost speed, and I wanted to let them know the number of icebergs on their track for the next 120

K

miles. My ship had no wireless, so I tried attracting attention by making Morse signals with sounds on my whistle, but finally had to give it up. Because of the fog I had stopped engines, but rather than be run down by a couple of battle-cruisers in a hurry I put my engine-telegraph at 'full ahead' to get out of their way.

But is it not strange how events shape themselves in spite of human effort?

The *Monmouth's* speed was very moderate indeed, yet within the next half-hour I drove her forefoot on to a beautiful iceberg! A certain amount of damage resulted, though daylight revealed that it might have been far worse, so I was able to carry on. Yet consider the sensation which would have been caused had the *Indomitable*, travelling at over twice our rate, crashed into a berg during that midnight thickness as the *Titanic* rushed to her doom a few years later. If the battle-cruiser galloped from Quebec to the south Irish coast in 60 odd hours, and broke every Atlantic record, one must admire the cool nerves responsible for her safety that summer's night, whilst admitting that luck does play a part in seafaring matters.

We steamed up the St. Lawrence to Montreal, effected slight repairs, loaded cargo, and started off for England. The voyage was uneventful until one day's run from the north Irish coast when—again about midnight—something happened. A vessel was burning signals of distress! Soon we steamed alongside and found her to be H.M.S. *Argo*, whose machinery had broken down. It did not take us long to get her in tow and the following day she was anchored safely in Moville Harbour, Lough Foyle; so she likewise had been fortunate. But her commanding officer? Captain Boyle T. Somerville, R.N., served for many years afterwards, and through the Great War, reaching the rank of Admiral. On retirement he went to live on his estate on south-west Ireland near to the sea, till assassination suddenly robbed him of life.

One day I had just taken the *Monmouth* out of port

outward bound for Montreal when a stowaway was discovered and brought to me on the bridge. From his appearance he appeared to be of the hardened criminal type, and I informed him that he wouldn't be able to land in Canada, so I should have to bring him back home when we returned.

"You don't take me back home," he protested.

He was put to work, and some days later we entered the St. Lawrence. I had some suspicion that the fellow might try escaping overboard and landing surreptitiously, so instead of hugging the land I kept 5 miles off. He would never escape under cover of darkness at that distance. When, however, daylight dawned, I gazed down from the bridge on to the deck below, where lay a bundle of clothes.

What did that signify?

I sent an officer to find out, and after examination it was concluded that they belonged to the stowaway. Search was made through the ship, but the man could be found nowhere. It transpired also that two lifebuoys likewise were missing, so with a little imagination we can reconstruct the attempt to float away from the *Monmouth* in the hope of eluding capture. Luck certainly was not with him that night, for he perished, and his body was a week later found on Fame Point. No other clue to him could be ascertained than the two articles which we brought to light from his clothing and manifested his choice of literature. These were a couple of 'penny dreadfuls': one entitled *Rejected*, and the other prophetically named *Doomed on the Deep*.

There was another occasion when the *Monmouth* unwillingly had to carry a stowaway across from England to the American continent, but this time the culprit did not get away. On making port, we handed him over to the authorities knowing that he would in due course be brought before a judge. Our mysterious passage-stealer had less the appearance of a tough villain than of a miserable human wreck, so thin and emaciated that a good honest meal might probably kill him. Whatever he might once have been, nature had left in him practically no 'kick,' and it was difficult to suppose there remained enough stamina for the smallest resistance.

After the poor wretch was landed, and the usual reporter swooped aboard to find a good story concerning anything which might have occurred on the trip from England, some of *Monmouth's* officers got busy.

"Carried a stowaway with us, this voyage," released one of them casually.

"Now that's real news," congratulated the journalist. "Where is the guy? Who is he?"

"Well," answered the Second Officer who enjoyed practical joking, "matter of fact, he's pretty tough. Champion Light-Weight boxer of England."

"Hell!" the news-hound enthused. "What's his name?"

"Known all over England as 'The Tipton Slosher.' But, in private life, John Nathaniel Griffiths."

(Now during the conversation neither I nor the Chief Officer had been present. The latter would have been more than interested, for that was his appellation.)

Next day the Press came out with great head-lines:
'England's Champion Light-Weight. Arrives On *Monmouth* As Stowaway. "Tipton Slosher" Is John Nathaniel Griffiths.'

You can guess the complications which ensued, especially when the stowaway was brought into dock by a couple of burly policemen. The case having been stated, the judge fixed his glasses and looked at the prisoner.

"Oh, yes! I've been reading about you in the newspaper. Young man, we have enough pugilists in this country, so you'll go back to England in the same vessel by which you came. And when you get home, you can fight your battles over there."

So the thin, delicate, delinquent was set free and we brought him to where he started. But what the judge meant by calling him a pugilist our guest could not comprehend, until we presented him with the full story.

CHAPTER XV

AFTER spending a couple of years in the *Monmouth* I was given command of the *Montrose*, and thus did fate contrive to bring about one of the most remarkable phases in any mariner's life. Little could I foresee that within a few weeks *Montrose* was to be on the lips of the whole civilized world.

At present the ship could not go to sea because of an extensive overhaul, but whilst standing by her in London there were plenty of things with which I could occupy my mind. And, not having ever seen the Derby run, nor having the most elementary knowledge of horses, I took advantage of the opportunity. On reaching Epsom I noticed an old tipster dressed up and wearing a white silk hat. For the price of one penny he was offering for sale a package of acid drops and a number of 'straight tips.' I risked the investment and didn't fare too badly for a beginner on the turf. Out of the six races he gave me no fewer than five winners and, what is more, I had no necessity to chase the bookmakers for my winnings.

So Derby Day, 1910, would have long remained memorable in my mind but for the much more important event that was soon to overshadow it.

Perhaps the reader may find the accompanying illustration of *Montrose* convenient in helping him to visualize her one bright summer's morning in the middle of July that year, as we were steaming down the Thames bound across to the Scheldt for Antwerp. Three decades have passed since then, much has occurred to alter the tempo of life, to extend transportation and improve distant communications. The use of wireless telegraphy was still comparatively rare, since only so recently as 1901

Marconi had succeeded in establishing connection between Cornwall and Newfoundland. Half a dozen years passed before public transatlantic service began to win favour, and even by 1910 barely sixty ships throughout the globe were thus fitted. It will be noted, however, from the illustration that *Montrose* was one of them.

Inasmuch as a new generation is supposed to replace its predecessor every thirty years, it may be well if I introduce here preliminaries of that story which during our voyage was to win the breathless attention not merely of British, but Canadian and American people. The Crippen case will never be forgotten, frequent mention of this exciting drama is still made in the Press ; but I now offer the following as the first, complete, and documented account by one who was privileged to be more than a spectator during the drama's climax.

Hawley Harvey Crippen was a little wisp of a man, aged 50, not more than about 5 ft. 4 ins. high, slight of body, with sandy hair becoming rather bald on the top; grey, big eyes and rather thick-lensed, gold-rimmed spectacles; somewhat slovenly of appearance, usually wearing a stand-up collar, frock coat, and (if you met him on the street) a silk hat. Add to these features a 'handle-bar' moustache, together with a curious habit of throwing his feet out when walking, and the composite picture suggests anything but romance.

In character he seemed quiet and retiring, simple in his tastes, gentle, and patient. He neither smoked, nor did he drink anything more potent than light ale. He cared not for late hours, he was no gambler, acquaintances rather liked his quiet gentleness, and there was something about this apparently unattractive personality which some people could never resist.

Secretly and at heart Crippen could be reckoned as a clever, crafty criminal. He possessed considerable plausibility, his remarkably cool and collected manner was able to help through at least one serious crisis, and he looked at you with a stare which sometimes roused suspicion. A citizen of the United States with an American doctor's diploma, he had lived in New York, Philadelphia, St. Louis, Detroit, Michigan, but now was representing in Albion House, New Oxford Street, London, an American firm owning patent medicines.

The domestic life of this little man was extremely unhappy. Married to a flashy, faithless shrew, loud-voiced, vulgar, and florid; known on the music-hall stage as Belle Elmore; he disliked her friends, hated her tastes, and gradually was drifting farther away into that lonely misery where danger threatens. Cora Crippen was not his first wife: he had been married twenty years previously to a woman in Salt Lake City, who died. As an artiste Belle Elmore was scarcely a success, yet she owned loyal friends among her theatrical associates, faithful to her memory long after Cora's death.

The Crippen home was in the north of London at 39 Hilldrop Crescent, Camden Town, where on the night of 31 January 1910 two friends came to dine and afterwards played Bridge till 1 a.m., when the guests departed. Whether Hawley and Cora Crippen next engaged in bitter quarrel that culminated in his terrible decision, we shall never learn, but Belle Elmore was never seen again. To stop inquisitive tongues, he gave it out presently that his wife had gone back to America and died in California, yet this statement created more suspicion than settlement.

Now, working in Dr. Crippen's New Oxford Street office was a 27-years old typist and shorthand-writer named Ethel Le Neve. Small, slim, with pale complexion and light brown hair, about 5 ft. 5 in. high, with large grey-blue eyes, this pleasant and quiet-mannered London woman was thrown by circumstances into a tragedy whereof she had taken no part. The lonely man in his wretchedness had won her sympathy, and from that it was an easy stage to affection. Before long Miss Le Neve was residing in the Hilldrop Crescent house, and so the spring months passed by without further news of

Belle Elmore's disappearance. Among the latter's music-hall friends suspicion now reached positive instinct that there had been foul play.

The matter was referred to Scotland Yard on 26 June, and on 6 July Inspector Dew went round to call at Hill-drop Crescent where he saw Miss Le Neve who took him down to New Oxford Street. This sudden visit naturally came as a great shock to the thin man, yet Crippen never lost his head, remained cool and collected, and finally admitted that he had lied as to Cora's death. To the best of his belief, she was alive in the United States.

One might have expected that the doctor's arrest would have taken place that same Friday, but a verbal promise to hold himself at the disposal of the police sufficed, and the Inspector departed. Crippen's guilty conscience now created uneasiness amounting to terror. The net was about to be cast in his direction, and could be avoided only by rapid flight. Ethel Le Neve would accompany him.

Neither possessed more than a few pounds, yet get clear of England this week-end they certainly must. Next day—July 9—was a Saturday, and there would be plenty of tourists going abroad; so, having completed their preparations, they slipped out of London at 1 p.m. and reached Brussels, where they put up at the Hotel des Ardennes. Not till Monday did Scotland Yard realize that Crippen and the young woman had made a clean escape: nor could they know that the typist, having cut short her hair and thrust her body into male attire, pretended to be a boy. At the Belgian hotel Crippen signed the register as 'John Robinson and son.'

So passed Sunday, Monday, and Tuesday: the interval before big events. On Wednesday, 13 July, 'Mr. and Master Robinson' had made up their minds to make for Canada, and that day commenced inquiries at a Brussels booking office. Crippen had shaved off his moustache

CAUSE AND EFFECT

The two people (*reading left to right*) are Miss Ethel Le Neve—disguised as a boy—and Dr. Crippen. This snapshot I took secretly from my cabin in the *Montrose* as they were promenading the deck. The cheque for £250 was afterwards paid me by the Metropolitan Police.

THE CRIPPEN CASE

(*Top*) The Pilot (centre figure) and Chief Officer on bridge of the S.S. *Montrose*. Crippen had just been arrested and placed in cabin.

(*Bottom*) Captain Kendall walking with Inspector Dew of Scotland Yard along the deck after arresting Crippen.

and was growing a beard, so a few days in retirement would not be amiss. On Friday he called again at the Brussels office, paid for the two fares from Antwerp to Quebec, which left them with less than £20 capital. Three days later (possibly with a view to economy) they forsook their small hotel for another address, yet early on the morning of Wednesday, 20 July, they were seen in Brussels, and by 8 a.m. were coming aboard the steamer at Antwerp.

Meanwhile a great sensation had been created in London. On the afternoon of that very day (13th) when the 'Robinsons' were inquiring about tickets, two police from Scotland Yard—Inspector Dew and Sergeant Mitchell—were searching the Hilldrop Crescent house and went down into the front cellar. Altogether they spent five or six hours. After removing some bricks they discovered human flesh six inches below, and further digging resulted in more remains, though whoever had set his mind to do this ghastly carving unquestionably was a practised hand. After dismemberment, he had then buried part of the flesh in pyjamas, but the bones he had disposed of elsewhere.

The reason for Crippen's hurried departure, and breaking of his promise, now became apparent. On the 16th the Metropolitan Police sent out 5000 posters in various languages with portraits and descriptions of the two fugitives. Newspapers, shipping offices, hotels, were informed, and three days later a reward of £250 was offered for information which might lead to arrest. The hue and cry had begun, newspapers were anxious to find out more about this Camden Town sensation, for it looked like a perfect and complete real-life detective yarn. 'Everybody enjoys a good murder story,' and this one promised the widest appeal: the mystery of a wife's disappearance, the long baffling of amateur sleuths, the mysterious flight of her husband and the 'other woman,' the evasion of Scotland Yard's experts at the last moment.

Sex, sentiment, suspense, adventure, mystery—everything was there to rouse the reader's excitement and maintain curiosity till the end. During the whole of modern journalism I doubt if any London crime ever attracted such universal attention. The names of Dr. Crippen and his typist Miss Ethel Le Neve immediately became common property, but whither they had fled was the great problem.

As usual, of course, many contradictory rumours spread themselves. Whilst one report insisted that the couple were hurrying across the continent, another statement alleged they were hiding somewhere in London, whilst the latest theory pointed to Crippen having been observed in Amsterdam. Yet a fortnight went by without yielding one genuine clue. Not all the resources of Scotland Yard, of watchers at railway termini and shipping ports, had been able to solve this urgent and intriguing puzzle.

Such, then, was the position on the date when we left London and were steaming towards the Scheldt. Next day, on arrival at Antwerp and indeed all the time *Montrose* waited there, I used to obtain the English newspapers on going ashore in the evening outside the Café Weber. On opening the pages, I turned eagerly to the Crippen affair, to learn that the latest opinion now definitely located him on the European continent. He had been traced to Brussels and the Hotel des Ardennes, his signature in the hotel register had been copied and a facsimile reproduced in the Press. Detailed description of his features was again offered, and it seemed to me that anybody with average intelligence could not fail to recognize Dr. Crippen when once confronted.

We were due to sail from Antwerp on 20 July with about a thousand passengers, of whom the most part were continentals. Representatives of the London police were searching every vessel before she left port, and this morning they scrutinized all those who came over *Montrose's* gangway. Of that embarking crowd not one person was detained or suspected, so without further complication we cast off about 10 a.m. and proceeded down the Scheldt bound for Canada.

I remained on the bridge till after passing Batts—a rather dangerous part of the river—left the pilot and walked into my cabin to light a cigar. Whilst so doing, I chanced to be looking through one of the cabin port-holes which gave out along the boat-deck. (See the accompanying illustration of *Montrose*.) There, behind the ship's lifeboat which was raised about 3 feet above deck, I observed the lower portions of two men, but one of them was squeezing the other's hand. For several minutes I continued to gaze and form certain conclusions, till the elder of the pair emerged clear of the lifeboat's stern and peeped along the deck. Was anyone looking?

He returned satisfied. They were alone.

I then, unobserved, walked through my cabin by the starboard door and down that side of the boat-deck, casually smoking my cigar. Then, crossing the after part of this deck, I returned towards the position where these two people were standing; but on my approach they both came away from the boat. With the intention of getting into conversation, I bid the older man 'Good day,' and we began discussing the river scenery—the low-lying Dutch and Belgian territory, the windmills on either side, the passing craft.

Now, throughout this while, I was taking great notice of him. His eyes protruded, there was a deep mark on the bridge of his nose, yet there were no spectacles. Clean-shaven, minus a moustache, he was obviously growing a chin beard. Still remembering the printed descriptions of a fugitive from New Oxford Street, I made a note that this traveller spoke with an American accent, but the 'boy' standing by his side never spoke at all until addressed. Very reserved was the latter's demeanour, and evidently not in the best of health, since he kept giving a rather harsh cough.

On this I could not help placing some notice.

"Yes," replied the 'father'. "My boy has a weak chest, so I'm taking him to California for his health."

"Good idea," I agreed and, after making a few complimentary remarks concerning the 'youngster,' I returned to the bridge—though only for the purpose of descending the other side into my cabin. Through the porthole I scanned them again, and by this time had become more than suspicious: in fact, I was little short of certainty. It was fortunate I had not destroyed that copy of an English newspaper, so on laying it in front of me and examining the photographs I reviewed the matter. More than ever was I convinced that Dr. Crippen and Miss Le Neve were these two passengers. In one respect they differed from Scotland Yard's description, which made the former in height '5 ft. 3 or 4' and the girl '5 ft. 5.' As they stood on deck, however, the doctor was quite one inch the taller, and I concluded that the girl when wearing high heels and the large hats (fashionable in 1910) must have seemed to possess superior stature. To-day, shod in a pair of boy's white canvas shoes, she did not completely tally with given facts.

However, that detail might stand over for the present.

A little later I went on deck to ask 'Mr. Robinson' if he had booked seats at table in the saloon.

"No," said he, "I have not."

"Then would you both care about sitting at my table?"

"Thank you very much," he answered. "We shall be glad to accept your invitation."

Whereupon I went below, saw the Purser, told him that the 'Robinsons' would sit on my right at meals; but also I took a look through the passenger tickets to find out where these had been booked.

Not England. But Brussels!

That agreed with the newspaper account.

Cabin 5.

This was a four-berth room! The ticket had been endorsed with 'Entire Room' written in red ink.

So 'Mr. Robinson' had been content to pay a higher rate to ensure having the 'boy' with him.

Shortly afterwards the bell went for lunch, and I stood at the top of the staircase till the pair passed along into the saloon. Then I waited just long enough for them to be out of the way, and betook myself to Cabin 5 in order to seek any further clues which might support existing suspicions. Any moment the girl might suddenly rush in for something, so I had to look around me quickly.

On the settee lay two hats. The former belonged to 'Robinson' and had come from 'Jackson's, Boulevard de Nord.' The other one was without a name, but around the rim had been packed paper to make it fit a smaller head. These two travellers had come aboard with a black box as their luggage, and this stood underneath the settee; but, since it was locked, and I could find nothing else to satisfy my curiosity, I was going out. At the threshold I glanced back, caught sight of something hanging from one of the toilet-hooks of the washstand, so proceeded to examination. This white rag had once been the sleeve of a woman's under-bodice. The 'boy' was using it as a face-flannel.

Another confirmatory clue!

Thus rewarded with a hasty visit, I went into the dining-saloon and took my seat at head of the table, the 'boy' being on the immediate right, with 'Mr. Robinson' on his right. This guarded 'Master Robinson' from having to converse with anyone save myself and her 'father.' I began chatting generally, at the same time maintaining a careful watch on their movements.

Now, according to the passenger-list, here was supposed to be a lad of 16, but it did not take me long to guess that my neighbour was a girl in the twenties! Why? From the general behaviour, firstly; but, secondly, from the careful handling of knife, fork, and spoon, together with the dainty fingering of fruit.

One more corroborating indication!

Lunch being over, the couple began promenading the saloon deck, and soon I was walking behind them, thinking out a ruse. If instantaneously I were to call: 'Mr. Robinson!' he would turn round at once—should that be his real name. If, on the contrary, he might be merely feigning a part, then more possibly he would be taken off his guard and forget.

And so did it turn out. Three times must I shout out his name before any notice was taken, and then only the 'boy' recognized. It was necessary for the latter to give 'father's' arm a violent shake ere identity could be remembered.

"I'm awfully sorry," the man apologized. "I didn't hear you. This cold wind is making me deaf."

And here it may be added that, when bound for the United States, every passenger has to fill up a manifest-form giving particulars as to themselves and their destination.

"Have you completed yours?" I inquired.

"Not yet," he admitted.

"Perhaps you might care to do so in my cabin? Save you from being troubled for the remainder of the voyage . . . in case you or the boy succumbs to sea-sickness before getting clear of the English Channel."

"Much obliged," he accepted, and they came inside.

Placing before him pen, ink, and the forms, I left them to get on with the job. Twenty minutes elapsed and they rejoined me on deck. Still promenading, I intentionally asked him about certain parts of the world, obtained the desired knowledge, then retired to my cabin where on the table were the forms duly completed.

He had fallen beautifully into the trap.

For now from a drawer I brought forth the English newspaper containing a facsimile of his handwriting in the Hotel des Ardennes register. I compared it with that which he had penned on these forms, and yet again no room for the slightest doubt seemed possible. Everything was working nicely, all the pieces of the puzzle fitting into their places with exactness, and (apart from that small item respecting the heights) not one bit of contradiction anywhere.

Unless some unforeseen incident upset calculations a steel net would shortly wind itself round 'Mr. Robinson.'

Sending for my steward, I now began to make sure that no loopholes could be possible.

CHAPTER XVI

THIS steward was a loyal and dependable young fellow, quite ignorant of the 'Robinson' business. I told him to go round the ship, look into all officers' and engineers' cabins, collecting every English newspaper he could get hold of. This he accomplished with great success, my object being to disarm everybody on board, and subdue any suspicion.

By this time we were heading towards the Straits of Dover, with no anxieties regarding weather. 'Mr. Robinson' and his 'boy' selected a couple of deck-chairs and stretched themselves out comfortably about twenty feet away from my cabin port-hole. Entering unobserved, I locked my doors and began operations.

First of all, I took the newspaper photograph of Dr. Crippen and pinned it on a drawing-board, then with chalk deleted both moustache and spectacles. Next, after watching the man through this circular opening (although he could not see me), I had no hesitation, on comparison, to declare silently: 'You are Dr. Crippen whom the police want for murder.'

But what about Miss Le Neve?

The printed illustration showed her as a girl with lots of hair and wearing a big hat. Instead of erasing these with chalk I cut out a circular hole in a piece of cardboard after measuring the face equally by dividers. Placing this frame over the portrait, so as to conceal hair and hat, I glanced at the real Miss Le Neve seated outside.

Yes: there could be no mistake. This was the 27-year-old typist.

Then sheer chance came to my aid. The wind began to freshen, the 'Robinsons' decided on a walk round when, without further preliminaries, a gust raised the 'boy's' coat a few inches round the waist, yet high enough to reveal one portion in the middle of the back where pants had been split so they might fit around the hips. And the joining was being held by that feminine article, a large safety-pin.

Final evidence as to who 'Master Robinson' might really be!

Yet, despite all these proofs taken separately and collectively; notwithstanding that every shred of doubt ceased to exist; it was my wish to make doubly and trebly certain before committing myself irretrievably.   The matter would be in any case far too grave for a bad slip through over-confidence. Other tests must be made and I should note the reactions. So that afternoon about four o'clock, when tea was served, I invited them both into my cabin. He arrived gladly, and I could see that so long as I gave him a lead he wasn't worrying about any other people in the ship; wherefore I continued to play the part of a simple 'Billy Muggins,' doubting nothing.

Over this meal I steered the conversation so that we could chat about various parts of the world, until gradually I could concentrate upon some particular place specified in the newspaper. One of these was San Francisco, where I had been during more than a single casual visit, as the reader knows from previous chapters. I began describing the Golden Gate Park, the Sutro Baths, Cliff House, and other places of interest; but, intentionally, placed the Sutro Baths where Cliff House should be, and vice versa.

This was to note if he would agree with me, or whether actually he did know 'Frisco.

Nor did he delay to correct me where I was wrong.

"And how d'you feel so sure about it?"

"Because . . . well, I lived there when I was 18 years old," he convicted himself further.

The paragraph stated that Crippen had lived in

L

Toronto, Detroit, and certain other cities. His conversation bore out this assertion: in fact, presently he satisfied
me on every point.

Not content with so doing he gratuitously made a
worse 'bloomer.' Whilst sipping tea, he asked if we used
distilled water.

"No," I answered. "We always carry fresh water
ample for the voyage. Distilled water wouldn't taste very
nice, I suppose. Have you ever had any experience
with it?"

"Why, yes. In my time I've used a great deal—for
mixing medicine."

By this last admission Dr. Crippen had pretty well
covered the whole category. One by one, out of his own
mouth, truths had been blurted in the most surprising
sequence, and (short of confessing his identity) there was
scarcely any point which had not been unintentionally
determined. One minor difficulty, other than the
question of height, still existed, and I wished to satisfy
my mind before final action.

According to the official description, Hawley Harvey
Crippen wore false teeth, yet throughout all our talks
I could not for the life of me realize that this was so :
and I continued most anxious to settle the doubt. What
could be done about it? Well, the only practical method
was to make him open his mouth wide. How? By causing
him to roar with laughter. I therefore related an amusing
anecdote, added story after story, sent him into a merry
mood, made him let go all seriousness. I can still see
Crippen lying on his back, his mouth wide open, yelling
with delight.

I looked again and again. Those teeth were not false.

Here, then, was a second item where Scotland Yard
had been slightly inaccurate. Weighed against the other
evidence, perhaps any impartial mentality might have
claimed that these minute errors possessed little value.
Later on, the police realized they had made a mistake:
in fact I have before me a copy of 16 July poster, to

which has been added in blue ink: 'Teeth Not False.'
But on board the *Montrose* I should have been glad to
learn this revision.

After dinner that same summer evening 'Mr. Robinson'
and I were standing at the entrance of the small lounge
yarning together, when a French lady sat down opposite
us. Now admittedly all this time I never eased observation on the man, kept alert for any further indication
by word or deed which might come from his activity.
Nevertheless it is impossible to prevent fate sometimes
intervening, and it did at this precise moment. The lady
was reading a copy of *Le Matin*, and as she opened this
newspaper there stood out in large black letters a thrilling
feature which neither he nor I could avoid noticing.
The three words ran: 'CRIMES DE LONDRES,' and underneath, 'LE DOCTEUR CRIPPEN.'

Out of the corner of my eye I snatched a look at him.
Clearly he was uncomfortable and agitated. What could
I do? Obviously, nothing but remain where we stood for
the present. The temptation to move away had to be
resisted: otherwise assuredly he would have smelt a rat.
The lady turned her paper over, our conversation was not
allowed to be interrupted, and the suspense died down.
It had been a painful moment.

So the hours since leaving Antwerp passed rapidly,
and I must now face a big dilemma before making a final
decision which would affect my future career for good or
bad. Put yourself in my place, and think out the matter.
I was 99 per cent sure that this was the fugitive whom
Scotland Yard wanted for 'murder and mutilation of Cora
Crippen.' To the best of my ability I had examined the
suspicious clues and come to a decision. That being so,
it was my duty both as a decent law-abiding individual
and shipmaster to let Scotland Yard know about these
mystery travellers. On the other hand, I was just asking
for a full measure of trouble should my opinion turn out
to be wrong. Suppose a detective from London was
despatched across the Atlantic on what might turn out a

goose chase? Apart altogether from the unprofitable expense, I should be accused of forming irresponsible judgments. And if the suspected passengers turned out to be above suspicion, who could say that some law action for damages might not result?

So, whichever way one looked at the problem, anything that I should do might be wrong. In those early days of wireless telegraphy, when it was the exception rather than the rule for ships to have facilities of talking across the sea, there had also to be reckoned the matter of distance. Modern radio-experts may be amused to learn that the greatest range *Montrose* owned for sending a message was 150 miles. Even for listening and receiving our limit was 600 miles, but on some occasions the intervening space could be bridged over from-ship-to-ship-to-shore.

It was 20 July when we left Antwerp, and now the afternoon of Friday, 22 July found me with my mind fully made up. Risk or fail, I intended taking the bold step of sending a wireless to England whilst still within the 150 miles. I would transmit it to Mr. Piers, the Managing Director of our Company in Liverpool, who would promptly get in touch with Scotland Yard, and whether my conclusions justified this extreme measure time alone would prove. In any case secrecy was the first essential.

I sent for my wireless operator, and took him into my confidence, entrusted him with the whole drama which had been going on these last forty-eight hours, and impressed on him that not one person aboard must receive so much as a hint. Otherwise the whole plan would break down. Instructing him that all messages sent to or from the ship—regardless of the persons—must be handed into my hands, I gave this youth a letter accepting all responsibility and easing his mind. We were less than 150 miles away from Poldhu, in Cornwall, and still to the south of Ireland, when at 3 p.m. (G.M.T.) this Friday I caused the following wireless message to be transmitted:

'PIERS LIVERPOOL—130 miles west Lizards—Have
strong suspicions that Crippen London cellar murderer
and accomplice are amongst Saloon passengers. Moustache taken off growing beard. Accomplice dressed
as boy. Voice manner and build undoubtedly a girl.
Both travelling as Mr. and Master Robinson.
KENDALL.'

I then notified my operator to listen for any news heard
over the long distance, and before 11 p.m. on Sunday he
came to my cabin with a most interesting message
intercepted by the *Montrose*. This was being sent by one
of our leading London journals, apparently to their
representative aboard the White Star liner *Laurentic*, and
you can imagine how it gripped my imagination:

'What is Inspector Dew doing? Is he sending and
receiving wireless messages? Is he playing games with
passengers? Are passengers excited over chase? Rush
reply.'

That was the first knowledge to reach me of the result-
ing effect from my Friday's telegram. So Inspector Dew,
of the Criminal Investigation Department, the officer
who helped to dig up the Camden Town cellar and later
interviewed both Le Neve and Crippen, had wasted no
time? On Saturday he caught the first steamer leaving
Liverpool for Canada, and of such superior speed that
she would reach the St. Lawrence River ahead of
Montrose. I had received no reply to my Liverpool radio,
but this casual intercept now relieved me of some anxiety.
Prompt action had followed, and the right man would
be waiting in Canada on our arrival. More than ever
was it become my duty to ensure that the 'Robinsons'
should not meanwhile disappear and make the Inspector's
trip useless.

Not till now did I know that the news of these two
being aboard *Montrose* had reached Fleet Street, or that
Dew was himself being shadowed on board the *Laurentic*

by a Press representative. Since our Marconigrams were
so infrequently received, how could I be aware that the
public had become keener than hitherto? Mere sensa-
tionalism had now risen to an absorbing drama watched
with breathless attention by the whole civilized world,
and the extraordinary situation was that meantime the
suspects were shut off by marine isolation from understanding so much. Never in the history of crime had a
hunted man been so closely watched whilst blindfolded.

The inquest had opened on 18 July, the date when the
'Robinsons' left the Hotel des Ardennes, but it was the
Montrose telegram which turned the Crippen mystery
into a thrilling romantic adventure. Liners racing across
the ocean, wireless for the first time employed in the
detection of a criminal, printing-presses waiting for the
latest twist in the story, Inspector Dew travelling as
'Mr. Dewhurst,' and all because of a guilty elopement!
Never was there such human interest.

Yes: but in two separate individuals afloat suspense was
greater still, though neither dared communicate this to
the other. In 1910 the practical side of wireless was still
imperfect, and anyone sitting on *Montrose's* deck could
tell by the crackling electric sparking that words were
being sent forth. Well do I remember Crippen seated
in a deck-chair looking aloft, listening to this noise, before
remarking:

"What a wonderful invention!"

Little did he understand that science was putting the
noose round his neck; or that I was nervous lest at the
end of our voyage he might jerk the loop aside. Mine was
the obligation that he should not escape, and I should be
accountable until the moment when Inspector Dew took
over. And if—as seemed fairly likely—Crippen was a
murderer, then justice demanded renewed vigilance just
now. Something might make the man break through this
outward calm. His nerves perhaps would not last out till
sighting the shores of the St. Lawrence. Suicide—another
murder, too—could not be ruled out as improbable.

So I had, like him, to maintain a pose and never relax. Night and day, meeting him frequently on deck and at mealtimes, pretending not to see through the girl's deception, still uncertain of the final phase, I played my role. By the Monday (25 July) we had got well clear of the Irish coast and, incidentally, were now out of wireless touch with all shore stations. Any further messages must be sent via other vessels eastward-bound whensoever they came within our 150 miles limit. At 2 a.m. to-day it became possible to communicate with our Company's S.S. *Montezuma*, and I transmitted to her Master, Captain Gillies, the following, asking him to post it as soon as he arrived in London:

'With reference to wireless I sent regarding Crippen I feel more fully convinced that it is him. All descriptions corresponding fully with information from papers and police report received in London. Is very reticent. Also accomplice. They have no baggage except a small cheap grip bought on continent. Is still letting beard grow but shaves upper lip. Managed to examine his soft grey felt hat while at lunch. Name inside Jackson's, Boulevard de Nord. Grey felt hat of accomplice no lining, packed inside of band to make fit. Both wearing brown suits and white canvas shoes. Crippen speaks with an American accent. Have also heard him speak in French when alone with French passengers. Noticed accomplice using safety pins in pants. According to conversations with him he has travelled all over the States. Up to present he has no suspicion of being watched on board. Keeping everything quiet. KENDALL.'

The purpose of this was to provide Scotland Yard with a clear summing-up of the present position. Next day, being now well out into the Atlantic, and in touch with the S.S. *Royal Edward*, I sent:

'12.30 a.m. Long. 30° West.
'Regarding Dr. Crippen and accomplice am now

fully confident it is them. Have sent full report by
Montezuma to post from London. Everything coin-
cides with police description wearing felt hat name
inside Jackson Boulevard de Nord. KENDALL.'

Throughout these summer days 'Mr. Robinson' was
taking things easily, promenading in the sunshine, reading
and sleeping in a deck chair, chatting; but the 'boy' talked
very little. There were times during meals when 'he' must
have felt more than embarrassed, as for example when a
young Englishman sitting opposite would discuss with her
football and cricket. Still, the girl was playing her part
well, even though outwardly in great distress. The strain
of make-believe, the suppressed excitement, the secret
anxiety, imposed on her a great mental and nervous
strain; so that one morning, whilst seated below my porthole, she swooned right away. Crippen was there, to
whom (as she revived) the sad admission fell from her
pallid lips: "I'm done for."

He, too, was putting up a stern fight, trying to maintain
her spirits besides his own optimism. Yet I think you
will agree that he foresaw, without any delusion, one
desperate and tragic scene vaguely imminent. That is to
say, it might come any hour before his feet touched
Canadian soil, but if Crippen were driven into a corner
he would do a very desperate deed.

Let it be understood that there were two Crippens, but
until about the fifth day out I was acquainted only with
the quiet-spoken little man who turned out to be one of the
most charming passengers I ever had with me. Well-
mannered, the very essence of politeness, a great reader,
always ready to hear a good story, a non-smoker and
(so far as I could see) total abstainer, his attitude towards
the girl indicated deep affection. Whether he exercised
over her a hypnotic influence I cannot say, but he would
scarcely let her go out of his sight.

Then on this fifth day, whilst walking round the deck,
there came a little puff of wind which blew the tail of

his jacket as it had once treated his 'son's.' This time I perceived that the gentle, reserved Dr. Crippen had another side to his character, for now his hip-pocket revealed the outline of a revolver. No mistake about it! He meant taking no chances when threatened with arrest, and there was not any need for him to threaten by words.

Silently I accepted the challenge, prepared for emergency, loaded my own revolver, and henceforth always went about with it in my pocket. My position was this: I had resolved to see this business through, but if he turned and fired on me I would shoot him dead. Why didn't I from the first day—or at least from to-day —place the pair under arrest on the high seas? Well, there were two reasons. Firstly, because of the difficulty in guarding them effectively and ensuring that they would not commit suicide. I had not enough staff to keep a thorough watch over them by night and day. But, secondly, the pair had not yet given me the slightest trouble, nor manifested any distrust. So it suited my purpose to continue as the complete simpleton.

But what a situation for novelist or playwright! Picture the three of us every day at 4 p.m. having tea alone in my cabin, playing our respective parts. Roars of happy laughter! Jokes swapped! Pouring out tea for each other in the friendliest fashion, yet one of the trio not a man at all, and the other two bulging with a gun ready to fire at the first display of truth!

Thus apart from my duties as shipmaster I was trying to be host and diplomatic-detective all in one. To keep the escapers' minds occupied, I furnished them with a regular supply of books, but the anxious time always occurred from about 10 p.m., when Crippen had the habit of coming up from his cabin and roaming about on deck among the shadows till midnight. I formed the opinion he was planning for an eventuality which might arise. All this diurnal and nocturnal tension was a little trying, and I must needs take my rest in odd snatches as convenient after 6 a.m. and before 8 p.m. By night I remained always alert, keyed-up, prepared for the unexpected.

The uncertain days dragged on, and each seemed as long as a week. The *Montrose* was not a fast ship, yet we were making the best of fine weather, and very soon now we should be in touch with the outside world again through Belle Isle wireless station.

What effect would the radiograms have on our future?

CHAPTER XVII

DURING our voyage from land to land—that is to say from Ireland to Labrador—the *Montrose* was steaming on a southern Great Circle whilst he *Laurentic* was following a northern Great Circle course. Although we could not connect by wireless, the White Star liner must eventually pass through Belle Isle Strait at least twelve hours before us, and flash thither a message for us from Inspector Dew. It would then be relayed to the *Montrose* as soon as we got within range.

Of course the notorious fog, as usual, tried to hinder our progress, but actually it made us more vigilant and we kept going, so that on Friday, 29 July (nine days out from Antwerp) we were talking to Belle Isle. Having been so long away from communication, we were inundated with messages telegraphed by the Press in all parts of the globe, as well as other senders. Some radiograms were addressed to Crippen from New York, and certain of these did not lack humour. One in particular invited him to conduct service ashore on Sunday after landing at Quebec! Doubtless this suggestion was due to the fact that some newspapers had asserted he was travelling as The Reverend Mr. Robinson. Other telegrams read: 'You are accused of murdering your wife in London. Please deny it. Wire a complete statement at once.'

Needless to say, Crippen was never allowed to see any of these.

Now the earlier despatch that I handled came from Inspector Dew, who on this Friday had just landed at a spot called Father Point (near Rimouski), about 200 miles up the River St. Lawrence on the southern shore. Here was the first message that I had received from the police, and it answered my initial one sent to Mr. Piers a week ago:

'Your message to Liverpool 130 miles Lizard Friday last will board you Father Point. Please keep any information until I arrive there. Strictly confidential. Dew Scotland Yard on board *Laurentic*.'

To this I replied at 1.45 p.m.:

'To Inspector Dew. Received wire will pick you up Father Point. He is ignorant of suspicion. Have made no arrest. Is cunning so be prepared. At present appears uneasy. Compliments. KENDALL.'

It may be mentioned that though Dew left Liverpool under an assumed name, and employed every possible effort to hide his identity, his presence aboard the *Laurentic* could not be concealed; yet by tacit consent fellow passengers for the most part respected his incognito. He made no friends, was never seen in the smoking-room and seldom in the lounge, much of his time being spent on deck playing games. In the dining-room he conversed no more with his neighbours than ordinary courtesy required, but when taken ashore there awaited him not merely Canadian police chiefs, but about forty of America's star-turn journalists representing the world's newspapers and Press associations. With no little persistence these gentlemen exacted from him promises of facilities. Such was the universal interest created by the advent of Crippen and Le Neve that from the little wooden telegraph hut at Father Point about 100,000 words relating to the case had already been transmitted. By way of comparison let me add that this volume which you are now reading contains 80,000, and during a normal week Father Point was wont to send out only a few *hundred* words.

Now, it was absolutely essential that this final phase of

our voyage and the meeting with Inspector Dew be effected with the greatest care. Here would be the very climax: the pivot between failure and success. And any bungling must have the most serious consequences. I knew this Canadian trade-route, its characteristics, and every bit of the environment by long years of acquaintance, whereas the Inspector was a stranger in a strange country. With a view to smooth working and avoidance of any possible error, I wirelessed the following suggested plan:

'9.50 a.m. July 30. To Dew Father Point. Should arrive Father Point about 6 a.m. to-morrow. Should advise you to come off in small boat with pilot disguised as one if possible. Pilot steamer with reporters if any could go ahead and board later. Suspect he is on the *qui vive*. Better communicate any boarding details to me. Arrangements must be mutual. Compliments. KENDALL.'

This method, I hoped, would prevent the fugitives becoming alarmed; for my intention was to keep them completely without knowledge until at the right moment a surprise was sprung on them.

During this Saturday afternoon all communication between *Montrose* and the Marconi hut on Father Point was severed from about midday till nearly 9 p.m. by a thunderstorm, but at 9 p.m. Dew replied:

'Thanks. Will speak to you later. Operator here will make arrangements. Meantime suggest suspects kept under discreet observation to prevent suicide. Compliments. DEW.'

Midnight passed, and at 1.40 a.m. (Sunday) I received:

'Suggestions made by you as to boarding your vessel will be acted upon. Compliments. DEW.'

Details now were almost completed, and it only remained for me to send Dew this final radio at 3.10 a.m.:

'Thanks for wireless. Tell pilot to come alongside starboard side in boat. This is imperative. Tell captain of pilot steamer to steam with reporters towards Bicque Island and not to approach my ship until I hoist the Canadian ensign at the mainmast head indicating you have made the arrest. Compliments. KENDALL.'

Six and a half hours later I received the Inspector's response:

'Everything arranged as you advise. DEW.'

Barring something sudden and unforeseen, I had now done all that was possible, yet even now a man fleeing from justice quite likely might stage a dramatic finale. During the past eleven days he had learnt nothing, yet his mind must have been full of activity and wonder; his nerves stretched almost to breaking. Doubtless from that first day aboard he had felt no little relief that the Captain looked after him and no detective had sprung out. Then the Atlantic days, away from all interference, had strengthened confidence after once settling down to new surroundings; but with the approach to land there could now be nothing except harassing suspense. And try as he might, Crippen could not conceal his anxious moodiness.

Human psychology may not be perfectly understood after the most watchful consideration, and I had begun to perceive that within this cunning criminal existed a strange flair for subtle effort. He was a light-weight physically, turning the scales at just over 10 stones; nevertheless, he possessed exceptional mental vigour and craftiness. Consider the following incident both as indicative of how his mind was working and as illuminative of his natural propensity.

Saturday. The day before we should reach Father

Point. I was seated in my cabin, back to the door, when someone knocked. Looking round I saw Crippen and invited him in. His hand was holding out a book, and his eyes were focused straight on mine.

"I have brought this for you to read," he began. "It will just suit you. A detective story."

"Yes? Whom is it by? Conan Doyle?"

"No," he answered. "By Edgar Wallace. It's called *The Four Just Men*. It's all about a murder in London, and £500 reward."

Pretty callous from one who had murdered his own wife!

You might say that his gesture to-day was to imply that, for himself, the Doctor had no reason to disclaim any connection with such crimes. But, personally, I interpreted the remark quite differently: he was trying to upset my equanimity before his supreme effort at bluff. If he had at last guessed that I knew his identity; if he knew that want of sleep and perpetual alertness were beginning to try my endurance; he would harrow my feelings by this 'thriller' just a little more to weaken the balance.

There, however, he made one of his mistakes. Daily and hourly as I lived the life of a hunter, association with Hawley Harvey Crippen had made me harder and more unfeeling. I quite expected any sort of trick, and was prepared to meet it. Something extra-subtle during these final hours would be required to catch me off my guard.

I turned to him.

"Thanks. Finished with the book? Want something else to read? Have you got anything?"

He replied:

"Only *Pickwick Papers*, but the young fellow [signifying Miss Le Neve] is reading it."

So, opening my bookcase and selecting a volume, I asked:

"Have you read that?"

"What's the title?"

"*The Murder of Delicia*, by Marie Corelli."

Perhaps it was the unexpectedness of this attack which pricked his conscience. For his face flushed crimson, he canted his head away from me, and gazed out through a porthole.

"Yes," I went on, "it's all about a man who murdered his wife."

Tense situation for the two of us alone! Anything might have happened that moment, and under stress of suppressed emotion he might have whipped out his gun. Instead, he raised his hand and started squeezing his lower lip.

"No," said he, "I have never read it."

A few minutes later Crippen went out. Each of us had kept a tight hold of himself, but both had 'gone through the hoop' just now, and it wouldn't have taken me long to slip the handcuffs on him.

Like all stirring dramas, the Crippen story grew more gripping in its ultimate development. The nearer we steamed towards Father Point, the more exciting seemed this secret contest. And nature intensified it all by environment. I was unceasingly watchful, every hair of my head 'on duty.' Above all, I wanted to gain Father Point with the utmost celerity, but on this Saturday night dense fog settled down and the air became full of weird sounds. Groping our way up the St. Lawrence, it would have been rough luck to have hit the shore or collided with another ship. All being well, I hoped to be off Father Point by 6 a.m. and to see Dew with Canadian detectives coming off in the boat. How could I prevent Crippen scenting trouble when not one, but several, 'pilots' came alongside?

I took a bold step, went up to the murderer and advised him to get up early if he wished to admire the St. Lawrence River; adding, quite casually, we should be picking up half a dozen pilots who were bound back to Quebec.

Photos Central News

(*Top*) THE TENDER *EUREKA* WHICH WENT OUT TO MEET *MONTROSE*
In the former were hidden forty pressmen until Inspector Dew, disguised as a pilot, boarded
the *Montrose* and arrested Crippen.

(*Bottom*) CRIPPEN (WITH TURNED-UP COLLAR) BEING ESCORTED ASHORE
BY INSPECTOR DEW AT LIVERPOOL LANDING-STAGE ON ARRIVAL
FROM AMERICA

S.S. *LAKE MANITOBA*

She was sister ship of the *Lake Champlain* and *Lake Erie*. The latter I commanded shortly after the Crippen case.

THE SHIP OF MYSTERY

This was really the C.P.R. S.S. *Ruthenia*, which I commanded before the War. But she was cleverly altered to resemble H.M.S. *King George V* in the famous 'Dummy Battle Fleet.'

That last night was dreary, anxious, unending, varied only by that other monotony of the fog-whistle. As I paced the narrow bridge, every now and again I glanced down to see the sinister figure of Crippen creeping about deck. Restless and uneasy, he had been putting finishing touches to those plans presently to be found on his person. The sea was smooth, we were doing our best to save time, and the Chief Engineer, Mr. Vine, was down below all night getting every bit of power from the engines. Sleep was out of the question, but one had become used to that: the last three days and nights had been without repose almost the whole period.

Only another few hours! And then the worry would be over.

By four o'clock Sunday the daylight was breaking fast, and through the thickness we identified the various points of land by listening to their fog signals. Keeping five miles away from the shore, we heard at 7 a.m. the distant moan of another station. It was Father Point, and did it sound good? No indication of the fog lifting, and since this had been thick for the last three or four days, I now trusted it would so continue all the morning, in order that Crippen might not observe the pilot boat—or, at any rate, recognize that self-same Inspector Dew who once called at Albion House, New Oxford Street.

Our luck, however, was clean out. We had got within five miles of Father Point when the wind sprang up unheralded from the west and blew so smartly that the fog vanished to leeward. It was like the sudden lifting of a theatre curtain which revealed the Canadian scenic beauty of background, whilst in the front appeared a white boat rowed by four oarsmen, but four others dressed as pilots were seated in the bows and stern. One steered, tiller in hand, whilst immediately on his left (wearing peaked cap) was 'pilot' Dew.

One mile ahead lay the pilot steamer *Eureka* (see accompanying photograph), with the forty Press representatives of the world, but at present forbidden to show

M

themselves. It was now between 8 a.m. and 9 a.m., the last day of July, and the sun shining brightly on the glistening river. Half a mile away on the port quarter lay the white rowing-boat, and now the big moment was here.

Everything was working smoothly according to plan. The *Montrose* stopped, went astern to take the way off her, then round by the starboard side came the rowing boat towards where the pilot-ladder was hanging. Crippen was pacing the deck uneasily, then halted a few moments with the *Montrose's* surgeon (Mr. Stewart) and leaned over the rail.

"Isn't it unusual for so many pilots to come aboard?" remarked the much-travelled murderer, but Mr. Stewart evaded the question.

Meanwhile I was covering Crippen from the bridge, whilst the Chief Officer (Mr. Sargent) had gone down to receive pilot and 'pilots,' who were brought along the after-deck, through the alleyway, to the staircase leading up to my cabin. Leaving the bridge, I entered the cabin, shook hands with Inspector Dew; Mr. Mcarthy, Chief of the Quebec Police; and Inspector Denis of that same force.

"Where is Crippen?" Dew at once requested.

I pointed through the porthole along the Saloon Deck.

"There—that's Crippen."

And off went the pilot-rigged Canadian police officials with a message that I wished to see the American in my cabin.

"Be careful," I cautioned. "He carries a revolver in his pocket."

But there was no delay, and along strolled the wanted man straight into ambush which awaited.

"Let me introduce Mr. Robinson," I turned to Dew.

At first the latter found it not easy to recognize the man who had discarded spectacles and moustache—any way, through the porthole such identification had scarcely been immediate. But now the Inspector shook hands, saying in strong tones:

"Good morning, Dr. Crippen!"

The effect was terrific. Stunned stupid, the escaper could not discern his enemy in that rig, so Scotland Yard's expert removed the peaked cap.

"I am Inspector Dew from Scotland Yard, and have come here to have you arrested in the name of the King for the murder and mutilation of your wife, Cora Crippen, on or about February 1st."

The two Canadian police then made the formal arrest, and one of the most dramatic moments in criminal history terminated.

Crippen quivered. Surprise had struck him dumb. All his six months' deception and carefully laid plans had been negatived in a flash of time. Ingenuity had ended in utter failure just when liberty seemed most assured, and a vast continent stretched wide for their entrance.

Emotionally overcome, hopes dashed to destruction, the guilty man was inclined to sob his grief, and sank back on to the settee whilst Dew still held his hand. Then did Dr. Crippen throw down all defence in one single utterance.

"Thank God, it's all over. The suspense has been too great. I couldn't stand it any longer."

That, obviously, indicated both the strain since Antwerp and the doubt in his mind of evading the shore authorities at Quebec. Handcuffs were immediately put on, and he was temporarily left in charge of Inspector Denis assisted by Chief Engineer Mr. Vine. Inspector Dew, myself, and Mr. Mcarthy, then went down below to arrest Miss Le Neve who was sitting in the four-berthed cabin reading a book. She looked up when the door opened, recognized Dew who had once called when she was at Hilldrop Crescent, and now fear seized her. After the warrant had been read out, we left her in charge of the Canadian detective and went to remove

Crippen into another cabin which meanwhile had been prepared. Here he was stripped of his clothes and changed into pyjamas.

This brought about a curious sequel. Stitched to his underclothing worn next the skin were discovered five of the murdered woman's diamond rings, but inside his pockets were notes which he had written to Miss Le Neve regretting that he had ruined her life and implying that he contemplated suicide. But was it really a preconceived idea to forfeit his own existence? Or were these letters meant to be found as another piece of bluff? My own opinion is that Crippen thought of hiding himself in the vessel between here and Quebec—some 157 miles up the river. These pencilled notes would convey the impression that he had drowned himself, and it would be waste of time searching anywhere along the vast St. Lawrence's banks. Then, under the cover of darkness at the first occasion after *Montrose* should reach Quebec, he would smuggle himself ashore, thereby dodging all awkward questioners.

As to his revolver, we never found it, and presumed that he thought it wiser to heave the article overboard than let it create difficulties on arrival. I wondered this forenoon—as I have wondered many times since—what Crippen imagined was going through my brain whilst plans were being worked out in his. Altogether it had been a unique voyage, and an entirely new sort of detective story. One journal in a leading article averred that 'never has there been such a situation in the annals of crime or of human affairs as this—that the hunted man is himself completely isolated from the world while the rest of mankind look on.' Other writers called attention to the unprecedented use of wireless as 'an invisible bloodhound following the scent over the high seas.' And certainly thus did the *Montrose* make history besides giving a great impetus to the general adoption by liners of Marconi's great invention.

But I experienced a great surprise when Dew turned

to me and in a quiet moment announced: "You get a reward of £250 for this. It's as good as in your hands." This was the first intimation, for not till twenty-four hours after we had sailed from Antwerp did Scotland Yard obtain the necessary departmental sanction.

CHAPTER XVIII

AND now we hoisted the Canadian ensign for pilot steamer *Eureka* to come alongside with her crowd of Pressmen, who were so eager to be first in obtaining the full story of detection and arrest, that most of them without waiting for the gangway climbed up by the ropes. The picture suggested nothing so much as a ship being raided by pirates. However, though it was necessary for the prisoners to be protected and kept from public gaze, our visitors by sundry means managed to obtain what they wanted despite our essentially impartial attitude; and many of them despatched long messages through the *Montrose's* wireless office.

We eventually were under way again, steaming up river with the genuine pilot in charge of the navigation and the 'pirates' back aboard the *Eureka* which hurried towards the telegraph hut at Father Point. And whilst thousands of words that Sunday were being flashed to distant newspapers in all directions, the villain of the play was taking matters quite calmly. Located in Cabin 8 he asked for another book to read, and I got him one: it was that popular *Letters from a Self-Made Merchant to His Son*, and evidently had a soothing effect on the nerves of Crippen, who after a while went off into a sound sleep.

Dew, likewise, was feeling at rest now that the eluder had been rounded up. Many criticisms as to why in the first place he ever allowed Crippen to escape had been asked both in England and America, but by July 8 the suspicion had not yet been sufficiently substantiated. Easy enough to find fault with another's judgment after the event? Yes: it is like the captain of a ship who takes a big risk in order to make a fast passage and break the record. If he succeeds, everybody calls him a very fine fellow; but if he runs his vessel ashore he is looked upon as a damn fool.

Before leaving Crippen in his new cabin it may be mentioned that on Sunday morning the Doctor had further modified his appearance. The upper lip still remained shaved, but the promising pointed beard had not sprouted with sufficient density, so he had removed it and in thus doing cut his chin. 'John Filo Robinson,' 'American citizen,' on his way to Detroit for a vacation of four weeks (as he informed some of his shipmates) was now for all time separated from his 'son John George Robinson.' On the former—apart from the diamond rings and a small watch—the only valuables found consisted of a 10-dollar bill (worth about £2 in those days), so that his resources for starting a new life on the American continent were not considerable.

As to Miss Le Neve, she had experienced the denouement with even greater shock, and almost fainted until brought round by brandy. To the head stewardess, Mrs. Heer, was entrusted the distasteful but most necessary task of searching this pretending 'boy' who kept weeping tears down her cheeks. Except for a brooch and 60 dollars (£12), she carried nothing of value. It was now my duty to make her as comfortable as possible, for she must have suffered misery during these three weeks' masquerading.

Notwithstanding her cut-off hair, the wide-awake hat, the boy's shoes and socks—apart from the ill-fitting suit (noticeable in the accompanying photograph which I secretly snapped through my cabin porthole one day whilst the pair were promenading on deck) and her studied reserve, it had been a hard tussle to maintain this make-believe. And one simple incident proved that in a crisis a woman's natural instinct will triumph above artificial untruths.

Among *Montrose's* passengers were a Belgian lady

who with her husband and small child one afternoon were on deck. Madame had always been suspicious of the Robinson 'boy' with such small hands and feet who occasionally would play with the Belgian child without ever speaking. The gentleness of manner and shape of 'John George's' figure roused certain questions which remained unanswered for some days. Then, one afternoon, by chance 'he' was passing along the deck when the little Belgian child slipped and might have fallen through the rails headlong into the Atlantic. Young 'Robinson' darted forth in time and saved the infant from death, but the narrow escape so startled 'him' as to release the most feminine of screams. "That decided the question for me," said Madame.

I was sorry for Crippen's companion and realized that she would be much less unhappy if restored to womanly garments, so I asked the stewardess if she could possibly give the girl a rig-out. Within very few minutes a complete wardrobe was forthcoming, but at this stage the Canadian detectives objected to any change being made: they wished her to be landed exactly as arrested, or there might be trouble with the authorities.

However, I had not been visiting Canada all these years without understanding the character of its people: their big-heartedness, their broad-mindedness, and respect for the opposite sex. Whatever steps I took on the girl's behalf would surely be approved, and it was encouraging to find that Inspector Dew's attitude fairly coincided with mine. Surely it was not the clothes which had been arrested, but the person inside.

But now came a problem. Whilst the girl changed her attire, she would be left alone with the stewardess, and we feared suicide. What was to be done? We put the matter fairly and squarely to the prisoner, who solemnly promised to attempt no such thing. Wherefore, having screwed up portholes and given the stewardess strict instructions, we left the cabin and remained waiting outside till transformation was completed.

Here was the real Miss Le Neve no longer pretending to be a boy. In 1910 women had not yet begun to bob their hair, and nothing could immediately restore her shorn tresses. Nor could the combined effects of past tension, present shock, and future fate manifested in that sad face be expected to disappear. During the ship's progress towards Quebec I spent a good deal of time with her, even relieving the detective at meal-hours whilst Dew provided a similar relaxation for the detective watching Crippen. No sort of doubt as to her innocence of crime remained in my mind. This was emphatically not the kind of girl who for weeks could spend all day alone in the Camden Town house knowing that below were the remains of the murdered Belle Elmore. Ethel Le Neve, under the spell of Crippen's fascination, believed that the wife had deserted to America. Not till the flight to Brussels was Crippen forced to invent other stories.

The *Montrose* got to Quebec about 3 a.m. on Monday, the weather being hot and sultry, but even at that hour some thousands of people lined the wharves to catch a glimpse of the prisoners' landing. Everything, however, was carried out expeditiously, and as I assisted Miss Le Neve down the gangway I was convinced she would ultimately emerge from the trial as an innocent person. Everybody has heard of Quebec's picturesque situation, its historic Plains of Abraham, where in 1759 the future of Canada was decided by clash of arms. When Crippen and the girl were being driven through the streets to the prison on the Heights of Abraham, I felt that one of the big crises in my life had passed and victory had come at the end of nearly a fortnight's constant worry.

Every nerve in me had been stretched to the utmost, and the most desirable thing in all the world just now seemed a good sleep. Henceforth no longer need I under the appearance of hilarity perform a detective's work, and life as a shipmaster could again be lived simply. For the first few days in Canada I kept in hiding from

the inquisitive.   On arrival at Montreal, Dew and I
went over to have a look at Niagara and fill our imagina-
tions with nobler things than a sordid tragedy.   Still,
if the latter had achieved nothing else, it provided wireless
with the most amazing advertisement; for, within six
months, the number of ships so fitted leaped from 60
to 600, and presently public opinion reacting on legisla-
tion made radio compulsory for all steamers except the
smallest.

Crippen was brought before Judge Panet Angers at
11.30 the same morning on being landed at Quebec.
Admitting his identity and that of his companion, he
stated that he was of American nationality, born in
Michigan and a graduate of that University.   He made
no objection to being extradited across to England.   The
girl, charged with being an accessory after the fact, was
too ill for appearance that day.   Later both were brought
across to London, and the trial concluded in October.
Ethel Le Neve was set free, but Crippen was found
guilty.   He had poisoned Belle Elmore with an alkaloid
known as hyoscine, and received the sentence of death.
Execution by hanging at Pentonville prison on 23
November 1910 was the final chapter in this amazng
tragedy.

But two points are to be mentioned by way of epilogue.
The first arose in connection with a startling assertion
made during the October trial in London before Lord
Alverstone, Lord Chief Justice of England, when
the following suggestion was made in Court:

"It was no surprise to Dr. Crippen that he was to be
arrested.   He knew that he was under surveillance and
that the wireless was hourly sending out a warning to
Scotland Yard officials.   The Quartermaster on the
Montrose told Crippen all the plans, while the other
officers of the ship thought they were closely guarded.
This same quartermaster agreed to smuggle Crippen
ashore in the vessel's cargo when it was disembarked in
Quebec.

"For a time Crippen acceded, but he knew he had nothing to fear, and finally decided to face arrest and show his innocence. It was while he was contemplating hiding in the hold of the steamer that he wrote 'suicide letters.'

"These letters were to be found when Dr. Crippen was missed, to blind the pursuers and prevent them from searching the vessel, where they might have found Crippen in the hiding-place selected by the Quartermaster. It had been planned that Miss Le Neve was to land openly, to be joined secretly on land by Crippen."

Apart from revealing a further unpleasant aspect of a bad man's character, this alleged incrimination against *Montrose's* Quartermaster was a very serious matter. As a matter of fact, we carried four men of that rank: E. Torell, G. Campbell, J. Ford, and A. G. Bentall, but all were indignant when the above accusation appeared in the *Montreal Daily Star* on 20 October of that year. The following repudiation in writing should be put on record to counteract Crippen's false insinuation:

' S.S. "Montrose,"
'River St. Lawrence.
'*Oct.* 24*th*, 1910.

'To whom it may concern,
'We the undersigned Quarter Masters of the above steamer do hereby deny emphatically the serious charge made against us by Dr. Crippen's counsel in his defence as read by us in the columns of the *Montreal Daily Star* of the 20th inst. and do furthermore deny having had any intercourse with the said Dr. Crippen on or during the voyage to Quebec.

E. Torell	Quarter Master.
G. Campbell	,, ,,
J. Ford	,, ,,
A. G. Bentall	,, ,,

The second item which impressed me after the Crippen voyage was the number of letters which came pouring in from all sorts of people. Some, doubtless, had been written by ex-convicts, for they contained angry threats. Others were penned by cranks blending a curious religious ardour with a morbid sex sentimentalism, as if the writers were not certain whether they should be in support of the moral law or prefer a mawkish insipidity. Whilst praising me for having delivered 'sinners up to justice,' I was accused of having 'rent two human souls asunder.'

Others were rich in humour, as, for example, that from an irate and neglected wife who wrote from one of the biggest cities in Canada, though I refrain from giving her name and address. Otherwise, the following is a literal copy:

'DEAR SKIPPER,
'My husband has run away with a Yankee woman. How much will youse charge to locate my man and that woman. Jim Boozer at the Opera House says you're is the smartest guy since Sherlock Holmes died. He says you sailors knows woman's ways and that's how it was you saw the doctor squeeze the girl's hand.
'Yours truly,
'_____ _____.'

Not less quaint was the letter written by a woman in Philadelphia making a proposal of marriage. I wrote and thanked her for the kind offer, but pointed out that I had three reasons for refusing, viz.: one wife, and two kids! She then replied expressing gratitude for my candour, and went on to remark that she had been divorced three times because her husbands were no good: but that if ever I went to Philadelphia and would ring her up on the 'phone [number given] she would see that I had the time of my life. However, I have not yet been to that famous city and, now that I am on the retired list, there is little likelihood of my crossing the Atlantic again.

Next followed a business proposition, tempting me with 20,000 dollars (£4000) on condition that I fulfilled a twenty-weeks' engagement in the United States theatres. This, likewise, had to be declined. Another man followed me round for nearly a week, dangling 500 dollars (£100) for a cast of my face to be exhibited among some wax-works, but I doubted whether mine was the kind of 'dial' suited for the collection! That happened almost thirty years ago, but it has never been altogether possible to shake off the publicity which so memorable a July inaugurated; for, at different times, and in divers places lots of questions are always being put to me by all sorts of people.

"What will you do, Captain, when you retire?" some one asked me a few months ago, but he got an answer very different from that which he expected.

"I expect to spend most of my time in the Chamber of Horrors with old Crippen, yarning about the grand times we had together."

Somehow the intention was disbelieved!

But it is difficult to convince some people even when one is serious. Shortly after this Crippen case I was transferred to command the S.S. *Lake Erie* whilst her Master was on shore undergoing an operation. This was one of the C.P.R.'s better ships and I went by train from Liverpool to join her at Glasgow. It was winter-time and we were bound for Boston, U.S.A. Wrapped up in a heavy overcoat and white muffler, I was seated waiting for the train to start, being the only occupant of the compartment, when a lady entered. She kissed her husband farewell, and away we started on the journey.

I was reading what might have seemed a venerable volume, though actually it was *The Comic History of England*, whilst the lady buried herself in a magazine. Nor did we exchange a remark until well on the journey and the train was rattling across a city's bridge. She inquired the name of the place, conversation ripened, and I learned with surprise that she took me for a parson. It was the first time in my life that had happened, but I played up to the respect which she bestowed. As the train drew into Kilmarnock, where she intended to alight, I asked how she could guess I was a cleric.

"Oh! Anyone could tell at a glance," she said.

"Your husband—is he a parson, too?"

"Dear me, no. He's a sailor."

"And so am I!"

But she seemed disinclined to believe me.

In the *Lake Erie* an uneventful voyage to Boston contrasted with another reminder of that bygone fortnight I was trying to forget. The manager of a local theatre had come down to the wharf inviting me and my officers for the following night. A new play was being presented, entitled *Caught by Wireless*, and a box having been placed at our disposal, we went to see it. This performance we discovered to be the whole Crippen case from Hilldrop Crescent to the gallows, but for us the first part of the story more than sufficed. During the interval, on to the stage marched the manager, who informed his audience that Captain Kendall was in the house sitting within that box.

Thereupon an enthusiastic uproar rose which caused us so much embarrassment that without waiting for the entertainment's second half we escaped to the nearest restaurant and concluded the evening with a good oyster supper.

CHAPTER XIX

BY the time I had made three voyages in the *Lake Erie*, her own commander had recovered, so back I went to the *Montrose* for a while. This time our route was to be into rather less northern latitudes, for the Government needed her as troopship. Off we steamed with a full complement to Bermuda, where the Governor boarded us and stayed to lunch.

Lieut.-General Sir Walter Kitchener will be remembered as the son of one soldier and younger brother of another, the famous Kitchener of Khartoum. After lunch the Governor, having entered my cabin for a smoke and chat, I mentioned that I had seen Lord Kitchener recently in the Royal procession on the day after King George V's Coronation, and looking very well.

"You mean that idiotic brother of mine from Egypt?"

I smiled, and asked:

"Why do you call him that?"

"Well, why shouldn't I? He always refers to me as that damn fool of a brother in Bermuda."

Both of these distinguished men have long since passed away, yet their names are still held in reverence.

It was after bringing *Montrose* home with troops for Southampton that this ship was laid aside for overhaul, and I took command of the Company's S.S. *Ruthenia* to open up a new service between Austria and Canada. Thus the Mediterranean and Adriatic introduced a fresh variety into our trips, but a link was strangely forged with the great European cataclysm that not one of us expected. We used to go right up as far as Trieste, and one day the Archduke Ferdinand of Austria sailed over from Miramar Castle to inspect the *Ruthenia*. He asked us to fire some rockets, as we went out, for his children to enjoy.

So, steaming clear of the long breakwaters, we let off from the bridge two rockets which detonated high in the air. Whilst we steered towards the Castle—a magnificent white building with a great tower at its seaward end—more fireworks shot up like a lively bombardment whilst the Royal party standing on a balustrade roof waved their hands in return to our salute. Then we swung to the southward and started down the Adriatic, but within an hour I received a wireless message from the Archduke thanking us for the ovation we had given; and later followed a message from the aged Austrian Emperor. Little did we imagine that within a few months the Archduke and his wife would be assassinated, thereby throwing Europe into the Great War.

The year 1914 for me personally promised to be more than ordinary, for I had been transferred to the Liverpool–Montreal route and given command of the finest ship in the C.P.R. fleet—the *Empress of Ireland*. It was no small honour to be Master of such a magnificent vessel, but one day the S.S. *Storstad* collided with us in the River St. Lawrence, and that was the end of the *Empress*. Even to-day this sad incident is too painfully engraved on my memory for me to enlarge on the matter. It will suffice if I state as a result of the inquiry, the Court found the whole blame rested on the *Storstad*. The Company then promoted me to Marine Superintendent and appointed me in that capacity temporarily to Antwerp whilst my immediate predecessor went on holiday. Nor had I been there more than a week when the threat of war became the prelude to fresh adventures. German troops were crossing Belgium's frontier, neutrality was violated in the short cut to France, for it had not been contemplated that any serious Belgian resistance would be offered.

But now, with deadly inevitability, grim fate was

marching. Shall I ever forget that historic occasion when hostilities were officially declared, and the bells of Antwerp Cathedral at midnight rang out their weird tones announcing that the climax had arrived? Those of us awake in the hotel went outside to ascertain the facts. Crowds were centred around the Town Hall; posts were being driven into the stones and notices attached summoning all able-bodied men to come and defend their country, asking also those left behind to look after the women and children. I recollect one Belgian citizen standing by me so overcome with grief that, observing my nationality, he threw his arms round my neck and exclaimed: "Now you and I are brothers."

Many were the sad scenes witnessed that night— incidents that I never wish to perceive again. The following days were occupied assisting foreigners to clear out of the country. Already every German had escaped over the frontier to rejoin his regiment, and all those German steamers which had been lying thick in the docks laden with merchandise for different parts of the world, received a sudden bidding to return home.

Belgium had to be defended, fortifications vast in size were thought to be impregnable until modern German artillery proved otherwise. Nothing could now stop the onrush of enemy troops, and it was only a question of time before they would be pouring into Antwerp. The day came when we must either remain and be German captives, or get away to England whilst the going was good. Most of the shipping had now departed, and hundreds of refugees were daily besieging the British Consul's offices.

Now it is curious how some vessels, like certain human beings, seem destined for adventure whenever and wherever it may suddenly occur. At this anxious August date there were two Canadian Pacific steamers in Antwerp: one was the *Montreal*—laid up. But the other was also out of commission undergoing an overhaul. She happened to be my old *Montrose*. What could be

N

done? There they rested inert, without steam, without crew.

One thing showed up perfectly clear: we could not desert them to their fate. Very shortly they would fall into German hands like ripe fruit that was dropping from the Belgian trees. The *Montrose* could be hurriedly refitted, engines made good enough for crossing the intervening distance to England, but what about the disabled *Montreal?* Exciting and exacting hours followed, fighting obstacles and fighting the clock. With the great assistance of the Chief Engineer, Mr. Vine (who had been with me during the Crippen voyage), aided also by the British Consul, we finally made the following arrangements. The *Montreal* would have to be towed, yet this powerless ship in her passage down the Scheldt with its strong tides, numerous shoals, and awkward turns, signified no easy problem. Aboard the *Montrose* we managed to place a scratch crew and raise steam.

Could we save British, American, and other refugees? I was able to tell our Consul that we would take as many as he cared to send, so next morning about five hundred joined us in a final effort at flight. Every sort and kind of person had availed himself of the chance— from millionaires to shoeblacks. The spirit of them all was admirable throughout, but very little food could be divided for the reason that none had been obtainable in Antwerp. Away started the *Montrose* down river: it was to be the last time she would ever see Antwerp, which she knew so well. A couple of tugs were in charge of the helpless *Montreal*, coaxing her through the narrow reaches, persuading her round the bends, dodging the sandbanks, until gaining the broad expanse abreast of Flushing where the North Sea was waiting, and tow-wires were connected with the *Montrose*.

Henceforth it became the latter's job hauling her sister over open waters. Of course we were unescorted, but fortunately neither raiders nor submarines interfered. On a pitch dark night the summer weather enabled us to reach the Thames mouth safely, but my uneasiness did not end there. British torpedo-craft were buzzing around us like a lot of flies, wondering who these two liners were, and why one was towing the other. Hours previously I had wired for a pilot to meet us off the Tongue Lightship, but by the time we were in that vicinity he had not showed up.

You will appreciate that under the circumstances of war, darkness, and possible alteration of the Thames buoyage, it was no pleasure to be hanging about in the tideway with a 12,000-tons ship secured to my stern. As any mariner knows, there are too many shoal patches hereabouts waiting to pick up all but the slight-draught vessels.

Therefore, after glancing at the chart, I carried on without pilot to the Nore Lightship off the Medway, chose what seemed a safe anchorage, and there left the *Montreal*. She had been saved from the enemy and could cause no further worry. I then continued up the Thames in *Montrose* till we got to Gravesend, where we disembarked our refugees. They had subsisted on ship's biscuits, porridge, salt beef—any odd food that we could scrape together—yet a happier and more grateful lot of people I never met.

Well, what now?

It had been strange to pace the *Montrose's* bridge again; to have once more left Antwerp alert for public developments; to have gone through with the task. But the final severance with my old vessel was quickly to be made. I brought her up to London, placed her in dock, and left her. Mr. Vine and myself both being officers in the Royal Naval Reserve, we set out towards the Registrar-General's office on Tower Hill to offer our services, but received a curious welcome. We were told that not one-fifth of the R.N.R. ranks would be required, as the War would last possibly only three months; but we could leave our addresses! So we walked out arm-in-arm, and afterwards reflected on the great risk of trying to prophesy. I proceeded to Liverpool and at the end of a few days the Admiralty appointed me to H.M.S. *Calgarian* as Commander under Captain Thomas Webster Kemp, C.I.E., R.N., who had been lately Commanding Officer of the battleship *London*.

Though at the time it was impossible to look ahead down the corridors of future years, this was to begin one more phase of life with a series of adventures culminating in approach to death far closer than when the *Empress of Ireland* nearly robbed me of life. Before asking the reader to share with me the War experiences afloat, he may wish to learn what happened to the *Montrose* ultimately. Not long after Dover settled down to become an important naval base with destroyers, drifters, trawlers, minesweepers, and all manner of craft, *Montrose* was sent thither. That harbour has two entrances, an eastern and western, but at an early stage of hostilities it was contemplated closing the western by sinking one or more block-ships.

To this end the *Montrose* was filled with stones and lay waiting alongside the Admiralty Pier at the harbour's western end, though the original decision fell through. But Dover is always an uncomfortable harbour at the best of times, and any southerly winds drive in a boisterous sea. One night a really severe south-west gale piped up and made the place like a boiling cauldron. Vessels at buoys were having a lively time, but through the western entrance, across which the tides run strongly and rebound from the massive breakwater, a heavy surge dashed in till suddenly *Montrose* snapped her moorings and tore out her bitts forward.

Then an incredible miracle happened. With no steam or crew, but merely a couple of scared men in her, she stampeded independently right amidst the moored shipping without sinking or even ruining them. She continued her mad caper, and through the black murk drove before the wind through the eastern entrance, again doing no damage. Tugs went off to search for this mysterious ghost ship, but both the *Ceylon* and the *Lady Crundall* realized that it would be easier to look for a nigger in a cellar. After an hour or more the wayward creature was located at the edge of the Goodwins Sands. The shrill blast of her siren and the burning of a small flare indicated that human life still was holding out for rescue.

But to go alongside this drifting ship in such a sea was to invite fatal collision under the most favourable chances. Furthermore, the *Montrose*, in readiness for the duty of protecting Dover from torpedoes, had been fitted with steel nets. The latter were now being washed about in all directions about her, making her practically unapproachable. Even the coolest and ablest seamanship could scarce prevent a tug's rudder or propellers getting foul of this invisible wire.

Yet, by dint of pluck and resource, *Ceylon* achieved the impossible, got near enough to rescue one man and after further effort picked up the second. Both were suffering from exposure, and had been snatched from the jaws of death. To do more than this, to attempt taking the *Montrose* in tow when her iron bitts had been carried away and her crinoline of steel wires hung around, was beyond the ability even of clever and daring tug-masters, so she betook herself to a sandy grave on the Goodwins which swallowed her up. Thus ended the career of 'Crippen's yacht,' but not a tear did men of the Dover Patrol shed. They had looked upon her as 'hoodoo' ship, and she had chosen her own demise wisely.

Yet who ever supposed that she could have committed suicide with such deliberation and such thoroughness?

CHAPTER XX

THE *Calgarian* was in peace-time a two-funnelled palatial Atlantic liner, with a cruiser stern, as will be seen from the accompanying illustration. Having been taken up by the Admiralty to serve as an armed merchant cruiser, she was completely gutted of inflammable wood and fittings, given eight 6-inch guns, together with a crew of nearly five hundred men.

And here it is necessary to let the reader understand something of Captain Kemp, one of those rugged sailor-men who had been born in the wrong century. In the days of Drake or Hawke—even so late as Nelson—he would have been at his best. A fine seaman, a genuine hard-case, brave as a lion, tough as leather, hard-bitten, a confirmed bachelor and woman-hater, he expected others to work as hard as himself—that is to say to the supreme limit of endurance. His zeal knew no bounds, hardships could not touch his courageous spirit, self-advertisement was entirely foreign to his nature, but deep down was a well of great kindness.

On the other hand a sharper disciplinarian never trod the deck of a modern ship, and very few naval martinets in the days of sail could have rivalled the vigour of his domination. Hasty-tempered, an independent thinker, neither tactful nor considerate of other persons' feelings, there was a period when to the Lower Deck he became no longer endurable. The climax began in September 1913, when Captain Kemp was appointed to command H.M.S. *London*, and some time later she went up the Medway to Chatham for her refit. His unpopularity reached such a pitch that a letter was signed by Chief Petty Officers and seamen, complaining of the excessive discipline ever since Captain Kemp took over. This epistle having been sent to the editor of a certain publication, an article appeared in the same paper calling attention to the men's grievance. Result—when presently the *London* was recommissioned, the Admiralty decided not to reappoint Captain Kemp.

The latter now found himself on half-pay, and brought an action against the editor, proprietors, printers for libel. The case created a considerable amount of interest, lasted six days, and in the end Captain Kemp was awarded £3000 damages. This vindicated his honour, and you will appreciate his character if I add that he tore up the cheque received for damages, yet it took him months before he could settle the last instalment of his law costs out of his slender means. In fact he was still discharging this debt meticulously month by month during most of the time he was in the *Calgarian*.

Now, that *London* incident ruined the Captain's career, the Admiralty informed him he would never be employed again; but a few months later the outbreak of war provided him with a rare chance when every officer's services were required, so that was why at the beginning of September 1914 he returned afloat to take charge of the *Calgarian* with myself as second-in-command.

He claimed to be a cousin of General French (Lord Ypres), for whom Kemp had no high regard. During the War one of the Captain's brothers served as a 'Tommy' in the trenches with the Canadians, but was killed; his other brother being a Brigadier-General. It was within twenty-four hours of Captain Kemp asking me to go as his Commander that the whole matter quickly shaped itself. I wished to be responsible for all navigation and handling of the ship, and he agreed with the suggestion.

We sailed from Liverpool under sealed orders, bound for the River Tagus, but it did not take long for me to realize that a tiger doesn't change his spots in retirement. The vileness of Kemp's temper apparently had in no wise altered since the *London* days: indeed before we had picked up the Bishop's light (south-west end of the Scillies) we already had our first 'dust-up.' It arose just as might have been expected of him. He began to 'wipe the bridge' with me in front of my juniors; and, inasmuch as I had only a few weeks previously been the sole Captain of a big Atlantic liner, I did not feel like 'taking his slack.' We went for each other 'hell for leather' till he left the bridge. Half an hour later he sent for me, began by referring to his hasty temper, and said he couldn't help it.

"Same with me," I answered, "but now that we understand each other perhaps we may be able to get along for a while. However, in any case, when the ship has finished with the Tagus and come to Gibraltar for coaling, I shall ask to be sent home."

I foresaw that things were not going to be pleasant, and had made up my mind that it would be better to separate rather than keep crossing swords all the time.

But this suggestion of leaving at Gibraltar quite upset the old man.

There was only one person whom Kemp feared, and that was Winston Churchill, First Lord of the Admiralty, who remembered him for the *London* affair.

"I hope, Kendall, you don't mean what you say; because if you leave me under the conditions which you mention, Churchill will put all the blame on to me."

Ghost of the past rising up!

No: I didn't want to see Kemp getting into more hot water, so we patched up our differences, I accepted his hand as a token of friendship, and in the future all went well. The longer I served with him, the better I got to like him, and to this day I think of that rough-hewn personality in one summing-up: A gentleman to the crown of his head, with a character straight as an arrow, and so fine a disciplinarian that had he ever taken the ship into action his crew would have fought as one man.

The *Calgarian* was under orders to join Rear-Admiral

A UNIQUE VOYAGE

When H.M.S. *Calgarian* escorted the first submarines in history to cross the Atlantic. Upper illustration shows the extraordinary combination of iceberg, submarine (H-class), and her oiler in one picture. Lower picture shows H.M. Submarine H-1 having her propeller repaired at the Azores.

CALGARIAN AND THE SUBMARINES

In one picture a boat has been sent off by H.M.S. *Calgarian* whilst in the Atlantic to pass a rope before taking the British submarine in tow. The other illustration shows one of these H-class types effecting propeller repairs whilst calling at the Azores.

J. M. de Robeck who was commanding the 9th Cruiser Squadron with his flag in the *Vindictive*. He had left Plymouth on 4 August to occupy the area between Finisterre and Cape St. Vincent, where he performed valuable work in capturing German steamers and keeping an eye on quite a fleet of other Teutonic liners up the Tagus off Lisbon; all anxious to break forth either as raiders or as supply ships for those other liners chosen to make raiding voyages over the Atlantic.

After the Tagus we were ordered farther south towards the Canaries, whence we patrolled the trade routes, going into Gibraltar for coal and stores. One day, whilst so occupied, there steamed into Gibraltar the battle-cruiser *Invincible*, flying the flag of Admiral Sturdee. She had just arrived from her victory at the Battle of the Falklands when on 8 December 1914 Admiral von Spee, together with the German squadron, suffered the heaviest defeat. Admiral Sturdee, who happened to be one of our Captain's oldest friends, came on board for a cocktail. You can imagine Kemp's expressed annoyance after pressing the bell and the steward entered with the admission:

"Sorry, sir, but we've nothing on board for making a cocktail."

"What! Then you ought to be sunk," commented Sturdee.

Among the world's roughest specimens of seafarers, the fireman (designated 'stoker' in the Royal Navy) is generally accounted the most turbulent; but Liverpool firemen have always been, for tamelessness, in a class by themselves. Yet it was characteristic of the severe Captain Kemp to relax stern discipline and impart kindness even when it seemed scarcely due to such a class as these. One day a *Calgarian* fireman approached with a special request. He had got a girl in trouble whilst in England, and would Captain Kemp allow him to go home on leave to marry her?

Privately Kemp asked my opinion.

"Not a genuine request," I answered. "Just a ruse to get out of the Navy."

But the old man, with his white hair and torpedo beard, thought otherwise. With great consideration he made arrangements for the man to have a passage in a ship bound for England.

"Go home," was the admonishment, "do the honourable thing, marry the girl, and in two months come back to your ship."

At the same time he slipped a sovereign in the man's hand as a wedding present.

Within two months—and greatly to my surprise—the fireman returned. A couple of days later the Captain sent for me.

"Well, Kendall, what about it? You never believed that man. But *I* did. And I consider he's shown the very meaning of honour."

I didn't want to upset Kemp, so let it go at that without disillusioning him. His knowledge of stokers was less than my acquaintance with firemen. There existed quite a different reason for the man's departure, and only one other person in the ship besides myself knew the secret. It had nothing to do with a wedding. And really there seemed a strange contradiction in the make-up of this officer who had ruined his career by inconsiderate harshness to his crew, yet could now be bluffed by all sorts of fairy-tales. The one practicable way of handling these Mersey firemen was to use that ultra-strictness which had been out of place among the disciplined, well-trained, chief petty officers and blue-jackets of the *London*. The time came when Captain Kemp went away from the *Calgarian* on ten days' leave, placing me in charge. On his return there was a surprise awaiting him.

Defaulters and drunks! They couldn't get away with their excuses just now. I had all the cells filled with the sweepings of Liverpool's dockside. For once they learned the meaning of cold, impartial, justice.

Thomas Webster Kemp passed away some years ago, but he has not taken with him all those stories which belonged to his life as a naval officer. Apparently he was ever somewhat 'difficult' in his younger days, and one of his shipmates told me the following anecdote when Lieutenant Kemp was serving in the Fleet and his ship with others lay anchored off Spithead. On a certain occasion H.R.H. the Prince of Wales (the future King Edward VII) had been visiting the ship accompanied by some friends, and was now to be taken ashore in the picket-boat. Lieutenant Kemp happened to be in charge of the latter and, before shoving off, had been given strict orders by his Captain to take every care of the Royal passenger.

On the journey shorewards Kemp, who was standing alongside the coxswain, looked round and chanced to see H.R.H. peeping over the canopy aft.

"Put your head down!" shouted the young lieutenant sharply, and the startled Prince meekly obeyed, though not without amusement.

That night the Prince and Admiral were dining together. The former spoke of his afternoon visit, and added:

"But I don't much like the officer sent in charge of the boat."

Next day the Admiral sent for young Kemp, who was ordered to give an explanation. This is what came forth:

"Before shoving off from the ship, sir, my Captain gave me strict instructions to take care of the Prince. I obeyed that command. On observing His Royal Highness looking above the canopy, I feared that he might get a clinker in his eye from the funnel. That's why, sir, I called out for him to duck his head."

Later on this story was related to the Prince, who more than appreciated the solicitous care for his person. Nor did he forget to express his thanks at the first opportunity which presented itself.

The *Calgarian* was kept busy all these months, on the go here and there. That initial employment with *Vindictive* off the Tagus mouth, keeping potential German raiders from sallying forth, was no less important than the work being done by three noble C.P.R. liners which at the beginning of War were out in the Pacific. The *Empress of Russia*, *Empress of Japan*, and *Empress of Asia* during August 1914 lay in Hong Kong, but on being taken over were armed and commissioned as merchant-cruisers. The first mentioned in the course of her normal passenger and mail service had left Vancouver, but now that portion of her crew consisting of Chinese was replaced in part by British Naval Reservists: yet there were not enough to go round. So what?

There were drafted to her (1) some British soldiers of the Royal Garrison Artillery, (2) some French naval gun-crews from Chinese river craft, (3) some Pathan Sepoys. And with this very mixed complement the *Empress of Russia* distinguished herself. It was she which, after steaming west, took over from H.M.S. *Sydney* the crew of the destroyed German raider *Emden*; and in conjunction with Indian troops the *Empress of Russia* captured the Turkish Red Sea fort of Kamaran. For twenty-three days this converted liner, by her four 4.7-inch guns, with her sister *Empress of Asia*, defended the Port of Aden till relieved by British warships, and afterwards reduced to ruins the Arabian fort of Salif which the Turks had declined to surrender.

The *Calgarian's* patrolling of the Atlantic trade routes was almost as monotonous as it was essential; for Germany's pre-War arrangements had been thorough, and the subsequent operations carried out with vigour. For example, every master of the North German Lloyd steamer on the eve of war was to listen-in to the Norddeich wireless station at 7 a.m., 1 p.m., and 11.10 p.m. A 'Cruiser Handbook,' containing a list of secret rendezvous where liners could make for and find other ships bringing them guns, was also issued. But equally detailed was the arrangement for Supply Centres in charge of Supply Officers. Such places as Las Palmas, New York, Rio Janeiro, Pernambuco, Teneriffe in the Canaries, and Horta in the Azores, were to be used for obtaining coal and stores.

At Las Palmas, where a number of German steamers had been interned, Korvetten-Kapitan Leonhardi was the energetic Supply Officer whose activities kept British cruisers continually on the qui vive. Not merely had German colliers from Cardiff and Barry come loaded into Las Palmas during the first week of war, but from Las Palmas, too, the S.S. *Duala*, the S.S. *Arucas*, and the S.S. *Bethania* brought their coal cargoes to the lonely north-west African anchorage of Rio d'Oro where the *Kaiser Wilhelm der Grosse* put in after the first week of her raiding voyage. This was the once-famous North German Lloyd mail steamer which became the pioneer Atlantic raider until H.M.S. *Highflyer* steamed also into Rio d'Oro and sank her.

But we in *Calgarian* never knew what might appear over the horizon any hour, or whence an S O S wireless call might indicate that another British vessel in the south Atlantic was being molested. So to speak, our cruiser force had to keep one eye on Las Palmas against any escape of the interned shipping, and another on the route which came up from South America. The wide entrance to the Chesapeake, before the United States entered the War, with Newport News as Supply Base, was a favourite locality for German and chartered neutral steamers to be coming and going.

On the whole it is surprising that German raiders down the Atlantic achieved so little, though the amount of sunken tonnage was serious enough. Not all of these enemies were armed liners, for we must not forget either S.M.S. *Dresden* or *Karlsruhe*. Our anxiety was concerned from the first by knowledge that at the opening of hostilities no fewer than 54 German and Austrian vessels lay in American Atlantic ports; and that New York

alone contained 9 large German liners such as the famous
*Vaterland, George Washington, Friedrich der Grosse,
Grosse Kurfurst,* and *Kaiser Wilhelm II.* On 21 August
the North German Lloyd S.S. *Brandenburg* was allowed
to leave Philadelphia under pretence of being bound
for Bergen. Actually she had been despatched by the
New York German Supply Centre to a rendezvous near
Newfoundland.

It was the four-funnelled North German Lloyd S.S.
Kronprinz Wilhelm which on the night of 3–4 August,
after coaling and provisioning for an extended voyage,
slipped out of New York, sped south, and was met by
S.M.S. *Karlsruhe* which supplied her with guns and
ammunition at a rendezvous 150 miles N.E. of Watling
Island. Of her long raiding cruise it is not necessary
for the moment to say more; or of the *Prinz Eitel
Friedrich;* or of the two voyages by the *Mowe* during
later months.

In searching for such as these, and protecting the
routes, weeks passed by, varied by periodical coaling;
but now the *Calgarian* was ordered to cross the ocean
and work on the New York patrol. Here was another
ceaseless vigil, which we kept up for months, sometimes
moving farther south to show ourselves off the Chesapeake
and let it be known that we were about. Curiously,
some people misunderstood our nationality, for, when
occasionally we used to obtain American newspapers
from British steamers, the *Calgarian* was always mentioned
as 'the big French cruiser.'

Time in its advance has a curious habit of bringing us
back to scenes once memorable during our earlier days.
And now the *Calgarian* in the summer of 1915 was sent
to the Gulf of St. Lawrence, which held for me so many
associations. After Antwerp, the Portuguese coast, and
warmer waters, it was like coming home when I returned
to the area of clammy fogs, but the reason can be reckoned
as unprecedented. Four submarines for the British
Navy—H-1, H-2, H-3, and H-4—had been built by

Vickers at Montreal and we were to escort them across the Atlantic to Gibraltar. I stress the occasion because this effort preceded by many months the first German submarine voyage over that ocean to America.

This H-class was 164½ feet long, and could do 13 knots on the surface in fairly smooth water. We got into touch and escorted them into St. John's, Newfoundland, which brought back memories of that night when I had been wrecked in the *Lusitania*. The *Calgarian* stayed at St. John's a few days merely to give the submarines opportunity for a good overhaul before making the long and trying trip. Then we put to sea, accompanied by a tramp steamer carrying all the oil-fuel which the quartette might require.

Just as modern aircraft have been known to make their journey from the United States to Europe via the Azores, as did the seventeenth-century ships sailing back to England after landing the early settlers in Virginia; so we six vessels of a modern age steered first towards the Azores hoping to get finer weather for our submarines. We experienced moderate conditions, sighted the island of Flores, and decided to anchor behind the latter. For one of the four had damaged a propeller against some floating wreckage.

It was inspiriting to watch keen young submarine officers working long and furiously to effect repairs. Half the time they were up to their necks in water, but nothing seemed too much trouble in their eagerness to arrive at the seat of war ready for action. The existence of these H-class boats had been kept wonderfully secret, so that, with the exception of the people at the Montreal yard and the Newfoundlanders, practically nobody knew anything about them. Thus were they destined to create a sensation sooner or later.

It came after we cleared Flores and were heading east for Gibraltar. One morning, as the little squadron was about half-way between these two places, a large English passenger steamer sighted us, approached, and suddenly the unwonted sight of four submarines sent the passengers into a wild delight, and their cheering became an ovation. Then followed the innocent but kindly signal: 'May we offer you our congratulations?'

They imagined we had captured a German nest!

Nor could we enlighten them any further than acknowledging their signal with thanks. A similar incident occurred later with another vessel, to our considerable amusement. By the day when the squadron had only 50 more miles to traverse ere reaching Gibraltar, three submarines asked permission to proceed independently at full speed. Having had twelve days at sea in these steel 'whales,' officers and men were longing to reach port. Request having been approved by Captain Kemp, the trio forged ahead, leaving us with the one somewhat lame duck.

The advisability of an escort on such a lengthy transatlantic trip, that crossed so many trade routes, became additionally confirmed shortly after the three quitted *Calgarian's* protection. They had proceeded about 10 miles ahead of us when a couple of tramp steamers bound south sighted with horror three submarines on the surface. In those anxious days all underwater craft seen outside British waters were regarded as enemy U-boats to be avoided at all costs or destroyed. And in 1915, when merchant ships in general were short of defensive guns, very few tramps possessed any sort of armament. So these two immediately turned right round and fled for their lives at full speed, belching out smoke plentifully.

Our responsibility ended at Gibraltar, and it is not without interest to note how three of these H-boats subsequently fared. H-1 (Lieutenant Wilfrid B. Pirie, R.N.) went to the Dardanelles, dived under minefields and nets, reaching the Sea of Marmora on more than one occasion. At a subsequent date she went to work in the Adriatic and on 28 February next year had the most annoying bad luck. It was not long after midday when H-1, being 10 miles west of Durazzo and sub-

merged, saw the chance of a million: in fact it was like
a young naval officer's dream of perfection. There on
the surface—and stopped, without any way—was an
Austrian submarine. Could an easier target be offered
in half a dozen wars?

Pirie flooded his tubes, got the enemy nicely ahead,
fired the lower starboard torpedo, expecting to blow the
enemy into fragments. The aim was immaculate, the
missile travelled in a straight line, but instead of hitting
dived under the enemy's hull. Why? Not because of
any fault aboard H-1, but through a technical Admiralty
error; war-heads of British torpedoes having in some cases
been made 40 lbs. heavier than the practice-heads
employed during exercises. H-2 was employed some
time in the Aegean as a decoy, but H-4 was the luckiest
of these transatlantic units. She, too, had been sent to
operate in the Adriatic and once, whilst making for
Brindisi, had a very narrow escape; for the British
drifters took her for an enemy, fired forty shells and only
just missed hitting at a distance of 5000 yards. Nevertheless, eleven days before Pirie suffered his disappointment Lieutenant H. E. Smyth, R.N., in H-4, when half-
way across between Brindisi and Cape Rodoni, shared
the same sort of angry surprise. He, too, sighted an
Austrian submarine on the surface stopped.

From a distance of only 700 yards Smyth loosed off
two torpedoes set for 5 feet; yet both these dived below
the enemy because of the same technical error. However,
during the War's last phase up the Adriatic H-4 (then
commanded by Lieutenant O. North, R.N.) received the
long postponed good fortune due to her. On 23 May
1918, about three-quarters of an hour before midnight,
North sighted the German UB-52, approached to 250
yards at full speed, fired a couple of torpedoes and both
were 'hits.' Down sank the German submarine within
fifteen seconds, but two survivors were picked up: one
the captain, and the other a petty officer.

o

CHAPTER XXI

FROM Gibraltar the *Calgarian*, having steamed thousands of miles north, south, east, and west, went to Liverpool for an overhaul. Only three weeks could be allowed for this necessity, but it enabled the different watches to go home on leave, and was not too short to prevent several of our officers getting married.

Back to the New York patrol we were bound, calling on the way at Bermuda where a hurricane held us up during ten days. Our next destination was Halifax, Nova Scotia, where our Skipper left us for another appointment. He was proceeding to take supreme charge of British naval operations in North Russia, a post that would suit his gifts in more than one sense. Somewhat of a Russian scholar, his tough personality presently was to surprise even the natives in that trying climate. And there survives to this day the story of Commodore Kemp holding the White Sea in such contempt that he considered it effeminate to wear extra clothing. At Archangel the Russians always remarked: "It must be a very cold day when the British Admiral puts on an overcoat."

He had been to St. Petersburg several times before the War, and on more than one occasion told me that, having noticed the approaching Revolution, he himself warned the Czar. Well, that yarn quite likely was true, and I can imagine old Kemp in St. Petersburg being the Czar himself, whilst the ruler of all Russia (for a time at least) would have to take a back seat.

Parting from our Captain after being shipmates for more than a year, was not made without regret. He had worked everybody, as himself, full out right from the first to the finish.   Continual target practice at various ranges up to five miles he had insisted upon till the *Calgarian* developed into a smart gunnery ship, but it was characteristic of him that he used up twelve months of ammunition during the practising of three months. Every officer in her, excepting himself, belonged to the Reserve—and just before leaving the *Calgarian* he sent for us and thanked us all together.   "When I joined this ship," he added in his blunt direct manner, "I had no damn use for an R.N.R. officer.   But you've changed my opinion entirely."

With all his faults, his harshness, hasty temper, and severity, there was yet some indefinable quality which attracted us all to him.   On the day when he finally walked down the gangway into the boat which was taking him ashore, the whole of *Calgarian's* crew cheered him to the echo—one of the greatest compliments which could ever be paid to a departing commanding officer, and the first time it had ever happened to this one.

His successor, Captain Robert Gwynne Corbett, R.N., was a big-hearted fellow who, without sacrificing efficiency, believed that life contained many opportunities for enjoyment which should be appreciated to the full. His nickname in the service was 'Shackles,' owing to the way his joints used to work when he strode along the deck.   For over $2\frac{1}{2}$ years he remained Captain of the *Calgarian*, and we took up our old position on the New York patrol, encountering all sorts of weather and having to keep an eye lifting for all the considerable traffic which goes in and out of that busy port.

And here I would like to give an illustration to show the reader how impossible it is to guarantee complete immunity by means of a cruiser patrol along an extended neutral coast.   Just as a policeman on his beat through the nocturnal hours cannot be everywhere at once, and he is unable to prevent a burglar occasionally breaking through into a house; so likewise when a handful of British cruisers was set to watch the vast area between

Nova Scotia and Virginia, with special regard to the approaches of Boston, New York, the Delaware and Chesapeake—apart altogether from the British possessions of Halifax and Bermuda—it was not impossible that occasionally a clever German ship might steal in or out.

Early in March 1915 there was a strong rumour that all the interned German liners in New York were ready to rush forth into the Atlantic. This would have been a serious matter for more than one reason. Firstly, the other German surface-raiders were nearly at their last gasp, and thirty fresh steamers with ample coal and provisions could have kept up the annoyance for most of another year in all directions; thereby still further lessening our mercantile tonnage on the high seas, and increasing the task of our overworked cruisers. From other theatres of war units would have to be recalled, and even then the results could not be satisfactory. But, secondly, the escape of one interned fleet might encourage another up the Tagus, or at the Canaries, to try the same experiment.

Our Commander-in-Chief at this date was no longer Admiral de Robeck—he had gone to command at the Dardanelles—but Sir George Patey, with his flag in the *Leviathan*. It was whilst the *Leviathan*, *Calgarian*, and several other cruisers were off the American coast that orders came to guard the approaches to New York. Certainly nobody could deny the wisdom of this decision, for in the neighbourhood of Hudson River not one American warship at that period was present for enforcing regulations.

We in the *Calgarian* asked permission to remain watching the Chesapeake entrance, as we believed that the New York rumour of thirty German ships raising steam was just a ruse to entice us away from the Virginia area. Our submission was not approved. But note the result. On 11 March that previously mentioned raider *Prinz Eitel Friedrich*, badly needing repairs to boilers and engines after seven months' continuous cruising and raiding, crept quietly into Newport News whilst we were away from the Chesapeake. The surprise of her arrival could not be denied: Americans and British were alike amazed. She never emerged to continue hostilities, for on 26 April the United States Government finally interned her. But by that time her sister-raider *Kronprinz Wilhelm*, under cover of darkness at 5 a.m. of 11 April, eluded H.M.S. *Suffolk* off the Chesapeake, and also got into Newport News, to suffer the same internment. When Great Britain made representations to the American Government about New York, this was acknowledged by sending the U.S.S. *Dolphin* (an old gunboat carrying two 4-inch guns) to that port, whilst another U.S.A. warship was dispatched to keep an eye on Boston.

One day, however, whilst patrolling off New York the *Calgarian* captured a steamer bound down the coast. She was flying American colours, yet really happened to be one of the German internees which had escaped. We placed aboard her one of our officers and prize party who were to take her into Halifax, the party, of course, being armed. From the first it was realized that this was going to be no happy yachting trip, and the Prize Officer had been cautioned against any tricky business which the disappointed Germans might set going.

In spite of his watchfulness, none the less they 'put it across' him. During the night his enemies plotted to prevent the ship reaching Halifax. She had on board only a limited supply of coal, though quite enough for reaching the Nova Scotian port, but it was not till late on in the dark hours that the officer realized how exceptionally busy had the engineering department been in dumping 'ashes' overboard. These 'ashes' were in fact so much perfectly good coal, so that he doubted if she would get further than the Nantucket Lightship.

Drastic orders now had to be issued, and the ship went steaming on whilst the officer wondered what shape the next trickery would take. Possibly they might now try to poison him? He accordingly declined to eat anything cooked by the Germans, and never quitted the bridge or the chart-room. We had supplied him with a chart—the only one aboard *Calgarian*—biscuits, butter, and marmalade; so that meals and navigation went on simultaneously on the chart-table, then he would return to the bridge. Now the only friendly creature to be trusted among the German outfit was the ship's cat, and even that animal 'did him down' in the end. For the officer on approaching the dangerous Nova Scotia coast entered the room to consult his chart.

Judge of his annoyance on finding that the cat had gleefully walked through a saucer of marmalade and then all over the precious chart.

"Heaven alone knows," he related afterwards, "how I ever got to Halifax through that sticky sea of marmalade."

One night when the *Calgarian* was patrolling off New York in a dense fog, another vessel collided with us. After the first impact the two ships drifted part. We could hear distant shouting. Men calling for help? We lowered two boats in charge of officers, and sent them to save the people in the other ship. After rowing some way through the fog, they suddenly met two other boats making for *Calgarian*.

"Where bound?" one of our officers hailed.

"We're off to save the people in the ship we've hit," came the answer.

"So are we. Who are you?"

She was a United States training ship with cadets making for New York. Luckily neither she nor the *Calgarian* received anything save the slightest damage, so we could carry on with our job—which incidentally was fairly thankless. Twenty-one days out, then into Halifax for coaling, then off again. Thus one month succeeded another, and any break of the monotony—no matter what its nature—was received with gratitude.

For reasons which would take too long if I were to explain, the *Prinz Eitel Friedrich* was from 11 March till her final internment on 26 April at Newport News a very uncertain item, and throughout those suspenseful weeks she might try sneaking out as stealthily as she had steamed in. We were back from our New York patrol and now keenly vigilant off Chesapeake Bay. A certain night seemed to indicate that the raider would try making for freedom again.

Aboard *Calgarian* all hands were standing by, all guns loaded, 40 rounds of ammunition on deck for each gun: in fact everything at the end of a split yarn ready for immediate action. It was not long before Captain Kemp had us keyed up, but the spring night was bitterly cold.

Suddenly the general alarm was rung and sounded through the ship. Gun-crews flew to their stations, officers in fawn duffle coats rushed on deck, guns were being trained through the darkness trying to locate the hidden foe. But whilst suspense continued supreme and men were waiting for the order to fire, one R.N.R. officer —a sizeable fellow of 16 stones—off duty down below was roused to wakefulness by the buzzer. He rubbed his eyes, recollected that he happened to be in charge of the after guns, and with one leap was out of his bunk, tearing towards his action station like the wind.

There he waited, and waited, like the rest. Yet never an order from the bridge. Ten minutes passed, the R.N.R officer gave a shiver without noticing it. Any moment would be issued the command for his guns to fire. He shivered again, still intent on nothing other than his duty, when one of the marines belonging to the gun-crew turned to him and said:

"Excuse me, sir. It's very cold to-night. Hadn't you better put on your trousers, sir?"

The officer glanced down, admitted that he wasn't feeling too warm. The truth is that in his eagerness and excitement he hadn't realized his scanty attire; but a minute or two later he was able to reach his cabin again, and the men to be dismissed. Old Kemp chanced not to be quite on the top-line that night. He had rung the alarm by mistake!

During the year 1917 when bigger, ocean-going sub-marines from Germany, heavily armed and with a wide radius of action, began to harass the trade routes far away from the coast, it became necessary for shipping to be escorted across the Atlantic in convoys. Thus, in lieu of steamers leaving port individually according to regular schedule, they sailed in groups with an armed cruiser or armed merchant cruiser to protect them. It was to be the most determined reply to Germany at the time when the U-boat campaign was nearing its peak; and historians tell us that no anti-submarine measure ever succeeded so handsomely, whilst U-boat captains admitted after the War that the convoy-system frustrated their efforts time after time. Occasionally some excep-tionally daring submarine officer would take a big risk and dive below the convoy, yet even at periscope depth whilst getting into position for attack, it was reckoned something of a nightmare as dozens of steel prows came rushing onwards. Either the submarine must play for safety, or the chance of being rammed was very high.

When the *Calgarian* received instructions to leave patrolling off the Chesapeake and New York there arose complete joy. We were to do convoy work now, and anything would be pleasanter than the old monotony, although we did not immediately appreciate either the importance or the dangers implied. That would come in time. Meanwhile let us get a clear notion of this new activity that was so familiar in the days of sail when old East Indiamen and other merchantmen voyaged in company during the Anglo-French wars.

Steamers and their escort must make as big a success as did their predecessors of past generations, but the basis of success again must be seamanship. Suppose, for example, we set out from Halifax eastward-bound to the United Kingdom with thirty or forty steamers. Each vessel would be given her allotted position at a preliminary meeting attended by each Master. And the fullest instructions would be plainly imparted.

Now to control a fleet of this size through day and
night, fine weather and fog during a distance of 2500
miles, through gales and danger zones of U-boats or mine-
fields, is no ordinary undertaking. The responsibility is
beyond all reckoning, for these vessels would have much-
needed cargoes of foodstuffs and munitions. Britain was
being sorely tried by a desperate enemy, too many
valuable steamships had been torpedoed, and the day was
approaching when our country would be within six weeks
of starvation. Therefore if the escorting cruiser were to
lose even one unit of the convoy, this was reckoned as a
nasty blow: so, besides good seamanship there must be
good fellowship—everybody pulling together on the
same rope.

The strength of a chain is its weakest link: the speed
of a convoy is that of its slowest steamer. Picture the
anxiety of the Captain in each of those forty vessels doing
a 10-knots average, coming along in a well-organized
crowd through a dirty Atlantic night without lights.
Each vessel, so to speak, is hanging on to the black mass
ahead, to port, or to starboard. A wrong order to the
helmsman, an error of judgment in the fog, would send
that ship and one other with two crews to their doom.
Seas would sweep over the bows and almost freeze into
ice before swishing on deck. Dark hours seemed unending and the dawn never coming. Yet if convoying
meant for us increased responsibility and keener solici-
tude, it was a new game which we learned to delight in.

Some of these vessels would be full of Canadian troops.
What would not a U-boat chance if he could be sure that
a couple of thousand soldiers might never reach France?
Yes: the bait was enormous and tantalizing. On the
other hand the safe passing of so many hundred ships in
formation, week after week, proved that convoying in
modern times was as sound theoretically as it had been
in the days of canvas and wooden walls. Many will
wonder why convoys had not been instituted earlier
during the Great War.

The answer is not quite so simple as might be expected. Admittedly there was some prejudice in high places, and some opinions were convinced that station-keeping would be impossible as a general rule—though this objection speedily vanished when once the matter came under practical test.

Quite another reason may be found in the trend of events. Until April 1915 the surface-raiders in different parts of the world, but especially in North and South Atlantic, brought so much damage that every available cruiser and converted liner was required for patrolling the steamer-tracks. Then came a period when surface-raiding was succeeded by submarine raiding within the Narrow Seas. Next a handful of daring specialists revived surface-raiding by such ships as *Möwe, Seeadler, Wolf;* but this demanded exceptional ability, immense nerve, and a great deal of luck for evading the Blockade ships off northern Scotland. Thus did less fortunate German raiders, such as the *Greif* and *Rena*, have to succumb without getting through into the Atlantic. But these were desultory affairs compared with the over-seas and intense U-boat campaign which marked the latter period of the War at sea. Older cruisers of less speed and value, ex-liners well tested in the Blockade Squadron, could now be employed more freely escorting transports and cargo—carriers after the United States enter the War; because the Blockade Squadron became no longer required and its units were available elsewhere.

Thus not against surface-ships but against submarines were convoys instituted after the former had done their worst. It affected my own career to the extent that henceforth to the end of hostilities I did nothing else than convoy. By a curious turn of circumstance I was back on my pre-War trade-route more nearly than might have been expected after all the changes and chances of previous months; but the essential difference was in regard to quantity. Not one single vessel, but many, had to be looked after throughout this period; not a few hundred passengers, but many thousands; not a chance load of bullion but millions of gold being transported west to pay for the stores brought east.

It will always be my pride that I was connected with ocean convoying as long as—but probably longer than—any other officer; since the period began at the beginning and ended with the end. During the whole of this period we never lost one ship that was being escorted, and only towards the finish did we lose our own vessel. This forms a separate story and, because of its drama, its hurling me nearer to death than I ever care to contemplate, I must reserve the narration till a later page.

So many people nowadays are wont to think of sea-power solely in terms of battleships that it is well to stress the need in wartime of cruisers, be they old or modern, genuine 'Navy,' or improvised from the great shipping lines. And if any doleful Jimmy insists that the disappearing of sail banished the art of ship handling, I would ask him to remember how minute was the percentage of accidents in the convoy fleets—despite the most difficult conditions which imagination could devise.

CHAPTER XXII

IT would be quite impossible to over-stress the importance of convoys for any nation largely reliant on overseas trade. Few countries are entirely independent of others, whether in times of peace or during war; whether because the cargoes are essential imports or the requisite conditions for monetary exchange. Germany's sea-borne trade was practically non-existent during the last war, as France similarly suffered during a previous generation when Britain was her enemy: but for the United Kingdom nowadays—more than ever throughout her long history—food and raw material fetched across thousands of sea miles are not less necessary to the nation than fresh air to the individual.

If the United States of America were engaged in hostilities with Japan, imports from over the ocean might not attain the importance mentioned, because America is far more self-contained. Yet even the U.S.A. might some day have to carry troops across the sea, through submarine zones, and there is no vessel which causes so much anxiety as a transport full of soldiers. For they compose a great crowd in a limited space without being of military value so long as afloat. Conversely the loss of life from one torpedo is proportionately larger than in the case of a freighter or ordinary passenger vessel.

Therefore this convoy problem is worthy of the closest study, but especially by those belonging to any country which possesses a Merchant Navy and (what follows) a fighting Navy. Occasionally the embryonic idea manifested itself in the early stages of the War when some specially important liner was escorted, though this was the exception rather than the rule. The policy of allow-ing even armed steamers to sail alone was proved to be wrong, and that of employing patrol vessels along an extensive route turned out to be both wasteful as well as weak. 'Union makes strength,' and there is mutual defence when (say) thirty armed steamships are voyaging together; but, likewise, instead of patrol vessels scattering their power, these are now concentrated ahead, astern, and on the flanks of the merchantmen.

Furthermore, the submarine finds this huge massed target more complicated than a series of separate ships, which can be dealt with in detail. The amount of con-centrated fire from the escorts' guns is something to deter many a plucky U-boat commander. Throughout the submarine campaign over and over again the German method of attack was typically that of the bully doing things on the cheap: that is to say, a U-boat would, from a long and safe range with a superior gun, begin to over-awe and intimidate the commercial ship by shelling and hoisting a signal 'M N' ('Stop Immediately'). Then the steamer would be ordered to lower a boat, row towards the submarine, who would send a party aboard armed with time-bombs. A few explosions, and down would disappear the steamship.

But the employment of convoy formation with escort ruled out these bomb tactics, and not for many minutes would even the biggest armed, long-range, U-boats care to engage in duel with escorts of still greater range having a steadier platform. Thus, if convoying did nothing else, it would reduce a submarine's method of attack to the torpedo alone: in other words, she must contend one-eyed, below the surface, instead of with full vision on the level. But that, as already mentioned, was full of risk and distractions when so many steel stems had to be dodged.

It was the F.C.T. (French Coal Trade) running across from the southern part of the United Kingdom to northern French ports which began to convince the Admiralty of the practical value of convoys, though these cross-Channel vessels were of small tonnage only. Now and again, in different parts of Europe, e.g. off the south of Ireland and up the Mediterranean, three or four armed trawlers would escort several steamers cruising together, and this also became a successful method. So, too, the Scandinavian convoys across the North Sea worked fairly well, though time was to show that the proximity to German bases fairly invited fast surface raiders to rush out and with overwhelming force fall upon the cargo-carriers.

But in the case of Atlantic convoying the possibilities were pretty well defined and may be summed up thus: (1) On the high seas, away from land, the chance of being attacked was improbable though not impossible. A surface raider such as the *Möwe* might get through past Scotland, yet the 'gate' was being so well guarded that she would need all the luck possible. True, one of the ocean-class U-boats might be encountered, but this type was slow at diving and a big, easy target for the escorts' artillery. (2) Much more to be feared was the following combination—a narrow channel after making the land; a concentration of two or three moderate-sized submarines commanded by really daring and determined officers. Any funnel-shaped confined waterway through which the convoy must pass like sheep through a door was inviting to U-boats who could lie in wait like a pack of hungry wolves. And such a funnel or gate was that stretch of water which is marked on our maps and charts as the North Channel, separating north-eastern Ireland from south-western Scotland. We shall come back to this area presently.

By February 1917 it is true, but strange to look back upon, that many shipmasters still agreed with the Admiralty that convoys in the steamship age would never succeed, because if they numbered ten or twenty instead of three or four, station-keeping would be too complicated and collisions must multiply seriously. And, certainly, we know from post-War German writers that our late enemies believed modern convoying was not practicable. But in history, as in fiction, curious coincidences do occur and the entry of the United States Navy happened at the right moment. Since the Blockade really boiled down to preventing Germany receiving goods from America (indirectly, via Holland, Denmark, or Scandinavia), it followed that when the United States became our ally, the Blockade 10th Cruiser Squadron could be removed and split up. The latter consisted of some of the best passenger liners, well-armed, able to keep the sea in all weathers, and possessing excellent speed. In other words, more than a match for *Möwes* and the biggest U-boats. And statistics revealed that in proportion as the convoy principle was established, so did the shipping losses diminish.

I have seen a convoy of merchantmen numbering 40 steamers zigzagging through the North Channel on a pitch-black night, and each vessel so close to each other at times that a biscuit could have been thrown on board. It was like a steel wall passing on its way between Ireland and Scotland. There could be no need to signal: 'Ships keep as close as possible to prevent submarine attack.' Master Mariners used their common sense and did it, well knowing that eager U-boats were lurking in the Channel for a torpedo chance.

Rightly and properly did the Merchant Service earn universal gratitude for their difficult achievement, often being compelled to make the best of indifferent material; for many of those old tramp steamers had been 'built by the mile and cut off as wanted.' Not easy to handle, they kept station with remarkable consistency though not without some narrow escapes. Valuable cargoes would be landed, away the ships would turn round and cross the ocean light, battering against westerly gales which not all the cruiser-protection in the world could alleviate.

In all this Atlantic ferrying there was plenty of dullness, and precious little variety for war-worn crews.

Censoring of letters was an important duty entrusted to a particular officer, who, of course, was regarded by the men as a 'nosey-Parker.' They resented this interruption of their privacy as much as he hated the necessity; and the consequence was that they put as little information in their correspondence home as would satisfy suspicious spouses at home. After a while the latter began to feel that all was not well: this absence of all expressed endearments seemed so extraordinary that doubting wives would write to the ship's commanding officer privately inquiring after husbands' fidelity. I remember old Kemp, during his period with us in the *Calgarian*, getting lots of these epistles.

He used to reply diplomatically explaining how sensitive the men felt in regard to their sentiments, but that censoring was the rule, and there need be no anxiety of their respective partners' faithfulness. In some of these armed merchant cruisers quite a large number of the sailors came from outlying villages of the Hebrides, and these simple fishermen did a very clever thing: they wrote to their wives in Gaelic, pretending their inability to write sufficiently well in English. Since no officer could read the Celtic tongue, censorship broke down utterly in that section.

It was remarkable that nothing could destroy the courage and persistency of such men who had left their nets and small craft; or others who had come from Newfoundland, from deep-sea tracks and all manner of ships. Some had been blown up by mines, some torpedoed more than once, yet they would be off to sea as soon as a new bag was packed and a new uniform obtained. One of these men whilst home on leave after enduring weeks of exposure to wintry weather on the Atlantic without ill effect, developed a sore throat through having to dwell in a house. Off he walked round the corner to see the local doctor.

"Gargle the throat with salt water," was the advice.

"Goodness me!" exclaimed Jack. "What, again?"

"And why shouldn't you?"

"Oh, nothing! But I've been torpedoed five times already."

One day after reaching Halifax later in the War we were informed by the Senior Naval Officer, Admiral Sir Montague Browning, that Their Royal Highnesses the Duke and Duchess of Connaught with Princess Patricia were to proceed homeward with us in the *Calgarian*, for the Duke's period as Governor-General of Canada was finished. Now a convoy escort with every bit of luxury taken out of her is not the sort of accommodation that such distinguished personages have a right to expect, yet nothing could have been more democratic than the way they adapted themselves to our make-shift preparations. And the responsibility of bringing these passengers through the danger zone was not lightly to be estimated. One torpedo into the *Calgarian's* hull and . . .

It was some comfort to know that H.M.S. *Drake*, a cruiser, commanded by Captain Fawcett Wray, R.N., would be sailing in company. But the Duchess was in failing health at that time, and U-boats regarded no person or thing with respect.

Without flourish or trumpets the *Calgarian* put to sea, an extra supply of food and luxuries had been taken on board to make our visitors less inconvenienced by the discomforts, but that grand old gentleman, the Duke, forbade any special fare to be placed on the table for his party. The same menu provided for *Calgarian's* officers was to be that for his family. Any lavishness he ordered to be swept aside; such articles as fruit must be declined till reaching England, but then sent to the hospitals for wounded soldiers.

During the voyage, every morning at breakfast food would be placed on the hot-plate for the royal trio to wait on themselves, the Princess looking after her mother. Then later, alert as a young man, the Duke would be seen promenading the decks, and in the afternoons the three would line up at boat exercise with lifebelts on like

P

any member of the ship's company. Fortunately, without event, we landed the party safely at Plymouth, and he left us not merely with happy recollections, but with a souvenir each for some of us: the final act of a memorable trip.

Within a few days we were off back with the new Governor-General, for the Duke of Devonshire, his lady and two eldest daughters, decided to entrust themselves to our care. If the previous fine weather was now to be absent, and a real hurricane blew all the way westward, this seemed all for the best: at any rate the risk from submarines would be considerably mitigated. So the *Calgarian* was able to bring this journey, also, to a good conclusion.

That made two very special occasions, yet a third had to be attempted. This was the carrying across of the Canadian and Newfoundland Premiers with their Ministers to an Imperial Conference in London. Having with us Sir Robert Borden, Lord Morris, and other illustrious statesmen, the *Calgarian* once more offered herself as a wonderful inducement for an enterprising U-boat to do her worst; yet risks are inseparable from war, and our best protection must be found in speed.

Of the latter we provided our utmost, and soon after clearing Halifax had worked up to 20 knots. So days succeeded each other and no torpedo struck us, but with a sense of relief we were able to deliver our passengers into England's safe keeping whilst the *Calgarian* received now a different set of orders. We were to escort a west-bound convoy through the submarine areas until in mid-Atlantic where possibility of danger would be remote. From that position the ships, after having been dispersed, might make their own way separately and individually to Halifax.

This arrangement was duly fulfilled, all went well until the *Calgarian* had only a few miles to steam when a wireless message sparked the most amazing news: Halifax had been visited by one of the worst disasters that ever afflicted a modern city. On 6 December 1917, within thirty seconds, the world's greatest munition explosion destroyed £4,000,000 worth of property, injured 8000 people, and mortally claimed 1500 other persons. Some reference was afterwards made in the English newspapers to this catastrophe, but so vast had been the occurrence, so depressing was its contemplation, that all the details did not become public until long after hostilities. Yet the cause of the disaster deserves to be borne in mind because of the terrible results which may recur from the simplest cause.

In those days Halifax gained a geographical importance never previously attained, for because of its unrivalled harbour (over a mile wide and six times that distance in length) this Nova Scotian Atlantic terminus became a sort of shipping clearing-house. Hither arrived the various steamers which gathered together before composing a convoy bound to Europe. Or, if you prefer a railway simile, here in this extensive goods-yard a long train of heavily-laden trucks was made up for its journey.

That accounted for the French S.S. *Mont Blanc*, entering Halifax on the momentous morning. Loaded with munitions for the battlefields in France, she was just arriving from the United States, whose factories were working hard to supply the armies' needs. Presently she would let go anchor among the other units, and be ready for the escorts. Now, to the north of Halifax lies Bedford Basin, entered by the Narrows formed by the city's shores, and Dartmouth, a suburb on the opposite side. In this Basin the number of east-bound vessels had begun to accumulate, but it happened that the Norwegian S.S. *Imo*, which had been chartered as a relief-ship for the Belgians, was also here. With the words BELGIAN RELIEF painted on either side of her hull, the *Imo* did not require escort. Carrying the charitable gifts of food and clothing to Antwerp for those made destitute by war, she expected that the Germans, whether in the Atlantic or North Sea, would give her safe passage.

About 8 a.m. imagine her, then, getting under way for the open sea. Meanwhile the *Mont Blanc*, which had been lying anchored all night at the harbour entrance waiting for daylight, was coming up to the Basin. We can picture her as having a grey hull with a deck cargo of benzol. In the holds were large quantities of wet and dry picric acid together with T.N.T. Thus, before quitting Sheepshead Bay, New York, the Frenchman had obtained about the maximum amount of dangerous material which space could contain.

Only one tiny item would suffice for an immense explosion.

Luckily this morning there happened to be no fog: it was one of those bright, sunny, frosty, winter days, and aboard either steamer was a pilot. But fate took charge of their direction, for when abreast the city's northern part and in about mid-harbour these two steamers collided, *Imo* running her bows into the *Mont Blanc* with such an impact that sparks were caused.

Easily it can be appreciated that the benzol began to leak along the deck, but whilst some eye-witnesses stated that the subsequent conflagration was brought about by the sparks, other opinions insist that the climax occurred when the benzol spirit reached the galley on deck further aft. The result followed within a few seconds, the time being nearly nine o'clock, and the *Mont Blanc* almost instantaneously developed into a raging furnace, whilst *Imo* drifted around the harbour out of control. Horror seized the Frenchmen as the fiery spirit took charge and they thought of the packed holds. Lowering a boat they crowded into it, rowing away quickly towards Dartmouth.

Then it stopped when they saw one of their shipmates had been left behind. Back the oarsmen pulled towards the floating hell, rescued him, hurriedly toiled at the oars, and managed to get clear. They had snatched an opportunity barely in time, for like an all-devouring demon the flames were making rapid consumption of masts, rigging, and were about to begin on the cargo below deck. Not any human power could overcome the devastating threat which awaited: neither those vicious tongues of flame nor the barely delayed explosions could be negatived now, and the Frenchmen saved themselves from certain death.

Meanwhile the drama was only beginning. If the *Mont Blanc* were no longer a danger to her crew, she offered peril to almost everybody else. Almost in the twinkling of an eye and quickly as thought can travel, she had become a blazing crucible at the mercy of wind and tide. People on shore crowded forth to gaze on this terrifying sight, as rare as it was spectacular. Business men came out of their offices alarmed, shipmasters feared for their vessels along the wharves wondering where the wayward *Mont Blanc* would collide again and bring death. That cruiser H.M.S. *Highflyer*, which we saw in an earlier chapter sink a German raider in a north-west African inlet, was lying near Halifax's naval dockyard, and the British commanding officer realized that something must be done without wasting even seconds. If the flaming Frenchman were to set alight to the dockyard with so many thousands of easily ignited articles, this would mean a tragedy for allied shipping. In Europe the shipyards could scarce contend with the overwork, and Halifax was more than a necessity in shouldering some of the repairs and refits. No: any interference with this Nova Scotian outpost in the middle of a big war would be more than a set-back.

So the Captain sent a couple of his boats to see what could be done. If the conflagration could not be extinguished, perhaps at least she might be brought to rest by letting go anchor, or hauled to one side. Already the munition-carrier was exuding such heat that despite the frosty atmosphere and the layer of snow on roofs and wharves, Halifax in one respect suggested an equatorial port.

You may guess how speedily everything happened, for by the time *Highflyer's* help got alongside the *Mont Blanc* it was only five minutes past nine. In about another minute the floating crucible collapsed, the arsenal inside this steel French hull burst with a convulsion so gigantic that superlatives cannot convey the full significance. The roar can be compared to that of a naval battle, but concentrated within moments; you may try thinking of the noise which a typhoon creates at its wickedest, but then multiply the sound many times, and the explosive effect was as if British, French, American, and German artillery had suddenly combined in endeavouring to wipe out the whole of Halifax.

Those brave men from the *Highflyer* vanished like dust before a rushing mighty wind; the Nova Scotian earth rocked as if shaken violently by earthquake ; the water which supported vessels at anchor and steamers peacefully tethered to quays, suddenly was transformed into an incredible tidal wave; wharves and streets were swept by lofty waves, gathering up men from their work into the boiling waters. Substantial buildings crumbled into rubble; citizens of all ages and both sexes were just killed as by a magic blight. Independent fires set up rival death-dealing efforts in different parts of Halifax, and from the universal distress it was as if some supernatural visitation had made this morning the beginning of doom.

And all because one moderate-sized ship had collided with another.

The *Mont Blanc* had been blasted into steel splinters which flew in showers over the city everywhere, the *Imo* had been cast ashore by the explosive force, everyone being killed including the pilot. Some of the facts and statistics seem so fantastic that the mere narration makes fiction commonplace and dull. Among the minor items were these: most vessels either wrecked in harbour or seriously damaged, the majority of crews killed, whilst within a radius of 2 miles every building was either razed to the ground or lacked such characteristics as roofs. Within 4 miles not a pane of glass survived, and even at 2½ miles the effects included demolition of a solid, concrete-built factory.

It was at this distance, too, that part of *Mont Blanc's* anchor travelled through the air, though that seems a mere nothing when we consider that 5 miles away from the explosion-scene other buildings were damaged. At 60 miles the shock was bad enough to ring church bells, and 160 miles off the inhabitants of Newfoundland experienced the concussion. Churches, dwellings, factories, shops, offices, foundries, railway station, schools, breweries, a sugar refinery, engineering plant, were all either wiped off the map or barely existed in ruins. The loss of a dry-dock, of a hospital, and much of the dock-yard meant a severe blow to naval efficiency in North America; yet there were oddly awful incidents such as that which happened to the city's fire-engine. It had been summoned at full speed when the burning *Mont Blanc* threatened to drift alongside the wharf, but the explosion just twisted it like a bit of cotton-waste and squeezed the life out of all the firemen except one. As if all this had not been enough for the few moments of a December day, Halifax was visited that night by one of the worst blizzards within the memory of man.

Next daylight dawned on a whited City of the Dead, thickly shrouded in snow, no fewer than 1500 of its 50,000 or 60,000 inhabitants having been snatched from life. Rescue parties endeavoured to drag wounded sufferers from burning houses and transfer them to temporary hospitals; but, because of the War, doctors and nurses were as inadequate as antiseptics and beds had become by reason of the disaster. Meanwhile into this harbour the *Calgarian* steamed, and immediately our crew were able to take part in rendering assistance, though the scenes of distress were beyond description. By this time the United States Red Cross organization was on its way with train-loads of doctors and nurses, yet so enormous were the numbers of surgical cases that for a while not all the latter could be dealt with. Temporary hospitals seemed to be fighting a losing game, the blizzard of that night, together with snowstorms during the next few days, increased the anxiety of homeless families and the painful quest of those who went searching for their dead. In fact not till four months later, and spring softened the ground, was the last body brought to its burial.

Yet survivors did wonders both to relieve suffering and to bring back new life into Halifax with its surroundings. Of course an official inquiry was duly held, and the suspicion that treachery had brought about disaster received no confirmation. It seemed surprising that, having regard to the fact of both pilots being old and respected Halifax citizens a collision in broad daylight should have been possible: yet both before and since that date ships have accidentally crashed into each other. Of these two expert seafarers one lived to narrate the colliding, and my own opinion agrees with the theory that the initial cause of trouble was the fracturing of steel-plates and sending out of sparks into the escaping spirit. After this chance ignition the rest followed inevitably, for it was confirmed at the inquiry that in the lower holds *Mont Blanc* carried between 4000 and 5000 tons of explosives. Mere chance selected a French vessel for victim, when quite as easily it might have been British. Equally possible the Norwegian might have been British also. So many of those steamers getting ready for the convoy were laden like the *Mont Blanc* that one may well wonder what *might* have happened.

If all the munition-cargoes had exploded, how much of Halifax would have remained more solid than dust, until snow turned it into mud?

CHAPTER XXIII

AFTER this sad visit to Halifax we took charge of
our convoy bound for England. Fortunately
the Atlantic trip developed no alarms or excitements, we were met nearer the land by destroyers who
took over, whilst a wireless message ordered *Calgarian*
to make for Portsmouth. At that busy base we spent the
next month refitting, and received a new skipper in
Captain Robert Newton, R.N. This officer, a comparatively young man, had been on the retired list some
time before the War and engaged in New Zealand sheep-
farming till summoned home by the European crisis.
'Bobby' Newton turned out to be 'one of the best,' a
really good shipmate and a most popular commanding
officer, whom every officer and rating would willingly
follow to the end. The *Calgarian* could never have been
more lucky in her leader, and this point is here specially
stressed because of what was fated to ensue.

A powerful drama not infrequently is prefaced by
light comedy, and so it began with us. Those four
weeks at Portsmouth, so restful and happy, so bright and
pleasant after boisterous seafaring in the Atlantic where
suspense and responsibility had been our daily portion,
certainly provided a notable contrast. *Calgarian's*
younger officers and midshipmen had made the best of
care-free days ashore; romance had cast its spell, and
'The Girl I Left Behind Me' was the theme which ran
through masculine minds as our ship steamed out past
Southsea bound for the same old ocean again, the same
old serious work of ensuring that fleets of merchantmen
might be able to bring in from North America the sinews

233

of war for our soldiers in France. Thus did we make a few more voyages.

But now, with that curious and predestined determination which sometimes controls human affairs, a totally new twist was to be given us in this armed merchant cruiser, but in order properly to appreciate the amazing juncture of cause and effect, let me begin by introducing U-19 whose career in the history of any war craft must always be regarded as unparalleled. It seems to prove that, despite all variations and obstacles at sea, a certain inevitability belongs to specific vessels. If some human beings find their path through life always along smoothness, direct and unhindered, there are those people to whom adventure comes continually even when least desired.

So it was throughout the history of this German submarine, whose career in the North and Irish Seas, the English Channel, the Baltic and Atlantic, is just one record of tightly packed adventure. Yet, at the beginning of War, U-19 was neither the biggest nor the newest underwater craft which our enemies possessed. We can visualize her as displacing some 650 tons when running on the surface, and 840 tons submerged. Completed in November 1913, she was fitted with a couple of torpedo tubes for-ard and another couple aft. These are quite important details, as the reader will presently appreciate, and whilst she possessed the endurance of 5200 miles for cruising on the surface at an average of 8 knots, she could increase to 15½ knots when circumstances justified uneconomical expense of fuel, her engines being Diesel.

It is to be noted that when travelling below the surface on her electric motors she could still do more than 9 knots, but whilst most of the German boats needed anything from 30 to 50 seconds for diving out of sight, the U-19 class required 75 seconds. Her crew of 4 officers and 35 men was up to the average number. Thus, in short, here we have a submarine technically of no outstanding capabilities, but of moderate attainments. At the best of

(*Top*) C.P.R. S.S. *METAGAMA*
Painted dazzle-fashion. Note paravane hanging from port side.
(*Bottom*) C.P.R. S.S. *EMPRESS OF RUSSIA*

H.M.S. *CALGARIAN*

(*Top*) The bridge whence a keen lookout for submarines was being kept.
(*Bottom*) About to leave St. John's, Newfoundland, during the War.

times submarines are tricky, uncertain creatures, which depend for their success or failure on personnel—particularly in regard to the commanding officer.

How did U-19 fare, then, after commencement of hostilities?

In August 1914 she and three others made a scouting expedition up the North Sea, but returned with no news. Her first adventure began a few weeks later when on the night of 24 October she was operating off the Dutch coast, but H.M.S. *Badger*—a destroyer—with sharp steel forefoot, rammed her. You can imagine the impact, the terrible shock to hull and men, the oncoming of a destroyer's high bows through the darkness, the deadly surprise. Any other U-boat would certainly have been cut through like butter by a knife, yet U-19 not only did not sink, but managed by her own power to reach Germany.

Here the dockyard people took her in hand, effected complete repairs, and before the end of January she was again prowling about the North Sea off the low-lying shores of Holland. On 21 January along came the British S.S. *Durward*, bound from Leith to Rotterdam, but U-19 was cruising about within 22 miles of the Maas Lightship, captured the *Durward*, placed bombs aboard, and so sent steamer to the bottom.

Pass over a few months and we come to the spring of 1915. On the night of 17–18 May the German cruiser *Hamburg* set forth on an expedition to lay a minefield off the Dogger Bank, but besides an escorting destroyer she was accompanied by a couple of submarines who were to torpedo any British ship that might interfere. U-19 with U-25 accordingly set out on what was to be a defensive rather than active project. That no opportunity for attack presented itself does not matter, but Germany was wont to let her submarine officers become specialists of particular areas, and U-19 was one of those boats already more than familiar with the North Sea as well as its merchantmen or its fishing vessels.

In June, then, this same pair of U-boats went forth up the North Sea with the intent to destroy every British fisherman they could find still carrying on bravely and the cruise ended with remarkable results: no fewer than twenty-seven trawlers were destroyed. Certainly U-19 was lucky, and not even change of skippers could alter her fortune. By the end of this summer her machinery had become worn out, but new engines now gave her a fresh lease of life, and though Lieut.-Commander Kolbe was succeeded by Lieut.-Commander Weisbach as her captain, she managed to go on sinking ship after ship till nearly 20,000 tons had vanished.

Then she made history on being transferred to Irish waters, which henceforth were to become her specialist area, additional to her North Sea region. For about 12 April 1916, in readiness for the Irish Rebellion due to begin at Easter, she was sent to carry Sir Roger Casement from Germany to Tralee Bay and she landed him in a collapsible boat during the early hours of Good Friday (21 April) on Tralee Beach. And whilst Casement was being arrested, U-19 was standing out to sea from the west coast, ultimately getting back home. Yes, once more had she been lucky, for the German steamer *Aud*, full of munitions for Ireland's rebels, had been caught by the patrols and subsequently sank herself whilst being conducted towards Queenstown.

The next job which awaited so adventurous an underwater war-craft was on the night of that still more historic 31 May. That evening had been fought the Battle of Jutland, when U-19 was lying up the Ems. Sudden orders came for her to shove off northward, and later she endeavoured to steer for the Scottish coast towards Scapa Flow with the object of torpedoing Grand Fleet units making for port after the battle. Just for once she did not enjoy success, since bad weather on 2 June caused her to turn back; but now comes one of those unexplainable features which no amount of logic can clear up.

Her skipper for many successful trips was Lieut.-

Commander Spiess, an officer of considerable experience, unusual technical skill and (as we shall perceive presently) quite consummate enterprise. Then he was promoted to U-52, a more modern, bigger boat, having on the surface another 1½ knots superior speed. Yet by some extraordinary perversity she appeared to be dogged by ill luck. Once U-52 nearly had a sticky end through her crew's error, and had to be salvaged with the utmost difficulty, her personnel being rescued only after the bows had been raised high enough for the inmates to get out.

Not surprisingly did Spiess go back to his old command, U-19, which during 1917 encountered a situation that happened during hostilities both to British and enemy submarines. It was known to Germany that British submarines were wont to lie in wait off the Norwegian island Üdsire and one day Spiess believed the opportunity was his for torpedoing such a craft. Evidently one of Britain's biggest types. So he stalked her, made ready, took a final glance through his periscope, but then hesitated. Several familiar characteristics about the stranger created in his mind a doubt. He, therefore, rose to the surface, made the challenging signal, which was promptly answered. She turned out to be not British, but the large U-155.

Spiess and U-19 had barely been prevented from destroying one of Germany's crack units. In the following August he waylaid one of the steamers belonging to my own Company. This was the C.P.R. *Miniota*, 6422 tons, 30 miles south-east of the Start, though it was not to be the last of our line against which he would direct his missiles. He and his boat by February of the following year had developed into rare experts in regard to the seas that wash Ireland, no fewer than 36,000 tons of shipping being sunk therein.

And now we come to the climax of this story, which but for the previous introduction would have been obscure. I mentioned on a previous page that narrow

bottle-neck known as the North Channel, separating
Ireland from Scotland, with Rathlin Island subdividing
the space further. Let it be stressed that during the
early part of 1918 the German U-boats were making
the most determined attack on convoys passing through
here, for the restricted sea-gland offered opportunities
nowhere else possible. Even the Straits of Dover—
apart from minefields and other artificial obstructions—
could not compare with the temptation which the North
Channel held out. Whilst British destroyers maintained
a ceaseless vigil, they could not be everywhere, though
the invisible U-boats had the advantage of keeping a
wary eye on all shipping movements.

It was on 5 February 1918 that UB-77 reached the
above channel and despite the attentions of destroyers
took up her ambush seven miles north of Rathlin Island
lighthouse, where also U-97 was waiting about. At
4.30 p.m. the two stopped and exchanged conversation,
but, half an hour later, UB-77 sighted an east-bound
convoy approaching at 12 knots, powerfully guarded by
destroyers. Lieut.-Commander Meyer, in charge of
UB-77, realized that unless he acted very promptly,
daylight would rob him of opportunity. He manœuvred
with no little skill and elapse of time: indeed that
immense cavalcade with the lively destroyers provided
many difficulties.

Eventually at 7.40 p.m. he did manage to single out
the largest of the targets, which was the two-funnelled,
14,348 tons, Anchor liner *Tuscania*. It meant trying a
long shot, but despite the range of 1300 yards his torpedo
hit *Tuscania* just abaft the second funnel. Low in the
water dropped the liner's stern, and down she disappeared
with the loss of forty-four lives.

One week later U-89, rather farther to the westward,
though on a course that would intercept vessels bound
for the North Channel, was hanging about and again
night had fallen. Another convoy approached, escorted
by H.M.S. *Roxburgh* (an armoured cruiser) at 8 knots.

The time was 11.20 p.m., the weather had been foggy, but ten minutes earlier it had suddenly cleared. Even now the darkness hung like a velvet pall.

All of a sudden Lieut.-Commander A. R. Smithwick, R.N., officer of the watch on the *Roxburgh's* bridge, sighted U-89 lying on the surface 150 yards off. Without wasting a tick of time, he starboarded, then steadied his ship straight for the enemy. There was a terrible crash as the weight of 10,850 tons crashed into 1000 tons like a train into a motor car. The noise resounded over the leaden waters, and the cruiser's speed became checked as if she had lost all way. Up rose German shouts, something flashed and exploded, then one part of the submarine floated along the port side before sinking, whilst two pieces of metal were afterwards found on *Roxburgh's* stem.

That incident, then, occurred on 12 February. But note the persistency with which the enemy still concentrated on the North Channel. They now sent that 'star-turn,' Lieut.-Commander Spiess, to see what he could do with his successful U-19, and the following is what happened.

On 1 March the *Calgarian*, escorting thirty ships, was steering in from the Atlantic towards the North Channel doing about 8 to 10 knots. We had been met by the destroyers, and now it seemed likely that a valuable armed merchant cruiser of 17,515 tons steaming at that slow pace through such a confined passage would be inviting trouble. We accordingly requested permission to proceed independently, and this was granted. Whacking up the *Calgarian* to 20 knots, we were approaching Rathlin Island, the weather being fine and clear. I was walking up and down the highest lookout-bridge, whilst the ship kept up a most confusing zigzag and a couple of destroyers protected us.

What with these circumstances plus our 20 knots, all danger—to me at least—seemed beyond possibility: we had nothing to fear from any U-boat. In fact I recollect remarking to the watch-keeping lieutenant alongside me that I should be quite pleased to shake hands with any German submarine officer who could 'plant' us under the prevailing conditions.

Scarcely had I uttered these words than the first explosion took place, a torpedo striking *Calgarian* between her two funnels, and within a moment we pair of officers became black as sweeps. The for'ard stokehold had been struck, and 29 men on watch killed. The ship heeled about forty degrees to port with the inrush of water, but the after stokehold was not affected inasmuch as the watertight doors were closed; so, given a slice of luck, we hoped to struggle on when the things had been put in order.

Volunteers were called for to go below, and it was not long before these were toiling magnificently to assist the engineers. Meanwhile 7 destroyers, 11 trawlers, and 3 sloops (a small type of cruiser built during the War) rushed forward to surround us, one destroyer steaming round us and making a smoke screen as additional protection. Nevertheless, U-19 was resolved on a desperate gamble. Spiess' first torpedo had been sent from a close range—about 550 yards—and now that he perceived *Calgarian* still afloat he dived below the screen of all these 21 vessels to fire two more torpedoes.

No liner ever built could endure so much. Steelwork and boats were blown to atoms when I arrived on deck after going below to close watertight doors with the help of some ratings. I looked round. Hardly a dozen men could be seen, for some had been blown overboard by explosions, whilst others had dived into the cold sea and were swimming about in all directions. I well remember about this time noticing a trawler come round *Calgarian's* stern. On the former's deck were dozens of our men who had been saved, and here came my chance of rescue at a critical moment. Sliding down a boat's fall, I was enabled to get by this rope to the trawler instead of being drowned.

The sight of men maimed and bleeding, though salved, did not lighten one's feelings. Nor was this trawler long permitted to survive, for the enemy got her too, though we were meanwhile taken off by another patrol vessel. Soon the unfortunate *Calgarian*, which to so many of us had been our home ever since the beginning of War, sank below the waters and another chapter in seafaring life came to its close. A fortnight later—on 15 March—not very far from where U-89 had been lying in wait, the Royal Mail Line S.S. *Amazon* (10,037 tons) was torpedoed and sunk by U-110, one of Germany's most powerful craft.

This steamer happened to be outward-bound, and before foundering was able to bleat 'S O S' on her wireless. The signal having been picked up by H.M.S. *Moresby* and *Michael* (both of them destroyers), *Moresby* went to rescue survivors and dropped four explosive depth-charges, whilst *Michael* continued the hunt. The enemy, frightened by the sight of these two very mobile vessels, dived to 130 feet and remained hiding below surface for a whole hour; but the depth-charges had shaken her so violently that the diving-gear was seriously damaged and U-110 could not be controlled. Like a fractious steed she leapt first to 300 feet down, and this depth caused so violent a pressure that her hull began leaking seriously. She then made a steep ascent to the surface, and (the hour being shortly after 11 a.m.) the vigilant *Michael* spotted her 5 miles away. Revenge now had its chance, for by this time the *Moresby* had returned and the submarine came under a merciless accurate fire from destroyers' guns which killed the German officer in the conning-tower. This was certainly the day when Germany got back something due for what she had done to others.

Commander Kroll, in charge of U-110, assembled his men on deck with life-saving waistcoats on and the crew began leaping into the sea, but a shell from *Michael* struck the submarine and caused a tremendous explosion.

Both destroyers were racing about at high speed under the impression that a second enemy was about, and during these evolutions U-110 was run over. Down went the latter for all time with Kroll and most of the men. Ten survivors were rescued, but the remaining thirty-three had gone. So U-110 had been less fortunate than when U-19 was rammed by H.M.S. *Badger*.

Spiess continued his amazing career, eluded all escorts and patrols, got back to Germany, refitted U-19 and actually returned to the North Channel area. He tempted fate severely and narrowly escaped being 'done in' this time, but mark the coolness of this intrepid fellow. During the War all sorts of silly stories were set going that submarine personnel from Germany occasionally landed on certain parts of the British Isles, though not one of these yarns has any truth—except that concerning U-19. She ran short of food whilst passing up the west coast of Scotland after her narrow escape, so that on arriving at St. Kilda, the solitary rock 40 miles west of the Outer Hebrides, Spiess sent some of his people ashore who shot a few sheep.

But to clew up the *Calgarian* story, many of us were landed at Larne and others at Londonderry. We had lost 49 of our comrades who for thousands of miles, through every kind of weather and anxiety, all over the Atlantic, had shared monotony and excitement alike. When, shortly, all survivors could be assembled, we held a memorial service at a little church on the sea-front, and that same night we who had been preserved crossed to England to report for the next duty.

I got into the train bound for Portsmouth, and a curious thing occurred during the journey. At some station *en route* I had to change, so I whiled the time away pacing up and down the platform. Another man kept staring rather closely as if weighing me up and I couldn't understand the reason. In came the train and I got into a compartment, but the inquisitive fellow entered too. Before long we were discussing the War.

Then he said:

"May I ask your name?"

"Kendall," I told him.

"Surely, you're not the Captain Kendall who caught Dr. Crippen?"

"Yes: I am."

"Well! That's damn funny!"

"Is it? Why?"

"I'm the man who executed him. That is to say, I was the Governor of Pentonville Prison."

CHAPTER XXIV

HAVING obtained a new rig-out, I was appointed to Whale Island at Portsmouth to do a course of Gunnery and Torpedo, but with so many vivid recollections of years afloat this interlude seemed intolerably dull. The only relief at all pleasant was on occasions when they sent me across to France with dispatches.

But one day in June of this same 1918 I was ordered to report at the Admiralty, and there the good news greeted me that I was appointed Commodore of Convoys. At this date the United States of America were helping the Allies with all their material and men. Troops were coming over the Atlantic in thousands and thousands, some transports being so crowded that soldiers were compelled to take their turn at sleeping. One man would occupy the bunk for, say, eight hours; then for the next eight hours another man would have it; and yet a third man would take his turn for the final period of the day.

But these keen warriors cared nothing for discomfort so long as they could reach the seat of war. Backed by America's wealth, encouraged by the American people's enthusiasm, these myriads of fine upstanding lads created a great impression on sailors now in their fourth year of hostilities. Some Commodores were British naval officers who had been retired years ago as Admirals, but a large portion were either retired or active senior officers from the Royal Naval Reserve, accustomed during long experience to the handling of steamships and conversant with the particular 'trade'—whether Atlantic, Mediterranean, West African, and so on.

To employ such accumulated practical knowledge was one of the wisest decisions ever made by the Admiralty.

Picked Master Mariners who had spent several decades backwards and forwards along a particular sea-track, could not fail to do good work or to shoulder such heavy responsibility. The fullest freedom and power were given to each Commodore, and the pay was excellent.

My first convoy as Commodore started from Plymouth and we were bound to the northern as well as southern ports of the United States. I had thirty ships to bring out of the Sound, being escorted by destroyers till well clear of what was reckoned the danger zone, when we all carried on for a couple of days well into the Atlantic. The time for dispersal to individual destinations would begin perhaps at 8 p.m., so that steamers having been given their respective courses to steer would, at the end of twenty-four hours, be out of sight from each other before making towards their separate ports.

The Commodore's ship varied from voyage to voyage. She was actually one of the convoy's merchantmen, but in practice usually the best and fastest of the group would naturally be selected. So now, in charge of what was officially designated the 'New York Convoy,' I began a new phase in my career and the routine was based on common-sense principles. At New York the Senior British Naval Officer, Captain Sir Lionel Wells, R.N., looked after arrangements. Having seen that all my vessels were safely moored, I landed with my staff and reported to him. Then followed a few days' rest and another convoy bound east from Newport News for the United Kingdom became entrusted to me.

This meant first taking a twenty-four hours' train journey southwards after being given that unbounded kindness and consideration for which American hospitality is famous. It would be impossible to detail all the exhibitions of goodwill and warmth of heart, the generosity and benignity. We were made honorary members in many of the leading clubs, invited to private homes—in fact time alone prevented us from availing ourselves of all the courtesies proffered, and these will always remain among my outstanding memories of the Great War.

At Newport News arrangements were made for Masters of every ship in the convoy to meet and discuss proceedings in a kind of heart-to-heart talk. Thereby I got to know them, they became acquainted with me as their Commodore, and learned to understand what would be expected of them. It was just a simple, sincere conference of mariners with no nonsense and the one aim of providing that every vessel should reach home with her valuable cargo safely.

On this first visit to Newport News I did, however, discover that the ship allotted to me was not quite convenient as senior. Her name? Oh, that was the best thing about her! No end of a swell, she sounded! Actually she was small and in my opinion would at sea be more like a half-tide rock. It did turn out, as suspected, that she had been chosen for Commodore because of her name and not of her suitability. However, that rectification caused no delay and eventually I installed myself aboard the largest and speediest unit. With a fleet of 40 different steamships I now proceeded out of the Chesapeake into the Atlantic. Such a number of vessels sailing in company for mutual protection may well cause the modern generation of seafarers to blink in wonder. Bad enough to be officer of the watch in a single ship coming along anxiously through black night and murky weather? But forty! And there would be complicated hours of zigzagging, too! As a sight from the sky all this amount of massed, moving shipping was something to surprise even the sea-gulls!

And before we leave this locality let me tell you what was related by one of my Captains in the convoy. You will remember in an earlier chapter how the raider *Kronprinz Wilhelm* crept into the Chesapeake? Well, neither American nor British sailormen wished her safe entry, and just then a British tramp steamer was in the Bay taking an American pilot aboard whilst not many

'ONCE A SAILOR ALWAYS A SAILOR'

Captain H. G. Kendall with the model he made of the sailing-ship *Lake Superior*. This fine old vessel belonged to the Beaver Line when passengers to Canada were still being carried across under canvas.

(*Top*) C.P.R. LINER PASSING UNDER QUEBEC BRIDGE
(*Bottom*) MONTREAL DEEP-WATER BERTHS

yards off the German raider had stopped engines for a similar purpose.

"Now's your chance," the first pilot advised the tramp skipper. "There's the German with no way on her. Put your helm hard over, ram her, sink her. And I'll say that your steering-gear had got out of order."

It was one of those opportunities which rarely happen in a long lifetime, and would have been a dramatic finale to the *Kronprinz's* marauding cruise. If the collision were not strictly legal, at least it could be said that an unwelcome visitor to Newport News had been kept out. And there are plenty of Master Mariners of the 'Captain Kettle' breed who would never have hesitated to do as the American suggested.

But the tramp skipper preferred to think rather of his own ship's welfare, and the profitable freights which the owners were gathering. Perfectly understandable! Yet what a grand occasion was missed of gaining fame in a great adventure.

To resume—we got clear of the American continent, and I now snatched a few minutes for the purpose of becoming more closely familiar with my ship. There was a four-foot deckload well covered over with deals, and I wanted to know what lay inside, so I questioned the Captain.

"Drums full of explosives!" he answered. "And pretty fierce at that. One drum would be enough to blow this ship into the next world."

On learning that we were carrying 400 tons of this commodity alone, I thought back on the *Mont Blanc* episode and wondered why at Newport News I had transferred from the 'half-tide rock.'

So I mentioned my apprehensions to the Captain with whom I talked. Said he:

"I don't see that we've any need to worry. It's loaded above the water-line, and if the damn stuff goes up, then the whole blessed convoy will go up too. Not a living soul within ten-miles radius will remain to tell the tale."

These munitions were badly needed at the Front, the freight was good, and he reckoned that in studying the interests of owners as well as troops, he had no cause for any further anxiety!

So with that sole consolation we headed on our course, and if a U-boat waylaid us in the manner that *Calgarian* was ambushed, this perfect floating arsenal would make a glorious bang.

But neither the dangers on deck, nor the unseen torpedoes below the sea completed the list of my uneasiness this voyage. That dread scourge of influenza had become rampant, men were going down like ninepins, and it was no uncommon occurrence when daylight broke for signals to be flying from many of the 40 vessels asking permission to stop a few minutes during the forenoon, so that some unfortunate who had passed away in the night might be committed to the deep.

Not a doctor was numbered in the whole fleet, since every steamer happened to be a tramp; so each Captain had to do his best with *The Shipmaster's Medical Guide* as his only aid. A rough-and-ready treatment on the high seas, when the disease was puzzling and defeating skilled medical men ashore? Well, we could but try and fail. In my own vessel I remember one fellow, standing his trick at the wheel and seemingly in the best of health. All of a sudden this quartermaster collapsed, so we took his temperature and found it very high. What to be done?

The steward suggested giving him a 'Dover Powder' to make the man sweat.

"No," I insisted. "We won't have any half-measures. Give him *two* powders, and if the flag has to be lowered there shall be a good reason."

Believe it or not, within a couple of hours we had three men down with the same trouble, and all of them partly delirious. To each we gave a couple of powders, the patients being wrapped up in blankets and placed in their bunks. At the centre of the cabin was placed another blanket previously dipped in carbolic, then the door was closed tight. Now, I reasoned, if any germ, parasite, or microbe from Germany, Paris, or Ireland can live in that condition, it would be remarkable. Every couple of hours we tepid-sponged our invalids, wrapped them up again within warm blankets, and less than forty-eight hours elapsed before they were on deck again. The cure had been drastic, the men had been fairly 'put through it,' but we now felt capable of curing the most obstinate of cases in future.

It called back to mind the technique of a ship's doctor years previously. After quitting port, when many of the sailors and firemen were still suffering the effects of having drowned their sorrows in good ale and indifferent whisky ashore, the crowd would amble along to this doctor complaining of the usual big head. Well did the expert understand cause and cure, so he never so much as attempted to diagnose. In his dispensary stood a large filter, on which was pasted 'B.F. Mixture,' and as each miserable complainant came in the tap was turned on. A glassful having been drunk, no other treatment had to be administered: the medicine sufficed.

One day I asked him what the lettering signified.

"'B——y Firemen's Mixture.' That's what it is. Black draught and Epsom Salts. Never fails to do the trick!"

Our voyage from the Chesapeake continued wearily, for the speed of the slowest ship was only 6 knots, which, of course, set the pace for the whole fleet and almost invited the attentions of submarines. This gave me reason for considerable meditation and planning against being waylaid. Quite rightly, wireless was strictly forbidden except in case of emergency: otherwise the enemy would not be long in locating our advent. I recollect one night listening to a ship 200 miles west of Ireland continually sending messages *en clair* to Queenstown something like this:

'I have 10,000 tons of sugar Stop please send destroyers to escort me.'

But the despatch of such protection became superfluous for the vessel played on her wireless so blatantly that a final message was not long delayed.

'Have been torpedoed.'

She never bleated again.

Many of our mercantile losses at the beginning of war were due through having made too light of enemy submarines, sailing trustfully along a steady course and not zigzagging. All very well to endeavour reaching port without wasting mileage, yet the Germans were only too thankful to know where they could definitely locate victims. But the restriction in regard to wireless must be reckoned as of prime importance, and this was the principle which Admiral Sturdee employed during that memorable secret voyage with his two battle-cruisers on the way from Devonport to South America. Everybody to-day knows how this silence effected the surprise which caused von Spee to stumble into defeat at the Battle of the Falklands, and when Sturdee on his return voyage called at Gibraltar the British Admiral was still harping on muteness. As previously mentioned, he came aboard *Calgarian*, and in conversation with Captain Kemp emphasized that wireless communication had been absolutely forbidden. It was this lesson, indelibly impressed on my mind, which made me when Commodore of Convoys insist on similar taciturnity. To that I largely attribute the fact that I never lost a ship under my care during the whole War.

So, despite its slowness, our initial trip from Newport News ended without disaster. It was long—extraordinarily long—but at the conclusion of twenty days all 40 vessels steamed safely into port. Another load off tired shoulders!

Only a very brief spell on land, then off we went again, but this time taking a big convoy of fast ships—16-knotters—bound from Liverpool to New York. The change in speed meant a general improvement all round: fewer risks, shorter time on the way, less troubles likely to develop except in thick weather. The slow convoy, which sailed the day previously, had been placed in charge of a Commander R.N. who was making his first trip as Commodore. Poor chap! He had the most unkind luck, for off the south-east Irish coast he ran into a submarine nest and lost several of his ships. On the following day we saw plenty of evidence as we steamed through considerable floating wreckage.

After arrival in New York I went a two-days' railway journey to Sydney, Cape Breton, and from that Nova Scotian deep bay fetched home another 40 steamers. Then it was England to New York with one more fast convoy and again up to Canada where I took care of more than 30 troop transports at Quebec. These, likewise, were fast ships, and it was a new experience to come through an old familiar area in charge of not one but many liners, bringing not hundreds of passengers, but over 50,000 troops who might never see France. Time in its stride plays strange pranks, and as we came down the St. Lawrence past Father Point the associations of a notorious murderer mingled curiously with present no less than future events. How was it all going to end.

The same old fog and ice awaited us, but twenty years' experience of those northern waters could not be dismissed as without value. Our escort was a cruiser under the command of Captain England, R.N., new to this part of the world. "I do like your optimism," he signalled me once as we groped our progress through thickness and dodging the icebergs hopefully. A seaman of the old school, he showed us so much thoughtfulness and consideration throughout the voyage that we almost began to feel as if convoy work was not such a hard life after all.

Now this homeward journey proved itself different from all its predecessors. An uncanny stillness filled the atmosphere that was never disturbed by one single sad 'S O S' message. Something had happened, or must be about to happen. The Atlantic Ocean in a curious manner had altered, and as we brought our transport fleet up the English Channel along a path brilliantly lit for us—or for submarines—the air was still silent. No warnings of U-boats! No hint of vessels being sunk! No new mine-fields!

Dover came and went, but when once in the Downs, and the convoy had been brought inside the defences, a trawler was sent to fetch me and my staff, though before landing us on Deal Pier, the trawler's skipper cleared up the mystery.

"They're just on the point of signing Armistice," he remarked.

Nor was the old fisherman far wrong.

I proceeded up to London, reported at the Admiralty, received orders with regard to another convoy. . . . But it never matured. Those days were over, the enemy had been beaten, the submarines had gone home.

No more zigzagging. No more steaming without lights. No more sailing in massed formation. A fresh freedom of the seas had begun, yet at first it was difficult to readjust oneself to this sudden transformation.

Before closing this chapter I must add the following story here, because it is, so to say, the final word on the sinking of *Calgarian*. Some time after the War I happened to be on a visit to Germany and was dining with a party of men who during hostilities had occupied impor-tant positions of authority. Among them was one who had been responsible for building 25 per cent of the U-boats, so I related my account of how the *Calgarian* met her doom. I stressed the fact that notwithstanding our 20 knots speed, our zigzagging, and the protection of a destroyer on either bow the first attack had been a success. Then I referred to the subsequent smoke screen and the flotilla of craft which came along to lend their protection.

"Yet despite all this," I added, "the U-boat got through and finished the job. A damn smart bit of work! And if that submarine commander is alive to-day I should like to shake hands with him."

The effect of these words spoken in all sincerity was remarkable.

Every one of those Germans rose to his feet by the table, bowed, and then followed a significant acknowledgment.

"Thank you, sir. Only an Englishman would have made such a generous statement, and we greatly appreciate it."

At the time I did not know—nor indeed till years afterwards—that U-19 had been my enemy. Spiess survived the War and the revolution which ensued, but I have not yet run across him. I should be interested to know what he felt like among all those steel-stems and revolving propellers.

Even the most intrepid submarine captain must have experienced an unpleasant nervousness amid this hunting throng.

CHAPTER XXV

WITHIN a few days of Armistice I was able to be released by the Admiralty and go back to the Canadian Pacific Line, becoming Marine Superintendent for the Company at Southampton until 1924. If this was a not unwelcome change after having brought 196 ships across the Atlantic during my period as Commodore of Convoys, let no one imagine that a Marine Superintendent is a man without heavy responsibilities. On the contrary, the same necessity for organizing, the same tact in handling personnel, the same vigilance over valuable ships still must be essential.

It was shortly after the War that I had to go down to Avonmouth and visit one of our vessels. The weather outside had been fairly bad and she was delayed, so I sat in the hotel trusting she might dock that night. Seated in an easy chair was an old man, typical specimen of the W. W. Jacobs characters, a regular ancient sea-dog with his tumbler of grog standing alongside him by the mantelpiece.

We drifted into conversation, though I had no idea of his identity, until the bell went for dinner, and I inquired of the waitress who this old fellow might be.

"Well," she replied, "at one time he was a sea Captain. But now he has a very soft job. He's a Marine Superintendent."

That shows how some of us can be misunderstood!

Looking back on those War years, it is a pleasure to remember the good comradeship which was generated between the Royal Navy and the Royal Naval Reserve. In the latter I served for about thirty-five years inclusive of the period 1914–1918. From Commanders-in-Chief down to the lowest rank I found they always gave one a square deal. If, as so many R.N. officers aver, the latter learned many things from us who had been brought up in the Merchant Navy, assuredly we learned a very great deal from the Royal Navy. I only wish that it was compulsory for both branches of the sea-service, men no less than officers, to spend annually a fixed period together. A certain amount of training in H.M. ships, every year, of Merchant seamen would make for better discipline, more efficient running of trading vessels, and provide a valuable personnel ready for national emergency.

Of course there will always be growlers and those who impute wrong motives through inherent, ineradicable suspicion, and there is on record that story of a certain Captain who one Sunday in port provided his sailors with turkey instead of beef.

"Mmph!" criticized a very incredulous fellow sticking his knife into the white meat. "Well, boys, I suppose that if this stuff wasn't cheaper'n beef it never would've come our way."

Far too long have I been connected with maritime matters to pretend that the seamy side does not exist; yet equally I can perceive that grumbling fails to get a man where he would like to be. The sorrows of a skipper were never really mine. I have enjoyed these years of seafaring with all the adventures in so many ships, meeting people of such vastly differing characteristics. It has been so full of interest, and so very much worth while doing your job to the best of your ability without worrying too much about the things which may never happen.

From 1924 until my sixty-fifth birthday in January 1939 I was Marine Superintendent of the Canadian Pacific ships in London, and now, if at last I have quitted seafaring to inhabit a 'stone frigate,' the call of ships and ocean can yet be heard. For no mariner, however long he lives, remains deaf to that powerful summons. Kipling understood this, and how to interpret it. Once, when I was Chief Officer in the *Empress of Ireland*, he and Mrs. Kipling were travelling across with us, and he graciously wrote a stanza of a poem in my album, whilst the ship hurried over the mid-Atlantic. Both author and his wife signed it, and I value these lines as among my most treasured possessions:

'Who hath desired the Sea?   Her menaces swift as her mercies,
The in-rolling walls of the fog and the silver-winged breeze that disperses,
The unstable mined berg going south, and the calvings and groans that
    declare it—
White water half-guessed overside and the moon breaking timely to
    bare it;
His sea as his fathers have dared—his sea as his children shall dare it—
  His seas as she serves him or kills!
So and no otherwise—so and no otherwise—
  Hillmen desire their Hills.'

CARRIE KIPLING.   July 1907.   RUDYARD KIPLING.

HURST & BLACKETT
GENERAL BOOKS

MEMOIRS OF MADAME PILSUDSKI. To many people Alexandra Pilsudski's career has been as rich and colourful, as romantic and adventurous, as that of her famous husband, Marshal Pilsudski, soldier and statesman. Side by side they worked in the same cause. She writes of their first meeting, of the love that was born of perfect comradeship; of the day when Joseph Pilsudski led his small force over the Russian frontier . . . "the poorest and shabbiest army in Europe". . . . Yet it put to flight the Czar's picked troops. When she left Poland last September with the noise of Stalin's guns thundering in the distance, her husband's famous maxim came into her mind : "to be defeated and not surrender, that is victory indeed". The story of one of the greatest romances of this age.
Demy 8vo. Illustrated. September Publication. 10s. 6d. net.

THIS FOR REMEMBRANCE. JULIA NEILSON. Few actresses of our time have had a more wonderful and faithful public than Julia Neilson. When Ellen Terry died they put Julia Neilson on her throne. Now she tells the story of her interesting life. Julia Neilson is a player who has moved millions because she understands to a nicety the psychology and technique of the theatre. For these and many other reasons her life story cannot help being a valuable document, and in it all those who love the theatre will find memories of absorbing interest. All through her career Julia Neilson has come in contact with the leading personalities of the English stage. *Demy 8vo. Fully Illustrated. September Publication.* 15s. net.

BUNCH : A Biography of Nelson Keys by his son JOHN PADDY CARSTAIRS, author of "Vinegar and Brown Paper", etc. Foreword by A. P. Herbert. With the passing of Nelson Keys the London Stage lost the greatest revue artist and mimic she ever possessed. Beloved by countless theatregoers, "Bunch", as he was affectionately known to his friends and fans, was, in his own inimitable work, one of the few real geniuses of the Stage : the late Sir James Barrie once said of him : "Here comes the whole Dramatic Profession in a nutshell". Behind the fascinating success story of this diminutive dapper star can now be told the incredible story of the little London Cockney who became the darling of London society.
Demy 8vo. Illustrated. October Publication. 15s. net.

GRANDMOTHER O KYO. ETSU INAGAKI SUGIMOTO, author of "Daughter of the Samurai", etc. It is a publishing honour to offer another of the distinguished books by one of Japan's greatest writers. Madame Sugimoto, with the short record of three books, the first of which, "A Daughter of the Samurai", has sold over 80,000 copies, is endeared to a much wider public than most writers attain with twenty. Writing quietly of the Japan that was and the Japan that is evolving, Madame Sugimoto gives an entirely foreign picture to the familiar one of newspaper headlines. Here is a picture of a great people living their lives apart from the savage rule of a minority at the top—an unforgettably sincere story of unwilling aggressors. The story of a Samurai grandmother who is approaching the celebration of her 88th birthday is an essentially simple one, depending for its impact on the beautiful style and endless subtle incidents. *Demy 8vo. September Publication.* 10s. 6d. net.

THE EPIC OF DUNKIRK. E. KEBLE CHATTERTON. The world needs little reminding that, in the amazing withdrawal from Dunkirk of the British Expeditionary Force, one of the greatest maritime feats throughout all naval history was performed. The incredible occurred, a miracle happened. Here is the full account of how that achievement was brought about, despite the enemy's myriads on land and his superiority in the sky, a narrative that will live through the ages as one tremendous act of bravery extending over ten terrible days. Mr. Keble Chatterton, who received official assistance in the preparation of this volume, and obtained first-hand information from participants themselves as well as a unique set of illustrations, has never had a more enthralling subject for historical writing. "The Epic of Dunkirk" is not merely a thrilling human story but a book of permanent and outstanding interest. *Demy 8vo. October Publication.* 7s. 6d. net.

ALL PRICES IN THIS CATALOGUE ARE PROVISIONAL AND SUBJECT TO ALTERATION

GREAT BRITAIN : An Empire in Transition. ALBERT VITON.
In this book an authoritative writer, well known as a severe critic of Britain's acts on many occasions, offers a unique and exciting study of the Empire—its structure, its strengths and weaknesses, the menaces from without, the forces of disintegration from within, the challenge of the current war, the problems that must be faced if Britain after winning the war is not to "lose the peace". With a comprehensiveness rarely before attempted, Mr. Viton surveys the nature and the problems of the entire British Empire. He shows how much more is at stake for Britain in the present war than merely the European conflict, and looks with great insight at the Empire's future. *Demy 8vo. October Publication. About 10s. 6d. net.*

FIGHTING THE U-BOATS. E. KEBLE CHATTERTON.
For many years Mr. Keble Chatterton has been at work on this important naval history, which must remain for all time a standard work. Full, complete and detailed, *Fighting the U-boats* is rich in colour, authoritative and a most thrilling account, essential to every sea-lover's library, but appealing alike to any man, woman and child who revels in dramatic true yarns more wonderful than fiction. The characters of U-boat commanders, the "tricks of the U-boat trade", are contrasted with the personalities and devices of British seamen ; British destroyers, cruisers, battleships, trawlers, drifters, Q-ships, armed yachts, motor craft—even sailing-ships and submarines—are shown actually contending with and vanquishing the German U-boats. *Spring Publication. Large Demy Fully Illustrated. 18s. net.*

THE NAUTICAL WEEK-END BOOK. JAMES HANLEY,
author of "Drift", "Boy", "Hollow Sea", etc. An exquisite collection of sea miscellanea covering every conceivable phase of life in, on, and even remotely connected with, the sea. It is essentially a hotch-potch and not a book of studied orderliness. Mr. Hanley has deliberately made it as unorthodox as possible simply because a mere handbook would give no idea of the glorious contrasts and surprises which are part and parcel of true seafaring literature. Here is what the author says : "This excursion off the beaten track has yielded many discoveries, and they are set out in this book for the reader's entertainment and information." *October Publication. Demy 8vo. Illustrated. About 10s. 6d. net.*

I KNEW THOSE SPIES. FELIX GROSS. Amazing Revelations of Secret Services in Wartime—German, French, Russian, English. No story is so topical today as the spy story, for thousands of aliens are still in our midst and of these a fairly large proportion must be considered as secret agents in the pay of Germany. Such at least is the opinion of Felix Gross, and it is based on first-hand knowledge, for in the course of his career he has come in contact with most of the master spies of the last twenty-five years and had excellent opportunities of observing their technique. Consequently his assembly of facts makes more enthralling reading than any fiction. *Demy 8vo. 12s. 6d. net.*

HITLER IS NO FOOL. KARL BILLINGER. The Menace of the Man and His Programme. Tearing away the veils of inarticulate mysticism which fog the pages of "Mein Kampf", the author of this book lays bare the grim purposes of the well-known Austrian paperhanger. This book does not purport to be another translation of "Mein Kampf". It is, however, an entirely accurate and faithful description of Hitler's world programme. We learn how Hitler came to power, why anti-Semitism is an inevitable part of Fascism, and why the real facts of Hitler's life are not told in his book. *Crown 8vo. Paper bound, 1s. 6d. net. Cloth bound, 2s. 6d. net.*

TRAWLERMAN'S "TOWN". JEROME WILLIS, well-known *Evening Standard* Reporter. Here is one of the grandest books ever written on the lives of those fearless seamen, the Trawlermen—men Earl Beatty was proud to salute. *Crown 8vo. Illustrated. 2s. 6d. net.*

ALL PRICES IN THIS CATALOGUE ARE PROVISIONAL AND SUBJECT TO ALTERATION

Standard Books on the Horse and Riding
Illustrated with photographs and diagrams.

CHAMBERLIN, LT.-COL. HARRY D.
 TRAINING HUNTERS, JUMPERS AND HACKS. *2nd edition. Demy 8vo. 12s. 6d. net.*
 RIDING AND SCHOOLING HORSES. *3rd edition. Demy 8vo. 10s. 6d. net.*

FILLIS, JAMES
 BREAKING AND RIDING. *5th edition. Demy 8vo 18s. net.*

HAYES, CAPTAIN M. HORACE, F.R.C.V.S.
 POINTS OF THE HORSE. *5th edition. Super Royal 8vo. 42s. net.*
 RIDING AND HUNTING. *5th edition. Demy 8vo. 20s. net.*
 STABLE MANAGEMENT AND EXERCISE. *3rd edition. Demy 8vo. 20s. net.*
 TRAINING AND HORSE MANAGEMENT IN INDIA. *7th edition. Revised. Cr. 8vo.*
 10s. 6d. net.
 VETERINARY NOTES FOR HORSE-OWNERS. *12th edition. Revised and enlarged.*
 Demy 8vo. 20s. net.

HITCHCOCK, CAPTAIN F. C., M.C.
 RUDIMENTS OF RIDING. *3rd edition. Pocket size. Cloth,* 2s. 6d. *net ; Rexine,*
 3s. 6d. net.
 'TO HORSE !". *3rd edition. Demy 8vo. 10s. 6d. net.*
 'SADDLE UP". *8th edition. Demy 8vo. 10s. 6d. net.*

LAMB, MAJOR A. J. R., D.S.O.
 HORSE FACTS *2nd edition Demy 8vo. 8s. 6d. net.*

LITTAUER, CAPTAIN V. S.
 THE FORWARD SEAT. *3rd edition. Crown 8vo. 6s. net.*
 MORE ABOUT THE FORWARD SEAT. *Small Demy. 7s. 6d. net.*

A LIST OF RECENT SUCCESSFUL BOOKS THAT ARE STILL SELLING

ADVENTURES ON THE HIGH SEAS. CAPT. H. G. KENDALL, R.D., R.N.R. 12s. 6d.
BARLOW'S JOURNAL, 1659-1703. BASIL LUBBOCK, 2 vols. 21s.
"BEHOLD OUR NEW EMPIRE"—MUSSOLINI. LOUISE DIEL. 10s. 6d.
BIOGRAPHY OF GENERAL CHIANG KAI-SHEK. HOLLINGTON K TONG. 2 vols.
BRITAIN'S JEWISH PROBLEM. M. G. MURCHIN. 5s.   [*Each* 15s.
CHARMINA ON THE RIVIERA. E. KEBLE CHATTERTON. 12s. 6d.
CHINA IN PEACE AND WAR. MADAME CHIANG KAI-SHEK. 16s.
COMMON-SENSE CONTRACT. LAURENCE H. KADE. 2s.
DRAGON RAMPANT. ROBIN HYDE. 8s. 6d.
ERRANT GOLFER, AN. E. P. LEIGH-BENNETT. 2s.
ESCAPE ON SKIS. BRIAN MEREDITH. 10s. 6d.
ESCAPE TO PRISON. ROBERT E. BURNS. 7s. 6d.
FIGHT FOR DIVORCE, THE. FRANCIS GRIBBLE. 3s. 6d.
FLY WITH ME. VICTOR RICKETTS. 1s.
GERMANY PUSHES SOUTH-EAST. DR. GERHARD SCHACHER. 7s. 6d.
GERMANY PUSHES WEST. DR. GERHARD SCHACHER. 10s. 6d.
GERMANY'S CLAIMS TO COLONIES. F. S. JOELSON. 8s. 6d.
GERMANY'S HITLER. HEINZ A. HEINZ. 5s.
GODOY. HANS ROGER MADOL. 5s.
HERMANN GOERING—The Man and His Work DR. ERICH GRITZBACH. 8s. 6d.
HITLER'S SPY RING. "E.7". 10s. 6d.
HOME IS THE SAILOR. WILLIAM BLAIN. 12s. 6d.
HOW TO WRITE BROADCAST PLAYS. VAL GIELGUD. 2s. 6d.
JOURNEY WESTWARD. WILLIAM ELLIS. 12s. 6d.

ALL PRICES IN THIS CATALOGUE ARE PROVISIONAL AND SUBJECT TO ALTERATION

A List of Recent Successful Novels—Continued

KING'S NURSE—BEGGAR'S NURSE. "BLACKIE" (Sister Catherine Black). 12s. 6d.
LEARN TO WRITE FOR BROADCASTING. CLAUDE HULBERT. 1s.
LIBEL FOR LAYMEN. M. A. MacKINNON AND J. ALLAN BELL. 3s. 6d.
LIMELIGHT. GEORGE MOZART. 18s.
MEIN KAMPF. ADOLF HITLER. 9s.
MEMOIRS OF WILLIAM HICKEY, 1749–1809. ALFRED SPENCER. Vols. I, II and III
each 15s. Vol. IV. 21s.
MISTINGUETT AND HER CONFESSIONS. HUBERT GRIFFITH. 15s.
MOSCOW-BERLIN SECRET SERVICES. VICTOR K. KALEDIN. 12s. 6d.
MY PART IN GERMANY'S FIGHT. DR. JOSEPH GOEBBELS. 7s. 6d.
PERSEPHONE IN WINTER. ROBIN HYDE. 3s. 6d.
PRACTICAL CARTOONING FOR PROFIT. WILL FARROW. 2s.
PRINCESS OR PRETENDER. MARY L. PENDERED AND JUSTINIAN MALLETT. 15s.
RED PILOT VLADIMIR UNISHEVSKY. 9s.
RESTLESS QUEST. JEROME WILLIS. 10s. 6d.
RIDDLE OF HELL'S JUNGLE. SCHULZ-KAMPFHENKEL. 16s.
SABU OF THE ELEPHANTS. JACK WHITTINGHAM. 5s.
SAHARA UNVEILED. PATRICK TURNBULL. 16s.
SAILING MADE EASY. RUFUS G. SMITH. 10s. 6d.
SAILING MODELS—ANCIENT AND MODERN. E. KEBLE CHATTERTON. 21s.
SCAPA FLOW. VICE-ADMIRAL VON REUTER. 6s.
SCRUFFY. CLAUDE BURBIDGE. 2s. 6d.
SEX AND COMMON SENSE. A. MAUDE ROYDEN. 4s. 6d.
SOUND AND FUEHRER. ROLF TELL. 2s. 6d.
SPICE OF LIFE, THE. GEORGE FOSTER. 12s. 6d.
"STAND TO!" F. C. HITCHCOCK, M.C. 7s. 6d.
"THEY ALSO SERVED". CECIL THOMAS. 8s. 6d.
TROOPER IN THE "TINS", A. R. A. LLOYD. 12s 6d.
UNDERGROUND DIPLOMACY. VICTOR K. KALEDIN. 15s.
UNKNOWN TO THE WORLD—HAITI. MABEL STEEDMAN, F.R.G.S. 15s.
UNDERSTANDING THE ENGLISH. JAMES HOWARD WELLARD. 10s. 6d.
VINDICATION OF CHARLES I, A. JOSHUA BROOKES. 3s. 6d.
WE SAW HIM ACT. H. A. SAINTSBURY AND CECIL PALMER. 21s.
WOMEN SPIES I HAVE KNOWN. "E.7". 12s. 6d.
WORLD OF WINGS AND THINGS, THE. SIR ALLIOTT VERDON-ROE, KT., O B.E., ETC.
YACHTSMAN'S PILOT. E. KEBLE CHATTERTON. 21s. [8s. 6d.

THE PATERNOSTER LIBRARY

In uniform fadeless cloth binding.   Demy 8vo.   5/- net each.

1. A DAUGHTER OF THE SAMURAI   ETSU INAGAKI SUGIMOTO
   (80,000 *copies sold in England and America*)
3. THE TUDOR WENCH   ELSWYTH THANE
   (*12th Thousand*)
4. MY AUTOBIOGRAPHY   BENITO MUSSOLINI
   (*58th Thousand*)
5. A MILLION MILES IN SAIL   JOHN HERRIES McCULLOCH
   (*10th Thousand*)
6. THE MENACE OF JAPAN   TAID O'CONROY
   (*33rd Thousand*)
7. THE BLACK TENTS OF ARABIA   CARL R. RASWAN
   (*6th Thousand*)
8 SCHIGGI-SCHIGGI : The Adventures of Leo Parcus in the Forests of Bolivia.
                                       FRITZ STRAUSS
   (*5th Thousand*)
9. THE LAND OF THE LINGAM   ARTHUR MILES (GERVÉE BARONTE)
   (*7th Thousand*)
10. A DAUGHTER OF THE NARIKIN   ETSU INAGAKI SUGIMOTO
   (*6th Thousand*)
11. JAPAN MUST FIGHT BRITAIN   LT.-COMDR. TOTA ISHIMARU
   (*11th Thousand*)
12. THE ROSE OF LONDON   GUY PAGET
   (*6th Thousand*)
13. K.14—O.M.66   COLONEL VICTOR K. KALEDIN
   (*8th Thousand*)
15. A DAUGHTER OF THE NOHFU   ETSU INAGAKI SUGIMOTO
   (*6th Thousand*)
16. MEMOIRS OF PRINCE CHRISTOPHER OF GREECE
   (*23rd Thousand*)
17. A CAGED BIRD   MAUREEN FLEMING (MRS. LARRY RUE)

ALL PRICES IN THIS CATALOGUE ARE PROVISIONAL AND SUBJECT TO ALTERATION

4